GLOBAL WHITE NATIONALISM

Manchester University Press

Racism, Resistance and Social Change

Global white nationalism

From apartheid to Trump

Edited by Daniel Geary, Camilla Schofield, and Jennifer Sutton

Manchester University Press

Published by Manchester University Press
Altrincham Street, Manchester M1 7JA

www.manchesteruniversitypress.co.uk

British Library Cataloguing-in-Publication Data
A catalogue record for this book is available from the British Library

ISBN 978 1 5261 4706 6 hardback
ISBN 978 1 5261 4707 3 paperback

First published 2020

Typeset by
Servis Filmsetting Ltd, Stockport, Cheshire
Printed in Great Britain by
TJ International Ltd, Padstow, Cornwall

For E, S, and U

Contents

Contents

Nostalgia for white rule

The far right in the Anglosphere

Contributors

Josiah Brownell is Associate Professor of History at the Pratt Institute in Brooklyn, NY, and is the author of *The Collapse of Rhodesia: Population Demographics and the Politics of Race* (Bloomsbury, 2010). He has written extensively on nationalism and white settlerism in central and southern Africa, and currently has a book under contract with Cambridge University Press comparing the failed independence bids of Katanga, Rhodesia, and South Africa's Bantustans.

Kyle Burke is Assistant Professor of History at Hartwick College where he teaches modern U.S. and global history. He is the author of *Revolutionaries for the Right: Anticommunist Internationalism and Paramilitary Warfare in the Cold War* (UNC Press, 2018) as well as articles, essays, and reviews in *Diplomatic History*, *Jacobin*, *Terrorism and Political Violence*, *H-War*, and *H-Diplo*.

Daniel Geary is the Mark Pigott Associate Professor in American History at Trinity College Dublin and author of *Beyond Civil Rights: The Moynihan Report and Its Legacy* (University of Pennsylvania Press, 2015).

Zoe Hyman is Lecturer in American History at the University College London Institute of the Americas. She is currently writing *Partnerships of Supremacy: American Segregationist Ideology and White Southern Africa, 1948–1975*.

Omar Khan was director of the Runnymede Trust from 2014 to 2020, in which capacity he wrote the Postscript for this volume. He has written widely on race and racism in the UK for two decades, and has a doctorate in political theory.

Kennetta Hammond Perry serves as the Director of the Stephen Lawrence Research Centre and is a Reader in History at De Montfort University, Leicester. Her research interests include transnational race politics and twentieth-century Black British history. She is the author of *London is the Place for Me: Black Britons, Citizenship and the Politics of Race* (Oxford University Press, 2016).

Camilla Schofield is Senior Lecturer in the School of History, University of East Anglia, and the author of *Enoch Powell and the Making of Postcolonial Britain* (Cambridge University Press, 2013).

Bill Schwarz teaches at the School for English and Drama, Queen Mary University London. He is currently engaged in completing his three-volume work, *Memories of Empire*, of which the first volume has been published: *The White Man's World* (Oxford University Press, 2011).

Evan Smith is a Research Fellow in History in the College of Humanities, Arts and Social Sciences at Flinders University, South Australia. He is the author of *No Platform: A History of Anti-Fascism, Universities and the Limits of Free Speech* (Routledge, 2020) and *British Communism and the Politics of Race* (Brill, 2018).

Jennifer Sutton is an independent scholar.

Stuart Ward is Professor and Head of the Saxo Institute of History, Archeology, Ethnology and Classics at the University of Copenhagen. He recent co-edited (with Astrid Rasch) *Embers of Empire in Brexit Britain* (Bloomsbury, 2019) and will soon publish *Untied Kingdom: A World History of the End of Britain* (Cambridge University Press).

Clive Webb is Professor of Modern American History at the University of Sussex. He is currently researching a book on the lynching of foreign nationals in the United States, funded by a Leverhulme Major Fellowship.

Series editors' foreword

Series Editors: John Solomos, Satnam Virdee, Aaron Winter

When we launched this series on *Racism, Resistance and Social Change* in 2018 we saw it as providing a forum for the publication of the highest-quality scholarship on race, racism, anti-racism and ethnic relations. As Editors we set out the core objectives of the series as being to provide a space both for theoretically driven books and texts with an empirical frame that seek to further develop our understanding of the origins, development and contemporary forms of racism, racial inequalities and racial and ethnic relations. As the series has developed, we hope that readers will agree that we are beginning to meet these objectives, although we are fully aware that the series is still in the early stages of its development.

As we made clear at the launch of the series, we welcome work from a range of theoretical and political perspectives, and as the series develops, we would ideally want to encourage a conversation that goes beyond specific national or geopolitical environments. While we are aware that there are important differences between national and regional research traditions, we hope that both early career scholars and researchers from a variety of disciplines and interdisciplinary frames will take the opportunity to include their research work in the series. We very much hope that scholars from the Global South and the Global North will be included in the list of books that we publish as the series grows and develops. Given the wider geopolitical context that has emerged over the past few decades we would very much like to see books in the series that address questions about resistance and anti-racism as well as the role of political and policy interventions in this rapidly changing social and political field. The changing forms of racist mobilisation and expression that have come to the fore in recent years have highlighted the need for more reflection and research on the role of political and civil society mobilisations in this field.

Now that the series has begun to establish itself, we would like to encourage potential authors to begin conversations with us and our publishers at Manchester University Press about ideas they have for books that could potentially be added to the series in the coming period. We are committed to building on theoretical advances in this growing field of scholarship by providing a forum for new and challenging theoretical and empirical studies on the changing morphology of race and racism in contemporary societies.

Preface

How does the police murder of an African American in Minneapolis spark the toppling of a statue of a slave trader in Bristol? As we put the final touches to this book in June 2020, many were asking this question. Decades of excellent scholarship has detailed the globally interconnected structures of racism that have persisted since the days of slavery and empire, and the ways in which anti-racist movements have forged ties and taken inspiration from one another. The question that motivated this book is a related but less explored one: in what ways has white nationalism also been a global movement, one that has sought to preserve racial hierarchy in the face of the powerful movements for equality that grew from decolonization and civil rights? In June 2020 those who defended the police against widespread calls for reform and fought to preserve monuments to slavery and empire made common cause across the oceans.

Center-right leaders scrambled to disassociate themselves from both the far right and the conditions that sparked the Black Lives Matter protests, but did so in ways that reveal the far-reaching influence of white nationalist sentiments and assumptions. Australia's Conservative Prime Minister, Scott Morrison, dismissed a demonstration in Sydney that linked the murder of George Floyd in Minneapolis to recent Indigenous deaths in police custody. He commented, "We shouldn't be importing the things that are happening overseas to Australia." Despite Australia's well-documented history of Indigenous slave labor, Morrison insisted on radio that "There was no slavery in Australia." Meanwhile, Britain's

Home Secretary Priti Patel channeled Richard Nixon in appealing to "the quiet law-abiding majority" of British citizens upset by incidents such as the toppling of the Bristol statue. As this moment demonstrates and as we insist throughout this book, white nationalism is not simply a movement of a small group of far right extremists, but an ideology that suffuses the mainstream electoral right and continues to structure widely held beliefs about history, law and order, and the limits of freedom in our societies.

If this book reached its conclusion in June 2020, it began at an earlier, though connected, historical moment in November 2016. The Brexit referendum and the election of Donald Trump convinced us that it was vital to understand the neglected transnational history of white nationalism in order to understand the world today. We cannot predict what will be happening by the time this book is published or by the time you read it. But we have little doubt that the profound challenge posed by the global mobilization of Black Lives Matter will be met with reaction from white nationalists, both in electoral politics and through radical acts of violence. The task of historicizing white nationalism will remain vital.

* * *

This book would not have been possible without the commitment and vision of those who participated in the 2017 workshop hosted by the Trinity College Dublin Long Room Hub Arts & Humanities Research Institute. We are grateful for funding for the workshop which came from the Hub, the Trinity College Dublin Arts, Humanities and Social Sciences Benefaction Fund, and the Grace Lawless Lee Fund. The Arts and Humanities Research Council (UK) also generously contributed to the making of this book with a leadership fellowship that provided essential research time away from the responsibilities of teaching. A project of this kind could only succeed as a collaboration, and we thank all our contributors. We also thank Thomas Borstelmann, Paul Kramer, and Stephanie Rolph for participating in the original workshop. The steadfast support and patience of Tom Dark and his colleagues at Manchester University

Press have made this book possible. We thank the anonymous readers for their careful attention.

We appreciate and thank all those who encouraged and supported us in this project, including family, friends, and colleagues. Royalties from the sale of this book will be donated to the Runnymede Trust.

Introduction:
Toward a global history of white nationalism

Daniel Geary, Camilla Schofield, and Jennifer Sutton

THE MORNING AFTER the 2016 Brexit referendum, Donald Trump landed at his Scottish golf resort and tweeted that Britons "took their country back, just like we will take America back." During his presidential campaign that summer, Trump forged a close alliance with Nigel Farage, leader of the United Kingdom Independence Party and the most prominent advocate of British withdrawal from the European Union. Farage already knew Trump's campaign manager, Steve Bannon, who hailed the rise of right-wing European nationalism as executive chairman of the alt-right website, Breitbart. In November, Farage was the first foreign leader to meet the president-elect; pleased with their successes on both sides of the Atlantic, they posed for a memorable celebratory photograph before a glimmering set of golden elevator doors in Trump Tower. Trump and Farage's image marked a victory in a struggle by linked resurgent white nationalists on both sides of the Atlantic to "take back" their countries from non-white immigrants and internationalist liberal elites.

Many observers have seen the surprise success of Brexit and Trump as similar but coincidental events. Few have recognized the historical connections. Similarly, many have been baffled by the international spread of white supremacist violence as authorities and the mass media wrongly depict such attacks as the work of isolated loners rather than as emanating from a dispersed political movement. Similar bonds, real and imagined, link Trump and Farage at the level of electoral politics and connect the 2016 assassination of pro-Remain Labour MP Jo Cox in Yorkshire by a neo-Nazi proclaiming "Britain First"; the 2018 killings at a Pittsburgh synagogue by a white supremacist who believed that Jews were orchestrating white genocide by abetting immigration from Latin America; and the 2019 murder of Muslims in Christchurch, New Zealand by an Australian white supremacist. Both the rise of ethnonationalism in electoral politics and of white supremacist violence in the English-speaking world need to be understood as related developments in a longer history of exchange among white nationalists in Britain, the U.S., and other former British settler colonies.

Because white nationalists are primarily concerned with the racial integrity of states, they have wrongly been assumed to be parochial in their politics, focused solely on domestic issues. In fact, transnational ties and transnational flows of culture and capital undergirded the pursuit of white racial nationalism long before the internet and social media helped enable such connections. International links, both real and imagined, have sustained white nationalists over the last fifty years. Global visions of whiteness have inspired local movements. The success of Brexit, for example, emboldened Trump's nativist supporters to see themselves as part of a global movement that could achieve power in the United States. Trump's victory in turn inspired the Christchurch killer who praised the U.S. president as a "symbol of renewed white identity and common purpose."[1] We need to understand the history of these connections if we are to grasp what has sustained white nationalism despite global trends toward liberation and equality, and we need to confront why such an outlook still resonates strongly enough for some to martyr themselves for its cause.

White nationalism is an ideology that asserts national identity and belonging in terms of European descent. Accordingly, white nationalists see their countries as threatened by immigration and social advancement by non-whites. They contend that national identity and belonging must be built around racial whiteness—rather than culture, language, or place—and that it is the *whiteness* of the nation's past, present, and future that ensures its continued historical development and survival. The fundamental ideas of white nationalists are hardly new. Yet they have been formulated since the mid-twentieth century as a politics of reaction to the promise of racial equality and decolonization. The term "white nationalism" was first coined in 1970 by white supremacists who sought to create a false equivalency with black nationalism. Though the numbers of self-identified "white nationalists" remain small, their ideas continue to resonate broadly, impacting contemporary debates about global demographic change, national identity, and mass migration.[2]

We treat "race" in this volume as an unstable social construct, originating in the colonial history of the dispossession, extermination, and subordination of native populations and in the transatlantic slave trade and establishment of plantation economies based on enslaved labor. The resiliency of white nationalist ideas around race, articulated at both the margins and the center of popular politics, makes sense when one understands that within living memory expressly racist policies were hegemonic in the U.S. and Britain's settler colonies. At the British Empire's zenith, its advocates claimed that the rule of law, free trade, and parliamentary sovereignty were natural virtues of the "English race." At the turn of the twentieth century, American elites shared with British imperialists a discourse of English racial heritage termed "Anglo-Saxonism" that was used to justify the subjugation of Native Americans, the subordination of African Americans, and the possession of its own overseas empire. According to Anglo-Saxonism, white, Protestant, English-speaking men naturally *made* modern nations. This racialized modernity is based on the presumption that only whites can govern and that the empowerment of non-whites is therefore an existential threat to white self-government. Though Anglo-Saxonism remained a prevailing ideology among British and American elites for much of the twentieth century, in different places and times throughout the English-speaking world, "whiteness" was defined differently, most broadly to encompass anyone of European descent.[3]

Anglo-Saxonism's cherished ideal of a "white man's country" reserving self-government and economic opportunity to whites may no longer be dominant as it was a century ago, but neither has it disappeared. Popular historian Niall Ferguson still maintains that British colonial settler culture brought "modernity" to the world.[4] Today some Brexiteers look to trade within an "Anglosphere" to reanimate this historical political tradition and harness racialized notions of "kith and kin" in the English-speaking world.[5] Indeed, nostalgia for a past period of national glory in which white rule was unchallenged is a signature feature of today's right-wing populists who seek to make their nations great *again*.

Any account of white nationalism's influence today must take account of this longer history and also recognize that profound and persistent structures of white supremacy remain deeply rooted (though too rarely acknowledged) in the English-speaking world. To understand the politics of racism in the present requires locating and examining the histories of modern white nationalism in global terms: as a response to decolonization, struggles for equal rights, mass migration, and postwar international institutions. This book aims to understand transnational relationships among white nationalists in the context of these major global events. As Western political and social elites professed a commitment to color-blind ideals, assumptions of white supremacy were challenged and reformulated.[6] The histories traced in this book show that the declining legitimacy of *overtly* racist political expression produced new international alliances and new populist claims among white supremacists.[7] As they saw themselves losing power locally, they looked abroad for allies. Countering liberal internationalist organizations such as the United Nations and the World Council of Churches, white nationalists increasingly adopted a rhetoric of ethnic populism, casting themselves as representatives of forgotten whites betrayed by globalist liberal elites. Even as they shifted their focus from opposing civil rights and preserving white rule in settler colonies to Islamophobia and opposing non-white immigration, they articulated a consistent mindset stressing the need to preserve the ethnoracial character of their nations as "white men's countries."

The roots of contemporary white nationalism

By the late nineteenth century English-speaking whites throughout the world were drawing a global color line that marked out their own nations as white men's countries. Their policies restricted immigration to "desirable" Europeans and limited non-whites' right to vote to ensure whites' ability to govern themselves. Though their aims were ethnonationalist, they developed ideas and policies in coordination with international networks. As historians Marilyn Lake and Henry Reynolds write, "The project of whiteness was thus a paradoxical politics, at once transnational in its inspiration and identification but nationalist in its methods and goals. The imagined community of white men was transnational in its reach, but nationalist in its outcomes, bolstering regimes of border protection and national sovereignty."[8]

In 1900, the ideal of the "white man's country" was broadly shared among whites of all classes even as it provoked tension between aggressive white settlers and cautious metropolitan elites. Nonetheless, the global color line was increasingly challenged over the course of the twentieth century. The industrialized slaughter of World War I undermined notions of European civilization's superiority. After the war, the colonized increasingly demanded self-determination and a new generation of intellectuals discredited the precepts of scientific racism.[9] World War II, which pitted the Allies against a fascist enemy, also did much to discredit notions of racial hierarchy and subordination.[10] The most important developments accelerated after World War II: the rise of national liberation movements and of movements for racial equality in existing nations. It was, as British Prime Minister Harold Macmillan put it to Australian Prime Minister Robert Menzies, "the revolt of the yellows and blacks from the automatic leadership of the whites."[11]

Many liberal elites, over the course of the twentieth century, evolved from a white nationalist perspective toward color-blind or multicultural conceptions of their nations. For instance, in 1944, the Carnegie Corporation published Swedish social scientist Gunnar Myrdal's *An American Dilemma*, an influential text calling for the gradual extension of equal rights to African Americans. In the 1920s, however, the foundation had funded studies to justify white minority rule in South Africa. Rejection of explicit white supremacy became one of the components of a new liberal internationalism, embodied in the United Nations. While the violence of apartheid and Jim Crow continued unabated, in 1950 the United

Nations Educational, Scientific, and Cultural Organization (UNESCO) released the first of its influential Statements on Race, drafted by an international team of prominent scholars and rejecting any notions of racial superiority. Many metropolitan elites also came to embrace decolonization, and thereby contain it, envisioning it as a historical step forward into modernity.[12] Those who adhered to explicit white supremacy, however, experienced this new racial liberalism as a "betrayal"; they shifted postwar white nationalism toward a populist perspective, arrayed against white elites—the "race traitors" within—as well as racial minorities.

The decades after the end of World War II saw the break-up of the British Empire as nations across the Global South won independence. As European empires dismantled, the U.S. extended its influence among newly independent nations. Despite losing its own major colony of the Philippines in 1946, the U.S. emerged from World War II as the preeminent world power, in many ways continuing the European imperial project of making the world safe for global capitalism.[13] The need to maintain good relations with new nations and win their support in the Cold War put considerable pressure on the U.S., U.K., and British dominions to dismantle domestic racial discrimination. As E. Franklin Frazier, the African American sociologist, anti-imperialist, and a principal author of the first UNESCO Statement on Race acerbically remarked in 1954, "The white man is scared down to his bowels, so it's be-kind-to-the-Negroes decade at last."[14]

Black activists and intellectuals in both the civil rights and anti-colonial nationalist movements saw themselves as fighting in a shared international struggle to dismantle white supremacy.[15] By the 1960s, though civil rights movements were unable to achieve their goal of full racial equality, they forced recognition of the formal legal equality of all citizens regardless of race. Landmark legislation prohibited racial discrimination. In 1963, the United Nations General Assembly adopted a Declaration on the Elimination on All Forms of Racial Discrimination; two years later, Ghanaian ambassador George Lamptey led the campaign to introduce a UN Convention against racial discrimination.[16] Steeped in the language of human rights, this Convention condemned colonialism and apartheid, affirmed equality before the law, and required its signatories to criminalize hate speech and institute national procedures to combat racial discrimination. The UN helped propel the extension of anti-discrimination laws globally. The U.S. passed the Civil Rights Act in 1964, the death knell to the Southern system of Jim Crow, and followed that with the Voting Rights Act of 1965, making "one person, one vote" a reality. The U.K. passed the Race Relations Act in 1965, Canada its Multiculturalism Act in 1971, and Australia its Racial Discrimination Act in 1975.

White supremacy was on the defensive. Yet ideas about whiteness and natural ability for self-government continued to shape understandings of global demography, anti-colonial violence, and uneven economic development. Racial anxieties ran through analyses of population growth in the Global South, for instance, echoing early twentieth-century panics about white "race suicide."[17] Anti-colonial violence was routinely de-politicized and depicted as an expression of savagery, a rejection of civilization.[18] Whites continued to assert themselves as natural agents of modernity via, for instance, international development; their authority now increasingly drawn from an emphasis on technical expertise rather than any explicit "white man's burden." Tenets of the "white man's country" were transmuted by technocracy to appear universal or colorblind.[19] Of course, the lack of explicit articulations of race is not equivalent to its true absence. As a vast scholarship has shown, whiteness derives its authority from "its seeming invisibility, its absence of particularity"; it is invested with "a universal register of value and meaning" as synonymous with civilization, the rule of law, commerce, the family, and freedom.[20] Thus, even as white nationalists found themselves on the defensive in a new "anti-racist" age and deeply at odds with liberal internationalists, they were able to continue to appeal to these racially coded liberal ideals.

Though white nationalism developed transnationally and in response to common international changes, it evolved asynchronously and asymmetrically according to different local logics. The U.S. has a history of slavery, mass immigration, and subjugation of Native Americans that contrasts with Britain's long history as an imperial metropole or the history of white minoritarian regimes in Rhodesia and South Africa. These differences are perhaps clearest in immigration policy changes and their demographic effects. The civil rights movement made the existence of racial quotas in U.S. immigration policy untenable, leading to the passage of the Hart-Cellar Act of 1965 which soon (unintentionally) led to a mass wave of emigration from Latin America, Asia, and Africa. Similarly, Australia dismantled its restrictionist White Australia policy in 1973, leading to a sharp increase in non-white immigration, especially from Asia. In Britain, however, the story was different. By the beginning of the twentieth century, Britain had small but established black communities, as well as larger racialized communities of Jewish and Irish settlement, in its major port cities. But it was in the aftermath of World War II that British subjects from Britain's colonies and former colonies, together with migrants from Ireland, Italy, Poland, Hungary and across war-torn Europe, began to arrive in increasing numbers in search of economic opportunity and security. This moment is often marked by the 1948 London arrival of the ship *Empire Windrush* which carried migrants from the Caribbean.[21] The non-white population in Britain increased tenfold by 1961. Then, as a result of domestic political opposition, the British government began to introduce migration controls.[22] To signal that these controls were part of a wider government effort to benefit "race relations," the government also passed new equality legislation modelled on that of the United States, but here the law accompanied the imposition of immigration restrictions rather than their relaxation. And in Rhodesia, the story was different again. Though the Rhodesian government restricted non-white immigration, it desperately sought white immigrants as an existential necessity to bolster the numbers of whites in its white-minority government.

In different national contexts, white nationalists adapted in similar ways to outlast the challenges against them: they persisted not simply by becoming "far right" fringe minorities but also by developing coded electoral appeals within major political parties. Everywhere, though, the array of forces against them led white nationalists to take up a defensive posture. In this new mode, white nationalists mobilized emotions of besiegement, resentment, loss, and nostalgia. As Bill Schwarz has written, "Those who found themselves embracing racial whiteness in these years, however, did not do so, like their colonial forebears, as heroic makers of history. On the contrary, they did so as representatives of a defeated people, betrayed by those charged to lead them."[23] White nationalists' sense of aggrievement came from what they perceived as their betrayal by national elites in giving in to the demands of non-whites. It also relied on an international consciousness of the global decline of white supremacy. The populist language of aggrievement white nationalists developed in retreat enabled them to capture broad appeal when new forms of political activism—on both left and right—challenged the legitimacy of the postwar order and the political establishment.

In response to the efforts to challenge white racial privilege in the 1960s and 1970s, a reactionary discourse emerged that rejected any liberal "guilt complex" over the long history of white supremacy and instead offered a counter-narrative of white victimization. Histories of "lost causes" were marshalled to this goal. As Paul Gilroy has examined, in Britain the loss of empire produced a melancholic attachment to the lost glories of the past. This widespread "postcolonial melancholia" led the British public, Gilroy argues, to compulsively revisit nostalgic versions of a heroic past—and, ironically, forget the historic ties of (an increasingly morally suspect) empire. In Britain, as in Australia and the American South, white nationalists turned away from acknowledging the atrocities of white supremacy in their nation's history; instead, their history is a history of heroism in defeat or, in Fintan O'Toole's words, "heroic failure."[24] Australia's Gallipoli campaign in World War I, America's defeated Confederacy, and Britain's potent myth of self-reliance at the retreat from Dunkirk in World War II all provide what Gilroy would call melancholic "dreamworlds" where white male heroism can be retrieved.[25]

A sense of resentment framed around the loss of "the nation" gave meaning to a wider set of social and political tensions in the period of decolonization and equal rights. The sexual revolution, student protests, and progressive legal reforms on marriage and abortion came to be viewed by many white nationalists as further examples of the destruction of national culture. Women's liberation and the moral revolution of the late twentieth century played into fears of a declining white population. White nationalism is replete with anxious visions of lost white male authority: the threat to patriarchy underscored the loss of the "white man's country." Opposition to gender equality was a midwife to the birth of modern white nationalism. But gender intersected with white nationalism in another important way, too. Defending white women and white domesticity functioned both in the colonies and the metropole as a means to defend white supremacy, colonial violence, and the dehumanization of people of color.[26] Updating a long tradition, white nationalists still promote fantasies of white women as victims; under threat from migrant rapists, black male sexuality, and Sharia law.

From the civil rights era to the present, white nationalists have found a home in right-wing political parties whose leaders appealed to racism despite formally renouncing "race." White nationalism fit within the broader constellation of ideas advocated by the transnational right whose critique of liberal internationalism also included asserting the place of social hierarchy, "law and order," patriarchal families, and fundamentalist Christian values, and attacking the legitimacy of the postwar social welfare state. In contrast to most studies of white nationalism, which focus on its most extreme exponents, this book examines the interplay between the far right and the electoral right. Though white nationalism is nurtured most intensely by a small group of activists and intellectuals, the electoral right throughout the English-speaking world has consistently appealed to racial fears among whites about loss of status. The electoral right receives much of its dynamism from the far right. Yet the existence of such far right groups makes the electoral right more respectable by contrast, able to appeal to white nationalist sentiment while disavowing violent and explicit racism, and thereby enabling it to assemble a broader political coalition. This dialectic of extremism and respectability operates not simply within national boundaries but in a transnational framework.

The birth of a nation

What distinguishes white nationalists is that they view self-government as a *natural and exclusive* white right that requires defending. In the post-civil rights era, there is no better example of this view than the solidarity movement that emerged to support the small state of Rhodesia, a movement that also demonstrates the global outlook and transnational connections among white nationalists. On November 11, 1965, Rhodesia announced its Unilateral Declaration of Independence (UDI) from Great Britain in order to preserve minority white rule. With British and American support, the United Nations declared Rhodesia an "illegal racist minority regime" and imposed economic sanctions; no government, not even South Africa, offered Rhodesia diplomatic recognition. Yet white nationalists around the globe mobilized in solidarity with the Rhodesian government, much as leftists had rallied to the republican side in the Spanish Civil War a generation earlier. Rhodesia won the support of a transnational community of embattled whites who saw the regime's existential struggle against a black liberation movement and a hostile international community as connected to their own local and national battles to maintain white privilege in the face of civil rights gains. They were inspired by Rhodesia's charismatic leader Ian Smith who forthrightly declared to a popular American magazine, "The white man is the master of Rhodesia ... [he] has built it and intends to keep it."[27]

Rhodesian independence excited disproportionate support among white nationalists throughout the English-speaking world compared to its neighbors, the Portuguese settler colonies of Angola and Mozambique, which fought contemporaneous battles against black liberation movements, and even its far more powerful and populous neighbor, South Africa. South Africa's introduction of apartheid, a system of institutionalized racial segregation, in 1948 showed the persistence of global white supremacy despite post-World War II decolonization and the formal anti-racism of the liberal internationalism associated with the United Nations. Apartheid galvanized anti-racists worldwide. It also inspired white supremacists to hold their ground, even if the anti-British component of Afrikaner nationalism complicated matters for Anglophone white nationalists. Yet white nationalists claimed Rhodesia as a critical front, or the last line of defense, in an imagined, globalized race war for white self-government.

Preparing the way for Rhodesia's emergence as the international symbol of embattled whiteness were the 1952 Mau Mau "emergency" and ensuing war in Kenya, which ended with independence from Britain in January 1960, followed by war in the newly independent Republic of the Congo between 1960 and 1965. The violent Mau Mau rebellion was perceived, from white British and American contemporary viewpoints, as targeting whites rather than as in fact an anti-colonial uprising that mainly divided Africans and resembled a civil war.[28] Popular representations of Mau Mau portrayed African decolonization as "impulsively savage," to use the words of a best-selling 1955 American novel about the rebellion, *Something of Value*. Its author, Robert Ruark, was a North Carolinian associated with the segregationist Citizens' Councils. Its success highlights how commonly whites accepted images of Africans as essentially irrational and thus incapable of self-government—in contrast, the rebellion inspired African American nationalists and others engaged in the global black freedom struggle.[29]

The international press similarly presented the Congo crisis in 1960 as a symbol of the seemingly inevitable violence and disorder of black liberation. In the U.S., a sense among White House officials that the Congolese displayed ingratitude toward the leaving Belgians contributed to a decision to oust the democratically elected prime minister Patrice Lumumba. Additionally, the crisis played into American fears of race war, or more precisely a slave uprising, as accounts of Congolese troops raping white nuns captured the attention of the press, the White House, the UN Security Council—and American segregationists.[30] "Don't wait for your daughter to be raped by these Congolese," proclaimed Leander Perez, a white supremacist leader from Louisiana.[31] The arrival of Soviet bloc technicians and matériel in 1960 convinced the Eisenhower administration that the Congo was a new front in the Cold War. By 1964, when UN peacekeeping forces were preparing to leave the Republic of Congo, Washington and Brussels began to fund white supremacist vigilante mercenaries devoted to halting "communism."[32] To white nationalists, the Congo crisis, coming on the heels of Mau Mau, seemed to justify their fears that decolonization would yield social disorder and violently destroy the white racial right to self-government not only through majority rule but also through communism.

These fears bolstered the Rhodesian government's appeal to white nationalists internationally following UDI, when it fostered support groups abroad to promote its cause, especially in Britain, South Africa, and the U.S.[33] In Britain, the Rhodesian issue was a crucial spur to the formation of a right-wing group within the Conservative Party, the Monday Club. The Monday Club became a leading platform not only for supporting white minority rule within (post-)colonial Africa but also for opposing non-white migration to Britain. It regularly trotted out Ian Smith's wartime service as an RAF pilot to generate support in Britain: Smith and even the UDI represented the *best* of Britain, its spirit of self-determination and heroism as the underdog proven in World War II. British rightists asserted that Britain had lost its "enterprising" spirit due to the postwar welfare state, yet in Rhodesia a heroic British culture could live on. According to Smith, if Winston Churchill were still alive, he would emigrate to Rhodesia.[34]

The Rhodesian cause also found significant support among Americans. Marvin Liebman, a conservative activist and paid lobbyist for the Rhodesian government, founded the American Friends of Rhodesian Independence (FORI) in 1966. By the end of the year, it claimed 122 branches and 25,000 members, attracting many who already belonged to right-wing groups such as the Liberty Lobby, the John Birch Society, and the segregationist Citizens' Council. The group appealed not only to anti-black sentiment but also to anti-communism and hostility to the "world government" of the United Nations that had imposed sanctions against Rhodesia.[35] Like other white nationalists during the Cold War, FORI conflated communism, liberal internationalism, and black rule while harkening back to notions of Anglo-Saxon ideals of self-governance. It had significant success in getting the American press to promote views supportive of the Rhodesian regime and in lobbying the U.S. government to scrap sanctions. In 1971, Congress passed the Byrd Amendment that allowed the U.S. to import chrome from Rhodesia in violation of UN sanctions. Though anti-communist rhetoric was crucial to the passage of the bill, it was hardly an accident that its sponsor was arch-segregationist Senator Harry Byrd of Virginia.[36]

It is telling that Rhodesian support groups referred to themselves as "friends" of the regime. Rather than invoking universal human rights, they appealed to kinship ties that bound white people together. Such ties of friendship and kinship were not always imagined. They were fostered through emigration to Rhodesia as well as visits to the country sponsored by support groups such as FORI, often with funding from the Rhodesian government.[37] The strongest support for the Rhodesian regime came from groups in Britain, South Africa, and the U.S., though the cause resonated elsewhere. The founder of a pro-Rhodesian group in Winnipeg, Canada, cited his eight grandchildren: "They're the ones I'm fighting for. No one is prejudiced against the black people. But what's the advantage of destroying white civilization?"[38] The right-wing Australian League of Rights took up the "Battle for Rhodesia," celebrating the formation of FORI groups in the U.S.[39] Especially after the intensification of armed struggle in 1974, the Rhodesian regime recruited mercenaries from abroad, especially from Australia, Britain, France, New Zealand, and the U.S.[40]

The Rhodesian regime fell in 1980 when Robert Mugabe, leader of the insurgent national liberation movement, proclaimed the Republic of Zimbabwe. Yet the failure of white minority rule in Rhodesia, followed over a decade later by the end of apartheid in South Africa, hardly dealt an irreversible blow to global white supremacy. White supremacists in the English-speaking world often succeeded in making Zimbabwe, which suffered under the misrule of Mugabe, into a morality tale of black majority rule. Shortly after Rhodesia's fall, *The Citizen*, the publication of the segregationist Citizens' Councils of America, printed several articles by Father Arthur Lewis, an English-born, Oxford-educated Anglican missionary who fled Rhodesia. Lewis denounced the purported mistreatment of whites by the Zimbabwean government, excoriated international organizations such as the World Council of Churches for their role in the downfall of Rhodesia, and pled for support for white Rhodesian refugees from friends in the U.S., Britain, Canada, and Europe.[41]

A romantic ideal of Rhodesia as an inspirational "lost cause" continues to seize the imagination of white supremacists. In 2015, Dylann Roof, radicalized by reading the publications of the Council of Conservative Citizens (the successor to the Citizens' Council), murdered nine people at a historic black church in Charleston, South Carolina. Roof styled himself "the Last Rhodesian" in his manifesto and attire. Puzzled commentators rushed to understand the meaning these symbols held for him. Rhodesian history and the glorification of white fighters in the 1970s war has grown online since 2015. In 2018, a gun manufacturer in Illinois planned to produce a "Rhodie tribute" automatic rifle. A clothing salespoint located outside Boston marketed a red-and-white patch proclaiming "Make Zimbabwe Rhodesia Again."[42] The memory of Rhodesia—nostalgia not only for a white-ruled state, but also specifically as a site of modern combat for white rule—continues to evoke white nationalism and the need to defend white self-government in transnational terms. And stories of violence against white landowners in southern Africa continue to excite white nationalists globally. For example, in 2018 Fox News pundits amplified conspiracy theories about a planned "white genocide" in southern Africa, leading President Trump to instruct the Secretary of State to investigate the purported "South Africa land and farm seizures and expropriations and the large scale killing of farmers." Though manifestly false, the familiar story continues to resonate with the crucial fear of white besiegement.[43]

Border crossings

Though the politics of white nationalism has focused on closing national borders (to non-whites), it has been nourished by the border crossings of leading white nationalists. Contrary to popular stereotype, white nationalists are hardly rubes ignorant of international affairs. Their leaders sought connections with counterparts in other countries, believing that they were involved in a shared struggle. For example, David Duke and Enoch Powell—two of the figures most famous for arguing the necessity of closing borders to keep nations white—crossed physical and intellectual borders to develop and advance their visions.

In March 1978, Duke traveled to England with the goals of increasing his profile, forming connections with like-minded Britons, and urging them to halt non-white migration to their nation lest they suffer the fate of the multiracial U.S. Duke's visit was widely publicized in the British tabloid press, which could not resist the figure of the youthful, handsome, articulate, and media-savvy Klansman. Eventually deported for inciting racial hatred, Duke managed to escape the authorities for several days, all the while remaining in the public spotlight, leading him to be dubbed the "racist Pimpernel" by British tabloids. The visit helped Duke, at the time relatively unknown outside Louisiana, to become the world-famous figure he is today.

Duke asserted that American and British whites shared a "special relationship" of racial affinity and sought to convince his American audience that non-white immigration was a mutual racial concern. Appearing on the BBC, Duke claimed that the U.S. was his "country" but that his "national origin" was British. Duke frequently appeared in front of quintessentially British locations. He posed for photographs wearing a heavily embroidered Klan robe—hood pulled back—near Big Ben. Later, wearing a coat and tie, he was photographed before Buckingham Palace, beside Beefeaters at the Tower of London, and (even while evading the authorities) outside Scotland Yard. Reflecting on his visit in an editorial for his newsletter, Duke wrote "in just about every western nation the White race is under assault. Our culture, values, heritage, economic well-being, and the very racial existence of our people are threatened by a tidal wave of colored peoples sweeping over our borders through immigration."

To Britons, Duke portrayed himself as "a Paul Revere in reverse, warning the British that their cities will become human sewers like ours if the non-White immigration continues." He told the *Evening News* he "came to help stop coloured immigration into this country." In fact, he proposed that Britons enact a "port watch" modeled on the vigilante patrol Duke's Klan had launched on the Mexican border in October 1977, running from Brownsville, Texas, to the Pacific. Duke sought connections among far right groups such as the National Front and hoped his visit would spark Klan branches in Britain, proclaiming, "someday we'll have more members in Birmingham, England than Birmingham, Alabama."[44]

Duke's mention of Birmingham, which he visited during his trip, evoked Enoch Powell, the British conservative politician who delivered his infamously racist and highly popular "Rivers of Blood" speech there in 1968, warning against non-white migration into Britain. A decade before Duke, Powell evoked the spectre of American racial chaos coming to the U.K., a vision fed by travels to Detroit the previous year where he toured the scene of one of the most destructive riots of the era. Powell's speech should be understood not only as a crucial moment in domestic British political history but also in white nationalism internationally. Powell's image as a man who courageously challenged elite opinion to stand against the "oppression" of white people resulted in multiple speaking tours outside of Britain. In 1973, Powell appeared on Australian television in a debate with Australia's Minister for Immigration, Albert Grassby. That year, the racially discriminatory aspects of Australia's 1958 Migration Act were officially overturned. Grassby initiated these reforms and introduced a national "multicultural" policy in Australia. As one observer noted, Powell in the debate made "a case for retaining a society that, in reality, never existed" in Australia; he seemed to "yearn for the mythical Anglo-Saxon England of days gone by."[45] Powell also captured the imagination of American segregationists. In 1971, the Citizens' Council, the leading organization fighting racial integration in the U.S., invited Powell to speak at its headquarters in Jackson, Mississippi. Powell's speech, which alleged that "whites are being held back to accommodate the Asiatics and blacks," met with widespread approval among an audience of Citizens' Council leaders and a host of local and state politicians.[46]

By 1978, Powell himself was no longer prominent in British politics. Having left the Conservative Party due to its support for Britain's entry into the European Economic Community in 1973, Powell turned to defending the cause of Protestants in Northern Ireland by representing the Ulster Unionist Party at Westminster. But Powell's ideas continued to inform British politics. As Stuart Hall observed in 1979, "Powell lost, but 'Powellism' won."[47] Margaret Thatcher, the Conservative Party leader in opposition at the time of Duke's visit, had earlier that year voiced her sympathy with white Britons feeling "swamped by people of a different culture." Her message all but destroyed the National Front in the 1979 general election, as the Conservative Party picked up the anti-immigrant vote in areas where the National Front had been most active.[48] Powell himself was perceived as too extreme, the National Front even more so, but their presence allowed Thatcher to gain power as a respectable alternative voicing much the same message that Powell and Duke had: non-white immigration threatened white Britons.[49] Though the tabloid press portrayed Duke the Klansman as a bizarre American curiosity, this framing occluded the tabloids' own key role in fostering the populist anti-immigrant sentiment exploited by Thatcher.[50]

Toward a global history of white nationalism

By tracing a variety of imagined ties like the "friends" of Rhodesia, and real border crossings like those of Duke and Powell, the essays in this volume analyze the entangled histories of white nationalism in the U.S., Britain, and former British settler colonies since the mid-twentieth century. The book is divided into four sections. In the first section, authors discuss how memories and forgettings of the long history of white supremacy enable white nationalism today. Kennetta Hammond Perry demonstrates how the popular memory of slavery in Britain today reproduces white supremacy. Stuart Ward shows how the history of settler colonialism in Australia helps explain the actions of the mass murderer of Muslims in Christchurch. Bill Schwarz demonstrates the profound ways in which British and American politics were shaped in reaction to global demands for black equality. The next three sections offer case studies of how particular instances of transnational exchange shaped the development of white nationalism globally. Clive Webb examines the importance of the U.S. to the development of Enoch Powell's ideas and the reception they received in the U.S., while Daniel Geary uncovers the importance of transnational networks of racist religious fundamentalists for Ian Paisley, the Protestant preacher and prominent opponent of

Catholic civil rights in Northern Ireland. Josiah Brownell shows how the Rhodesian government used Powellite imagery of Britain swamped by non-white migration to recruit white immigrants, while Zoe Hyman reveals how both Rhodesia and South Africa provided American segregationists with "an alternative future where white supremacy persisted." Evan Smith examines how different groups in the Australian far right looked to the U.S. and U.K. for inspiration, while Kyle Burke shows how skinhead culture fed into hypermasculine and paramilitary cultures of the far right in the U.K and U.S. Both Smith and Burke make clear that contemporary white nationalism in the Anglosphere continues to draw from a fascist, anti-Semitic tradition.

What follows is best understood as a collective and preliminary effort. It is necessarily a collection of essays because it requires the expertise of scholars working on different geographical areas. It is necessarily a provisional effort because of the newness of studies of this kind. As such, our book inevitably has several lacunae. Despite its effort to internationalize our understandings of white nationalism's history, it remains limited geographically. Though we claim that there is a specific intensity and character of relationships among white nationalists throughout the English-speaking world, any truly global history of white nationalism would obviously have to include continental Europe and other former European settler colonies, not to mention former British settler colonies not treated here such as Canada, Kenya, and New Zealand.

This book focuses on the activities of white nationalists themselves, rather than on organized opposition to their activism; the actors in these histories are, therefore, largely male and white. Women played essential roles in the social reproduction of white nationalism, but with some key exceptions they typically worked behind the scenes. Though gender runs throughout the chapters of this book as a category of analysis, an entire volume could be dedicated to the work of gender in the transnational history of white nationalism. It warrants further sustained examination. Though the chapters in this volume focus primarily (though hardly exclusively) on how white nationalists responded to black empowerment, it should be noted that at different times and places white nationalists have been equally or more concerned with threats posed by Asians, Latin Americans, indigenous peoples, Muslims, Jews, or even southern and eastern Europeans. Tracing the history of white nationalism up to the present would especially require more attention to developments since the 1990s, when Islamophobia has become an increasingly prominent component of white nationalist ideology. It is our hypothesis that recent Islamophobic movements have been grounded in the earlier period of white nationalism. White nationalism, after all, is best understood as a consistent mindset rather than a reaction to particular groups of people.

One of the key issues involved in understanding global white nationalism is whether it should be perceived as a marginal political movement or as part of the mainstream of contemporary political culture. We think white nationalism should be understood as *both* constitutive of our societies and as a specific political movement of the right whose fortunes are now resurgent. Given the deep ways in which notions of "white men's countries" structured Britain, the U.S., and British settler colonies just a century ago, it is hardly surprising that a foundation of white supremacy remains under the edifice of societies that have formally renounced racism. This is particularly true given the partial defeat of movements for racial equality as reflected in the continuation of vast systemic inequalities and institutional anti-black violence. We invite readers to heed the warning of David Theo Goldberg not to confuse "the end of racism" with "no more than being against race."[51] The persistence of white supremacy in our societies has provided a strong platform on which white nationalists can stand, and it must be dismantled.

We also believe that white nationalism needs to be understood as a specific political movement of the right, though one hardly limited to just a handful of extremists. The successes of anti-racist movements in the twentieth century were only partial, but they were enough to spark a powerful reaction from those who wished that their nations were still white men's countries. White nationalists share a sense of dispossession rooted in incomplete changes to the racial order. Yet their feelings of loss, cloaked in the mainstream as calls for a return to national greatness, serve as scant cover for white supremacy.

Combatting contemporary white nationalism requires truly grappling with the long history of white supremacy and white nationalism's roots in the global history of slavery and settler colonialism. It also requires understanding white nationalism today as a specific historical formation which emerged in reaction to the global black freedom struggle. This is the central project of this book.

To many observers, Brexit and Trump made it seem as if an atavistic ideology was suddenly resurrected. This book shows that white nationalism has remained a consistent presence in transnational political culture. While rooted in the older ideal of the "white man's country" associated with Anglophone settler colonialism, it has adapted to the challenges posed by decolonization, civil rights, and liberal internationalism. Those seeking to explain white nationalism's renewed political strength in our own time should then ask why it has begun to have greater appeal. To the minority who explicitly identify with white nationalist ideas, their sense of victimization and desire to return to an imagined past era of national glory has everything to do with the decline of white dominance. To many other white people, white nationalists' rhetoric of betrayal, nostalgia, and denunciation of non-white immigrants and internationalist elites has increased appeal in a period of financial crash, depressed wages, and precarious employment. The lack until recently of a significant left-wing challenge to neoliberalism has moreover made ethnonationalism the main political form in which anti-establishment sentiment can be articulated.[52] The adaptations that white nationalists made after 1945 have enabled it to broaden its appeal in our time. White nationalism, the following chapters show, is a worldly ideology. Its future may be uncertain, but its resilience should never again be underestimated.

Notes

1 "White House Dismisses Trump Mention in Christchurch Shooter Manifesto," *Guardian*, March 17, 2019.

2 We use the term "white nationalism" here instead of related terms such as "white supremacism" and "White Power," both of which are apt terms for many of the

phenomena we discuss. However, while underlining links with earlier notions of "white men's countries," "white nationalism" also suggests a historical specificity in the post-civil rights and post-decolonization era that "white supremacism" lacks. "White nationalism" also captures the essential importance of ethnonationalism to its appeal. In her excellent book *Bring the War Home*, Kathleen Belew rejects the term "white nationalism" in favor of "White Power." Her terminology is certainly appropriate for the small number of individuals (10,000–25,000 in her estimation) who actively support violent resistance, many of whom speak of building a new white ethnostate. However, Belew tends to confuse anti-statism with a rejection of nationalism, thereby missing the key populist element of white ethnonationalism that counterposes the white "people" of the nation against the traitorous elites who govern it. Unlike "White Power," "white nationalism" also captures a broader set of ideas evident in both extremist movements like White Power and in mainstream politics. Though this book treats white nationalism as a historically specific species of ethnonationalism, we recognize that ethnonationalism need not be expressed in terms of "whiteness," as evident for example in the contemporary ascendance of Hindu nationalism in India. See Kathleen Belew, *Bring the War Home: The White Power Movement and Paramilitary America* (Cambridge, MA: Harvard University Press, 2018).

3 Paul Kramer, "Empires, Exceptions, and Anglo-Saxons: Race and Rule Between the British and United States Empires, 1880–1910," *Journal of American History* 88 (2002): 1315–53. The use of Anglo-Saxon medieval symbols and references in recent white nationalist rallies also reveals the persistence of these ideas. See the contemporary debates surrounding the field of Anglo-Saxon medieval history: Hannah Natanson, "'It's all white people': Allegations of White Supremacy Are Tearing Apart a Prestigious Medieval Studies Group," *Washington Post*, September 19, 2019.

4 Niall Ferguson, *Empire: How Britain Made the Modern World* (London: Allen Lane, 2003).

5 Duncan Bell and Srdjan Vucetic, "Brexit, CANZUK, and the Legacy of Empire," *The British Journal of Politics and International Relations* 21.2 (2019): 367–82. For more on the racial politics of the Anglosphere, see Srdjan Vucetic, "A Racialized Peace? How Britain and the US Made Their Relationship Special," *Foreign Policy Analysis* 7.3 (2011): 403–21; Michael Kenny and Nick Pearce, *Shadows of Empire: The Anglosphere in British Politics* (Cambridge: Polity, 2018).

6 For the significance of racial equality in the human rights revolution, see Steven L. B. Jensen, *The Making of International Human Rights: The 1960s, Decolonization, and the Reconstruction of Global Values* (Cambridge: Cambridge University Press, 2016).

7 While specific expressions of racism and intolerance were increasingly represented as morally reprehensible or as signs of deviant extremism, discrimination against

"outsiders" and racist beliefs remained widespread and accepted in certain political formulations and within particular cultural and economic practices. As we note elsewhere in this introduction and as is discussed throughout this book, we are not arguing that racism itself was defeated by the politics of racial equality, mass migration and decolonization.

8 Marilyn Lake and Henry Reynolds, *Drawing the Global Colour Line: White Men's Countries and the International Challenge of Racial Equality* (Cambridge: Cambridge University Press, 2008), 4.

9 Michael Adas, "Contested Hegemony: The Great War and the Afro-Asian Assault on the Civilizing Mission Ideology," *Journal of World History* 15.1 (2004): 31–63; Marc Matera, *Black London: The Imperial Metropolis and Decolonization in the Twentieth Century* (Oakland, CA: University of California Press, 2015); Erez Manela, *The Wilsonian Moment: Self-Determination and the International Origins of Anticolonial Nationalism* (Oxford: Oxford University Press, 2007).

10 See, for instance, Wendy Webster, "The Post-war People's Empire," in *Englishness and Empire, 1939–1965* (Oxford: Oxford University Press, 2005); Christopher Hilliard, "Words that Disturb the State: Hate Speech and the Lessons of Fascism in Britain, 1930s–1960s," *Journal of Modern History* 88 (2016): 764–96; Frederick Cooper, "Afterword: Social Rights and Human Rights in the Time of Decolonization," *Humanity: An International Journal of Human Rights, Humanitarianism, and Development* 3 (2012): 473–92.

11 Harold Macmillan, "The Commonwealth: Reflections on Commonwealth and other changes in the post-war world," personal telegram (reply), Mr. Macmillan to Mr. Menzies, February 8, 1962, PREM 11/3644, T51/62.

12 For an excellent discussion of this strategic embrace of decolonization, see Todd Shepard, "Introduction," in *The Invention of Decolonization: The Algerian War and the Remaking of France* (Ithaca, NY: Cornell University Press, 2006), 1–16. See also Camilla Schofield, *Enoch Powell and the Making of Postcolonial Britain* (Cambridge: Cambridge University Press, 2013), 76–139.

13 See Wm. Roger Louis and Ronald Robinson, "The Imperialism of Decolonization," *The Journal of Imperial and Commonwealth History* 22.3 (2008): 462–511.

14 As quoted in Harold Isaacs, *The New World of Negro Americans* (New York: John Day, 1963), 332.

15 There is a rich literature on black internationalism in the Cold War era. See, for instance, Rob Waters, *Thinking Black, Britain 1964–1985* (Berkeley, CA: University of California Press, 2018); Nicholas Grant, *Winning Our Freedoms Together: African Americans and Apartheid, 1945–1960* (Chapel Hill, NC: University of North Carolina Press, 2017); Robin D. G. Kelley and Stephen Tuck

(eds.), *The Other Special Relationship: Race, Rights, and Riots in Britain and the United States* (New York: Palgrave Macmillan, 2015); Matera, *Black London*; Kennetta Hammond Perry, *London is the Place for Me: Black Britons, Citizenship and the Politics of Race* (Oxford: Oxford University Press, 2015); Nico Slate (ed.), *Black Power Beyond Borders: The Global Dimensions of the Black Power Movement* (New York: Palgrave Macmillan, 2012); Penny von Eschen, *Race Against Empire: Black Americans and Anticolonialism, 1937–1957* (Ithaca, NY: Cornell University Press, 1997).

16 David Keane and Annapurna Waughray, *Fifty Years of the International Convention on the Elimination of All Forms of Racial Discrimination: A Living Instrument* (Manchester: Manchester University Press, 2017). For the importance of leadership from the Global South in the human rights revolution, see Jensen, *The Making of International Human Rights*.

17 Karl Ittmann, *A Problem of Great Importance: Population, Race, and Power in the British Empire, 1918–1973* (Berkeley, CA: University of California Press, 2013). On "race suicide" in the early twentieth century, see Gail Bederman, *Manliness and Civilization: A Cultural History of Gender and Race in the United States, 1880–1917* (Chicago: University of Chicago Press, 1995). The racist nature of discourse about world population was not always hidden during the later twentieth century. For instance, in the 1960s, American, British, and South African eugenicists launched the pseudo-academic journal *Mankind Quarterly* in a "shared campaign to defend white supremacy against liberal egalitarianism." The journal was rejected by the vast majority of academic institutions and by the "liberal elite" it pitted itself against. Saul Dubow, "Rhodes Must Fall: Brexit and Circuits of Knowledge and Influence," in Stuart Ward and Astrid Rasch (eds.), *Embers of Empire in Brexit Britain* (London: Bloomsbury, 2019), 111–20 (115).

18 Wendy Webster, "'There'll Always Be England': Representations of Colonial Wars and Immigration, 1948–1968," *Journal of British Studies* 40.4 (2001): 557–84; Frederick Cooper, "Mau Mau and the Discourses of Decolonization," *Journal of African History* 29.2 (1988): 313–20. On the racialization of "modernity," see also Luis White, "The Utopia of Working Phones: Rhodesian Independence and the Place of Race in Decolonization," in Michael D. Gordin, Helen Tilley and Gyan Prakash (eds.), *Utopia/Dystopia: Conditions of Historical Possibility* (Princeton, NJ: Princeton University Press, 2010), 94–116.

19 Joseph Hodge, *The Triumph of the Expert: Agrarian Doctrines of Development and the Legacies of British Colonialism* (Oxford: Oxford University Press, 2007).

20 Haynes, "The Whiteness of Civilization," 325. Recent critical analyses of whiteness and its international dimensions include Gurminder Bhambra, "Trump, Brexit and

'methodological whiteness,'" *British Journal of Sociology* 68.1 (2017): S214–S232; Moonie-Kie Jung, João H. Costa Vargas, and Eduardo Bonilla-Silva (eds.), *State of White Supremacy: Racism, Governance, and the United States* (Stanford, CA: Stanford University Press, 2011).

21 See Perry, *London is the Place for Me*. An extensive literature challenges the notion that black Britons "arrived" with the *Empire Windrush*; see, for instance, the canonical text: Peter Fryer, *Staying Power: The History of Black People in Britain* (Edmonton: University of Alberta Press, 1984). Yet there is little doubt that the 1948 arrival of the *Empire Windrush* has taken on mythic proportions in British cultural memory as the origin story of multiethnic Britain, especially after the mistreatment of black British migrants in the recent "Windrush Scandal."

22 While the 1948 British Nationality Act enshrined into law the right of migrants from the British Empire and the independent states of the Commonwealth to live and work in Britain, it is important to note that restrictions in the 1960s against these migrants were preceded by earlier migration restrictions against British subjects that reveal the long history of racialized logics of Britain as a white nation. See, for instance, the discussion of the Coloured Alien Seamen's Order of 1925 in Laura Tabili, "The Construction of Racial Difference in Twentieth Century Britain: The Special Restriction (Coloured Alien Seaman) Order, 1925," *Journal of British Studies* 33.1 (1994): 54–98.

23 Bill Schwarz, *The White Man's World* (Oxford: Oxford University Press, 2011), 12.

24 Fintan O'Toole, *Heroic Failure: Brexit and the Politics of Pain* (London: Apollo, 2018).

25 Paul Gilroy, *Postcolonial Melancholia* (New York: Columbia University Press, 2004).

26 Wendy Webster, *Englishness and Empire 1939–1965* (Oxford: Oxford University Press, 2005).

27 "Rhodesia: Christmas Postponed," *Time*, November 6, 1964.

28 David M. Anderson, *Histories of the Hanged: Britain's Dirty War in Kenya and the End of the Empire* (London: Weidenfeld and Nicolson, 2005), 3–4. In fact, only 32 civilian deaths were European, compared to 1,800 Africans murdered.

29 Ibid., 1. The novel led to a 1957 film starring Rock Hudson and Sidney Poitier. See David M. Anderson, "Mau Mau at the Movies: Contemporary Representations of a Colonial War," *South African Historical Journal*, May 2003, 71–89; Gerald Horne, *Mau Mau in Harlem? The U.S. and the Liberation of Kenya* (New York: Palgrave Macmillan, 2009).

30 Thomas Borstelmann, *The Cold War and the Color Line: American Race Relations in the Global Arena* (Cambridge, MA: Harvard University Press, 2001), 128–32.

31   As quoted in ibid., 130.

32   Piero Gleijesis, "'Flee! The White Giants Are Coming!': The United States, the Mercenaries and the Congo 1964–1965," in Tom Young (ed.), *Readings in the International Relations of Africa* (Bloomington, IN: Indiana University Press, 2016), 153–64.

33   Enocent Msindo, "'Winning Hearts and Minds:' Crisis and Propaganda in Colonial Zimbabwe," *Journal of Southern African Studies* 35 (2009): 663–81.

34   Schwarz, *White Man's World*, 394–438.

35   Vernon McKay, "The Domino Theory of the Rhodesia Lobby," *Africa Report* (June 1967), 55–8.

36   Gerald Horne, *From the Barrel of a Gun: The United States and the War against Zimbabwe* (Chapel Hill, NC: University of North Carolina Press, 2001).

37   Ibid., 69.

38   "Unfriendly Friends of Rhodesia," *Macleans*, September 3, 1966, 4.

39   *On Target*, June 9, 1967, https://alor.org/Volume3/Vol3No21.htm (accessed June 11, 2019).

40   Kyle Burke, *Revolutionaries for the Right: Anticommunist Internationalism and Paramilitary Warfare in the Cold War* (Chapel Hill, NC: University of North Carolina Press, 2018), 108–12.

41   For example, see Arthur Lewis, "The Zimbabwe Nightmare," *The Citizen*, November 1982, 16–22.

42   John Ismay, "Rhodesia's Dead—But White Supremacists Have Given It New Life Online," *New York Times Magazine*, August 17, 2019, www.nytimes.com/2018/04/10/magazine/rhodesia-zimbabwe-white-supremacists.html (accessed April 15, 2020).

43   "Trump tweets the word 'Africa' for the First Time as President—In Defense of Whites in South Africa," *Washington Post*, August 23, 2018.

44   Tyler Bridges, *The Rise of David Duke* (Jackson, MS: University of Mississippi Press, 1994), 68–71. Quotes from clippings included in *The Crusader*, March 1978. Duke's 1978 visit did not lead to any lasting organizational connections but paved the way for his later alliance with Nick Griffin, who in 1999 became leader of the British National Party. Duke impressed on Griffin the need to appear more moderate and respectable to win electoral success; in 2009, the BBC exposed the two of them at a joint conference advocating ethnic cleansing but stressing the need for white nationalists to use more palatable language.

45   Graham Coddington, "Getting to Know Mr. Right," *The Australian*, February 25, 1998.

46 Daniel Geary and Jennifer Sutton, "Resisting the 'Wind of Change': The White Citizens' Councils and European Decolonization," in Manfred Berg and Cornelius Van Minnen (eds.), *The U.S South and Europe* (Lexington, KY: University of Kentucky Press, 2013), 265–83.

47 Stuart Hall, "The Great Moving Right Show," *Marxism Today* (January 1979): 14–20 (19).

48 Camilla Schofield, "'A Nation or No Nation?': Enoch Powell and Thatcherism," in Ben Jackson and Robert Saunders (eds.), *The Making of Thatcher's Britain* (Cambridge: Cambridge University Press, 2012), 95–110.

49 For an early discussion of how Powell unleashed a new populist politics that would transform British conservativism, see Andrew Gamble, *The Conservative Nation* (London: Routledge and Kegan Paul, 1974).

50 James West, "Hunt the Wizard," *Journal of British Studies*, forthcoming.

51 Due to this confusion, or this assumption that "racial refusal" is synonymous with the end of racism, Goldberg asks, "What residues of racist arrangement and subordination—social, economic, cultural, psychological, legal, and political—linger unaddressed and repressed in singularly stressing racial demise? What doors are thus closed to coming to terms with historical horrors racially inscribed, and what attendant expressions of racial grief and group melancholia, one the one side, and racial self-assertion and triumphalism, on the other, are left unrecognized?" David Theo Goldberg, *The Threat of Race: Reflections on Racial Neoliberalism* (Malden, MA: Blackwell, 2009), 1.

52 Bart Bonikowski, "Ethno-nationalist Populism and the Mobilization of Collective Resentment," *British Journal of Sociology* 68 (2017): S181–S213; Magne Flemmen and Mike Savage, "The Politics of Nationalism and White Racism in the UK," *British Journal of Sociology* 68 (2017): S233–S264.

In the shadow of slavery and empire

1

Black pasts, white nationalist racecraft, and the political work of history

Kennetta Hammond Perry

IN MARCH OF 2016, the then 15-year-old Zyahna Bryant made a successful petition to the local city council in Charlottesville, Virginia to remove a monument of Confederate General Robert E. Lee. In her letter to local leaders, Bryant noted that in addition to being a public site that evoked memories of "physical harm, cruelty, and disenfranchisement" associated with histories of enslavement, it was also a place that represented "the selective display of history in the city."[1] In a later interview she went on to explain her petition was both a response to what the statue represented and a challenge to the "romanticized" historical narratives that she had been exposed to about the Civil War which transformed personalities like Lee into figures for uncritical celebration rather than scrutiny and rebuke.[2] Essentially, Bryant understood that the presence of the statue as part of the design of the city represented an ongoing battleground of ideas and memories which framed a larger story about race, and more specifically, histories of white supremacy in America. And it was this deeply rooted political contest over history, history making, and the uses of the past that underpinned the racist violence of the Unite the Right rally which ultimately resulted in the death of Heather Heyer on August 12, 2017.

Originally published in 1935, the final chapter of W. E. B. Du Bois's *Black Reconstruction*, aptly titled "the propaganda of history," offered a scathing critique of the state of historical writing about the Civil War and Reconstruction.[3] By foregrounding the role of slavery and the perspectives of freedpeople in shaping this transformative period in American history, Du Bois's magisterial study challenged the dominant historical consensus at the time. In his closing chapter, he drew critical attention to a consistent refrain in the historiography that regarded Black people's contributions to and presence within American history as negligible at best, but more often than not, maligned or completely absent. Beginning with a survey of textbooks from the era in which he was writing, Du Bois outlined recurring themes in the historical scholarship on Reconstruction that portrayed its failures as the fault of ignorant and incompetent newly freed people in the South, unfit and ill prepared to be a part of American governance. Likewise, he argued that the lack of emphasis on the centrality of the future of slavery as the underlying cause of the Civil War, and the omission of the role that freedpeople played as architects of their own emancipation, created a flawed, inaccurate, and "dangerous" interpretation of one of the most transformative moments in the history of American nation making.[4]

For Du Bois, narratives of Reconstruction provided an important barometer for measuring how the historical profession—as both a set of disciplinary practices and practitioners—contributed to a broader civic ideal of cultivating a citizenry empowered to aim for a more democratic, anti-racist future.[5] And in that regard, he insisted that historical writing as a professional enterprise had failed. Du Bois highlighted what he judged as a persistent tendency to craft history in a way that glossed over unpleasant realities and omitted ugly and or unflattering truths. Inviting his readers to consider the stakes of whitewashing history in a way that "paints perfect men and noble nations, but … does not tell the truth," Du Bois argued that the consequences of selective remembrance had implications in the present.[6] To illustrate this point, he explained that one could easily go through the American education system "without any idea of the part which the black race has played in America; of the tremendous moral problem of abolition; of the cause and meaning of the Civil War and the relation which Reconstruction had to democratic government and the labor movement today."[7] In Du Bois's view, this could be attributed to a persistent and ahistorical refusal to acknowledge the value of Black humanity. And this was indeed an epistemic issue that he believed reflected myths of Black inferiority that were then weaponized to imagine Black people as a problem to be controlled, disavowed, and left barren of rights in an effort to uphold the socio-economic infrastructure of a type of racecraft rooted in the white nationalist ideology that underwrote the post-slavery regimes of Jim Crow America.[8]

Writing more than five decades after the publication of *Black Reconstruction*, in the introduction to his now classic text on race and nation, *There Ain't No Black in the Union Jack*, published in 1987, Paul Gilroy deployed Du Bois's insights on the relationship between Black people's imagined "problem" status and the ideological fictions about the past—or what Du Bois termed "the propaganda of history." Citing Du Bois's original formulation of this issue in his 1903 text, *The Souls of Black Folk*, as he asked his readers to ponder "How does it feel to be a problem?," Gilroy insisted that racism lived and regenerated itself in various forms over time in part through its "capacity to evacuate any historical dimension to black life" and continually strip Black people of any degree of historical agency or social value.[9] Acknowledging the differences in time and space that separated the world of 1980s Britain from that of Du Bois in early twentieth-century America, Gilroy nonetheless found a degree of continuity in the ways in which an assemblage of systematic exclusions, "strategic silences," and intentional denials of the historical conditions of Black life operated to inform how racism worked as a vehicle to marginalize, demean, and invalidate claims to citizenship and other forms of political and cultural participation in civil society.[10]

In wrestling with the cultural politics of race and nation that positioned Blackness as a contradiction to Britishness, Gilroy's work did not necessarily center an historical recovery of the presence, contributions, and experiences of Black people in British society. However, he most certainly offered fertile ground to consider how the histories that we do and do not tell are signifiers of a broader racialized power structure that can shore up one's ability to imagine and access belonging, rights and cultural space within the political economy of nations. To be sure, Gilroy was indeed critical of the homogenizing and reductive effects of thinking with and through the frame of the nation. But it is important to note his insistence on turning toward Black cultural formations as a means of exposing and countering the limits of what he described as forms of "ethnic absolutism" that oftentimes accompanied notions of national belonging in ways that bolstered ahistorical ideas equating whiteness with Britishness. In this sense, rather than completely dispensing with nation, Gilroy calls for a re-examination of British culture and history that accounts for the imperial, diasporic, and global encounters, interfaces, networks, and relations of power that have shaped the formation of race and racism, as well as the idea and experience of national un/belonging in Britain over time.[11]

Anticipating later work, including Michel-Rolph Trouillout's *Silencing the Past*, Du Bois and Gilroy grappled with how the questions we ask, the stories we tell, our methods of inquiry and interpretation, the constitution of the historical guild, as well as our conception of the past and its utility in the present have political consequences.[12] Moreover, their work speaks to the ways in which these dynamics are deeply implicated in the ideological artifices that structure how racism and white supremacy have operated over time to (re)create, rationalize, and routinize inequities and denials of justice, inclusion, and the civic rights and privileges associated with national belonging. This essay invokes Du Bois and Gilroy's ideas about the politics of historical praxis to examine the cultivation and proliferation of what I am terming white nationalist racecraft. While Barbara Fields and Karen Fields introduce the concept of racecraft to capture the ways in which the illusion of race is made and retrofitted in different sociohistorical context through the work of racism, here I would like to dwell on the ways in which particular fictions about race, nation, and the attributes of whiteness are mobilized in and through the circulation and retellings of historical narratives about a collective national past where the conditions of Black humanity are disavowed—known yet unspoken—and/or rendered inessential or absent.[13] While the following chapters largely explore white supremacist ideologies activated by individuals and networks with a stated or explicit political interest in Black disempowerment, this essay raises questions about how whiteness, as a proxy for claim making, is produced discursively through the craft and creation of historical writing and assemblages where Black people and their lived experiences are repressed, negated, or misremembered.

On October 18, 2018 the Royal Historical Society released the findings of research undertaken by a special working group convened to study and develop recommendations to address the persistence of racial and ethnic inequality in the discipline of history with particular attention to higher education in the U.K. Unsurprisingly, the report insisted that "a White-centred and Eurocentric curriculum is a racial problem within the discipline."[14] In highlighting these concerns, the RHS report offered a series of timely recommendations aimed at spurring action on a range of different levels. Citing an acute underrepresentation of Black students and staff in departments, in terms of specific curricular interventions that could potentially have cascading effects on the overall landscape in the profession, one of the recommendations included addressing the curricular "absences of Black British history." The report found that while over 40 percent of all U.K.-based historians specialize in British history, the representation of histories of Black and racially minoritized communities in Britain remained largely absent in the curriculum at all levels. When those histories did appear, as Paul Gilroy suggested two decades earlier, the report explained that Black people often entered the narrative only through the narrow prism of an abolitionist-oriented history of colonial enslavement and exploitation.[15]

If we take Black history in the terms outlined by Du Bois and Gilroy as a means of acknowledging the existential value of Black humanity and engaging the conditions that have shaped the making of Black life as ingredients for understanding the contours of the nation, one has to consider the stakes of the relative absence of Black British history as an institutionalized field of inquiry and as an educational and political resource in British society.[16] What does this absence tell us about the status of Black people in British society and how race and racism work in relation to the idea and historical portrayal of Britain as a white nation in our present moment? How can attending to and interrogating the making of these absences provide a site to begin to map some of the structural impediments that prevent a basic recognition of long-standing racial inequalities? And what does Black Britain's absence from historical narratives of the nation inhibit in terms of a collective reckoning with the violence and precarity associated with the racialization of citizenship and modes of national belonging and unfreedom, past and present?

The RHS report's recommendations offered little more than a call to go beyond some of the limited frames in which Black people typically populate British history. However, here I would like to explore some of the particulars of imagining the content of a historical praxis that centers Black lives and lived experiences as both agents in the making of Britain as an imperial nation-state and as conduits for interpreting the relationship between race and claims to citizenship and other pathways of national belonging and civic inclusion.[17] Just as Du Bois recognized that the narratives that defined our collective understanding of the significance of chattel slavery and the terms of abolition could be mobilized as proxies for legitimating and retooling white supremacist claims and structures over time in an American context, the remainder of this essay explores this idea in relation to Britain. British historians including Catherine Hall have called for a more rigorous reconsideration of Britain's "massive debt to slavery" and self-congratulatory narratives of British abolitionism as a means of historicizing the links between race and nation.[18] I want to take this up to explore how the very process of producing narratives of slavery in Britain tethered to anti-slavery and abolitionism is a project that has been mired in constructing, authorizing, and memorializing the imagined virtues of whiteness—moral, benevolent, innocent, and humanitarian— as integral to the story of the British nation. To be sure, this national myth making is predicated on silencing and/or misremembering the experiences of the enslaved and the racialized violence of enslavement as a means to bolster and rationalize white supremacy as a logic of governance. And as a result, conventional narratives of British abolitionism disavow or fail to reckon with a national Black past rooted in the entangled colonial and metropolitan geographies of empire that accounts for the violence, disenfranchisement, and forms of social and civic death that survived the ending of slavery and continue to shape a legacy of anti-Black racism and precarious Black freedom in Britain in the present. This too is part of the unwelcomed and unreconciled indebtedness that Britain has to slavery which informs how race structures the present and anticipates the future.[19]

* * *

Unquestionably, 2007 was the year of abolition in Britain. From the highest reaches of government to locally sponsored events including community discussions, film screenings, and public exhibitions, commemorations of the bicentenary of the passage of the Abolition of the Slave Trade Act in 1807 abounded as sites of national interest. In addition to the opening of major exhibits in Parliament, the British Empire and Commonwealth Museum, the Docklands Museum, the Royal Navy Museum, and the newly minted International Slavery Museum in Liverpool, timed to open during the bicentenary, commemorations of the abolition of the slave trade also took place as part of a national service of commemoration held in Westminster Abbey, at local events including a ceremony at the tomb of an enslaved African, Scipio Africanus, in Bristol, and on the big screen with the release of the major box office feature, *Amazing Grace*.

At the heart of many of these projects was a desire to highlight the role that British anti-slavery advocates played in pressuring Parliament to outlaw the international trafficking of human beings and indicting the conditions that made the slave trade possible and profitable as a business venture. In this vein, the cause of anti-slavery was remembered as a campaign that mobilized a broad cross-section of British society including well-known political figures like William Wilberforce and Thomas Buxton, as well as men and women of the working classes.[20] Moreover, in addition to framing abolitionism as a mass movement and a national campaign that drew support from virtually every sector of British society, many of the most prominently reviewed exhibitions gave special attention to the efforts of freed Black abolitionists, including Olaudah Equiano and Ignatius Sancho, as well as the overt resistance of the enslaved in forwarding the cause of abolitionism. In an official publication released by the Department for Culture, Media and Sport, the British government declared, "The people who fought against slavery came from all walks of life, including slaves and former slaves, church leaders and the countless ordinary British citizens who signed petitions, marched, lobbied and prayed for change."[21]

To be sure, a key theme in the scholarship on the abolition of both the slave trade in 1807 and the institution of slavery in the British Empire with the 1833 Abolition Act involves a set of historiographical debates that have largely turned on discussions about the interests of a widening sphere of stakeholders—the enslaved, evangelicals, capitalists, humanitarians, freed black activists, politicians, disenfranchised workers, women, and most recently, those who applied for and received compensation for lost property under the terms of the Abolition Act of 1833.[22] In many ways the terms of this ongoing debate within the historiography can be traced to the publication of Eric Williams's seminal study, *Capitalism and Slavery*, in 1944. Arguably, while there are aspects of Williams's text that have undergone significant scrutiny in the historical scholarship—namely his contention that slavery as an economic institution was in a state of decline in the years leading up to British abolition—there are several pillars of his thesis about the relationship between slavery and the rise of industrial capitalism that continue to hold sway.[23] In particular, there is an ample body of scholarship that supports Williams's argument that chattel slavery and the transatlantic slave trade laid the foundation for industrial capitalism.[24] Likewise, as it relates to the question of abolition, Williams's framing of abolitionism as an ideological, political, social, and economic project that involved competing interests and a variety of stakeholders, including the enslaved, rather than being a battle of wills between "saints and sinners," stands as a critical touchstone in understanding both the evolving scholarship and commemorative practices related to British anti-slavery activism in the late eighteenth and early nineteenth centuries. Upending the dominant historiography of British abolitionism in an age of decolonization, Williams's magnum opus stands as one of the first scholarly appraisals to challenge self-congratulatory Victorian narratives of abolitionism predicated on recalling an anti-slavery past in which white, Christian, bourgeois reformers like William Wilberforce rallied tirelessly in opposition to the amoral and inhumane exploitation of Black bodies. Instead, Williams argued that "the inhumanity of West Indian slavery" was not always at the forefront of anti-slavery advocates' agendas, and persuasively demonstrated that abolition did not unfold as a strictly humanitarian cause but was championed by those deeply vested in the entangled routines of empire, racial capitalism, and white supremacy.[25]

In the aftermath of the 2007 bicentenary, a number of historians have taken stock of what the nation remembered about the history of slavery and abolition, and what was obscured, forgotten, and disavowed as part of the democratization of the legacy of abolitionism as an all-encompassing national cause.[26] What is notable is that even as national narratives of abolitionism have become more adept at depicting slavery and, in particular, the business of the slave trade as institutions that engulfed all aspects of British life, the memory of abolition persists as a redemptive liberal political achievement of freedom, a turning point of sorts, that absolved the nation of its former sins. In a reconsideration of the memory work associated with bicentenary events held throughout the British Isles, historian Diana Paton notes that even in the midst of concerted efforts to take heed of Eric Williams's contention that the efforts of the enslaved were critical in effecting abolition, those seeking to represent the past should still "be concerned about the ease with which a teleological story of slavery into freedom slips from the pages of history into museum galleries, school curricula and political speeches" as part of narratives of abolition. More specifically, in her final evaluation of the ways that the activism of enslaved people and freed Black anti-slavery advocates was co-opted into the national story of abolition, Paton surmised,

> The year 2007 demonstrated the relative ease with which the stories of enslaved resistance and black abolitionism can be integrated into a wider narrative that emphasizes liberal humanitarianism. Other stories which emphasize the damage done by enslavement, the problematic outcomes of anti-slavery governmental action and the power relations that remained in place after slavery in its Atlantic

form was left behind have proved much harder to present as public history, yet are at least as significant.[27]

Paton's insightful observations draw attention to the ways in which the framing of Britain's relationship to slavery through the narrative lens of abolition has created a limited field of vision for understanding the conditions of enslavement and the perspectives of the enslaved as people who had the closest proximity to the transitions that abolition signaled. In this paradigm, rightfully, the role of the enslaved, typically by way of their overt resistance to the conditions of slavery or their involvement in anti-slavery activism, is acknowledged as pertinent to the campaign for abolition, but only in as much as it serves to realize the end of slavery and a clear break from all that slavery entailed. In the process, the experience of enslavement, and more specifically the violent and exploitative imperial racial order that survived and thrived in new forms after abolition, is at best not fully accounted for; and at worst, it is a history that is silenced or disavowed as part of a memory-making process that continually relegates the institution of slavery and its remnants as something "past."

Essentially, in these terms, abolitionism functions as a means of marking a temporal line of demarcation—a before and after—that provides a type of national absolution for slavery and the racial regimes that it simultaneously depended upon and reinforced, without any attention to the continuities in the organization of imperial power.[28] For the formerly enslaved, abolition engendered what Thomas Holt described as "the problem of freedom," a post-emancipation conundrum that reconstituted the racial prescriptions of white colonial power that defined enslavement to render Black lives vulnerable to violence, alienated from rights and legal standing, and on the periphery of civic representation as an ongoing condition to preserve a social system and everyday routines premised upon the maintenance of white supremacy.[29]

So how do we work to rewrite and decolonize British histories of slavery and abolition in a way that reckons with enslavement and its connections to the conditions of Black life past and present? How do we write against a vindicationist history of nostalgic white abolitionism to center the experiences of the enslaved and open up ways of mobilizing Black histories that account for the persistence of white nationalist racecraft and anti-Black racism in the present as a part of the racial inheritance of slavery?[30] How do we begin to read the conditions of Black life historically as an opening to understand the failures of abolition?

In her 2012 work, *Sites of Slavery*, Salamishah Tillet posits that the sites where histories of slavery are commemorated materially and/or ideologically are contested spaces that can offer crucial links between a sense of the collective national past and the extant realities and contradictions of race, citizenship, and national belonging. Not only do they recover histories of slavery in and for the present, but she argues that the ways in which they are claimed and interpreted can also provide a type of national recognition for the enslaved and for those still grappling with the racial legacies of slavery through contemporary forms of "civic estrangement" that reproduce alienation from the legal parameters of citizenship as well as the social, cultural, and affective modalities of national representation and recognition.[31] Tillet's work provides a number of object lessons for reclaiming, reinterpreting, and recontextualizing the "sites of slavery" beyond an abolitionist end, that acknowledges the utility of Black lives in British history as conduits for understanding the structure of race and the colonial order on both sides of the Atlantic during and after the period of enslavement.[32]

In exploring the purchase of Tillet's arguments regarding the relationship between the ways that we interpret the sites of slavery's representation and the types of political claims that can be articulated in the present about the historical dimensions of contemporary anti-Black racism in Britain, one of the sites that might be considered is *The History of Mary Prince, A West Indian Slave*, one of the earliest narratives of enslaved life in the British Empire published by a Black woman.[33] Mary Prince was born enslaved in Bermuda and spent several years in Antigua before she was brought to London as the property of James Wood in 1828. Laboring unwaged in London, she remained in the Wood household in London for less than a year before leaving and finding refuge in the local Moravian church, where she eventually met Thomas Pringle, an active member of the Anti-Slavery Society. With Pringle's urging, Prince agreed to have her life chronicled and published in 1831 as *The History of Mary Prince*, a text that remains one of the few slave narratives in the Black British literary canon.[34] In 2007, the Nubian Jak Community Trust honored Mary Prince with a commemorative blue plaque in Bloomsbury where she once resided. Additionally, in that same year as part of the commemorations of British abolitionism, the Docklands Museum exhibit *London, Sugar and Slavery* recognized her as "an author who played a crucial role in the abolition campaign."[35] But just as Prince's history is remembered as part of the British anti-slavery campaign that appropriated her narrative to forward an abolitionist cause, it can also be read as a text that places the institution of slavery, the condition of the enslaved, and the limits of Black freedom squarely within the landscapes of metropolitan Britain.

Much of what has been written about the *History of Mary Prince* has focused on issues of authenticity, narrative voice, and depictions of slavery in the Caribbean.[36] However, an alternative reading of Prince's story, focused on what it reveals about the precarious nature of Black freedom in metropolitan Britain—precisely when it was imagined by anti-slavery advocates as a locale where slavery was intolerable and incompatible with the prescriptions of English common law—offers a means of seeing it as a post-abolitionist commentary. In this light it can be read as a text that foreshadowed the inability of the legal abolition of slavery to rectify the abject status of the enslaved, as it kept the racial hierarchies that governed empire intact in the colonies and the metropole. Just as anti-slavery advocates campaigning in the world where Prince told her story of enslavement used constructions of slavery and freedom to mark the boundaries between colony and metropole, throughout the narrative Prince juxtaposes her life as a slave in the Caribbean colonies with her life in England. In contrast to the violent punitive conditions that she recounts defining her enslavement before her arrival in London, she asserts an awareness that the metropole conferred a somewhat different status for the enslaved. When faced with a decision to remain in the Woods' household under conditions that involved enduring verbal abuse and physical labor that often left her body riddled with excruciating pain due to her rheumatism, she declared, "I knew I was free in England, but I did not know where to go, or how to get my living; and therefore, I did not like to leave the house."[37] Likewise, in the text, as Prince debated whether or not she should "go and try what freedom would do" for her in England and flee the Wood household, she makes it clear that Mr. and Mrs. Wood were also conscious of the contingencies of Black freedom in England that presented obstacles to her survival, including being a stranger and having no attachments.[38] And despite having to operate as slave owners under a different legal structure from the colonies, they too were still well aware of how the precarities of Black freedom in the metropole reinforced their power as property owners who could continue to exploit, demean, and exercise violence against the enslaved.

Mary Prince's story reminds us that slavery was not a British imperial institution that happened in the colonies. Instead, from its inception, it was something that was also a part of metropolitan life.[39] In rethinking her narrative as one that depicts the contingencies of Black freedom as shaped by the ongoing stain of her formerly enslaved status rather than simply a call for abolition, historians might be able to erect British histories that would emphasize the machinations of violence, pain, dislocation, and terror as well as strategies of resistance, protest, and survival that marked the conditions of Black life over time and in the transition from slavery to what many might consider a still-elusive Black freedom. If one begins to write against an abolitionist end using the lives of the enslaved, one can more clearly see how the demise of slavery transformed legal codes, but merely recalibrated the imperial social order that relegated Black people to an inferior status, with ideas of freedom hanging in the balance. Using the conditions of enslavement as a starting point, rather than as a means to a predetermined abolitionist end, we can see with greater clarity how the acquisition of wages did not necessarily equate to freedom for the formerly enslaved. From this vantage point, we are in a better position to ask more about what stayed the same and persisted over time rather than what ended. Essentially, in reckoning with the imperial conditions of enslavement—with enslaved people's lives at the fore—we open up some of the dangerous foreclosures that have attempted to write the conditions of white supremacy that produced anti-Black violence and dispossession out of British history. Ironically, it is precisely this erasure that provides currency for sustaining the relationship between imagining the virtues of whiteness and Britishness that systematically and strategically excludes histories of Black Britain from the cultural and political life of the nation.[40]

* * *

In August of 2019, as part of building a platform to launch his bid for re-election in 2020, London mayor Sadiq Khan publicly endorsed a proposal by the Fabian Society to establish a British slavery museum in London, which he described as a "timely" resource for fighting "racism and hatred in all its forms."[41] In outlining the proposal, Omar Khan, director of the Runnymede Trust, one of Britain's most influential race equality think tanks, explained that the museum's potential cultural and political work would be twofold. Not only would it offer a site of knowledge about and acknowledgment of the fundamental role that cities like London and imperial nations like Britain played in facilitating and benefitting from the atrocities associated with centuries of involvement in the transatlantic slave trade, but it could also provide a historical context for cultivating the necessary political will to address the persistence of racial inequities that maintain white privilege. Whereas commemorations of (white) British abolitionism abounded in the national narrative, Omar Khan suggested that this new project should speak directly to "the history of enslave-ment." In doing so, he suggested that in the process of grappling with the conditions of enslavement, contemporary audiences might be better equipped to identify the "historic origins of racism" and make connections between the racial logics that were devised to justify the exploitation of colonial laborers and those which continue to work in the present to struc-ture discriminatory practices, policies, and institutions to the detriment of people of color in Britain.[42]

One could easily argue that the presence of a museum dedicated to countering the myth making that has positioned British abolitionism as a national triumph is not an antidote for the entrenched structural pro-cesses and frameworks that undergird how racism works as a function of

Western capitalism to produce disparities in access to public resources, earning potential, rights, routes to social mobility, and a sense of security.[43] However, one cannot dismiss the role of knowledge production and justice-oriented educational praxis as a tool of anti-racist political engagement. At its best, it provides a powerful means of consciousness raising that can stimulate a more critical interrogation of the evidence that frames the terms of the debate about what the nation is, how its power has been constituted over time, and whose interests its collective resources should be designed to serve and perhaps redress. Likewise, as this essay has attempted to suggest, the absence of counternarratives portends its own political project that can be wielded to shore up the distortions and denials that white nationalist racecraft breeds to justify its existence and claims to legitimacy.

It is useful to think about recent public discussions regarding the representation of histories of slavery and the conditions of enslavement as part of an ongoing dialogue about how racism operates through sites of knowledge production and exchange. In 2015 this debate gained widespread media attention in the U.K. in the wake of protests by Oxford University students adopting the Rhodes Must Fall movement. Like a number of campaigns in recent years at institutions in the U.S. including Brown, Harvard, Rutgers, and the University of North Carolina at Chapel Hill, which invoked critiques of the built environment as a proxy to open up a wider dialogue about the legacies of slavery and the machinations of institutional racism within the higher education landscape, the Rhodes Must Fall movement began at the University of Cape Town in South Africa in an effort to remove the statue of Cecil Rhodes.[44] As a figure who unabashedly trafficked in nineteenth-century white supremacist discourses of manifest destiny to justify the plunder, conquest, and exploitation of southern African land and labor, for students involved in the campaign, Rhodes's statue served as a physical space marking the university's investment in commemorating a legacy of anti-Black imperial violence, one with residual effects that were still a palpable part of the student experience in the present.[45]

As this movement took shape and began to attract attention internationally, one of the core issues focused upon the need to decolonize the curriculum to re-examine the content, narrative schemas, pedagogical approaches, academic representation, and underlying disciplinary conventions driving knowledge exchange and production in the university setting.[46] To capture this multifaceted dialogue, one of the guiding questions became "Why is my curriculum white?," as organizers identified the curriculum as a field of power relations that reinforced racial hierarchies. In this process, whiteness—in the form of a Eurocentric curriculum delivered as universalist in a higher education landscape with an abysmal number of non-white staff—assumed a position as the most legitimate purveyor of knowledge and an agent of an imperial benevolence that had been graciously extended to lesser races through various British colonial projects.[47] By marking the whiteness of the curriculum—its design, its architects, and its underlying narrative structure—these campaigns continue to serve as a stark reminder of the various ways in which ideologies of white supremacy get articulated and reproduced as a commonplace feature of an educational system invested in cultivating redemptive national myths about a colonial past-present where the conditions of Black life are rendered illegible, inconsequential, or peripheral to understanding the collective historical foundations that constitute what the nation is, and perhaps more importantly what it should be. Therefore, at a conjuncture when the terms of reference for making claims of citizenship and belonging within the body of the nation are in a perilous state of flux, engaging with what is absent in our histories of the nation is an urgent and necessary agenda for the present.

Notes

1 Zyahna Bryant, "Letter to the Editor," www.change.org/p/charlottesville-city-council-change-the-name-of-lee-park-and-remove-the-statue-in-charlottesville-va (accessed February 7, 2020).

2 Amdé Mengistu, "This Teenager Made History and Pissed Off Racists Everywhere," *Vice*, February 27, 2018, www.vice.com/en_uk/article/8xdkj5/this-teenager-made-history-and-pissed-off-racists-everywhere (accessed February 7, 2020); see also Julian Maxwell Hayter, "Charlottesville Was About Memory, Not Monuments: Why Our History Educations Must Be Better," *Washington Post*, August 10, 2018,

www.washingtonpost.com/news/made-by-history/wp/2018/08/10/charlottesvi
lle-was-about-memory-not-monuments/ (accessed February 7, 2020).

3 W. E. B. Du Bois, *Black Reconstruction in America* (New York: The Free Press,
   1992), 711–29.

4 Du Bois, *Black Reconstruction*, 723.

5 Other works that have taken up some of these issues about the role of history and
   historians since Du Bois include Marc Bloch, *The Historians' Craft* (Manchester:
   Manchester University Press, 1992); John Lewis Gaddis, *The Landscape of History:
   How Historians Map the Past* (New York: Oxford University Press, 2004); John
   Tosh (ed.), *Historians on History* (New York: Routledge, 2018); Peter Novick,
   That Noble Dream: The 'Objectivity Question' and the American Historical Profession
   (Cambridge: Cambridge University Press, 1988); Joan Scott, *Gender and the Politics
   of History* (New York: Columbia University Press, 1999); Lynn Hunt, *History: Why
   It Matters* (Cambridge: Polity Press, 2018).

6 Du Bois, *Black Reconstruction*, 722.

7 Du Bois, *Black Reconstruction*, 713.

8 Karen E. Fields and Barbara Fields, *Racecraft: The Soul of Inequality in American
   Life.* (London: Verso, 2012), 19. Fields and Fields employ the term racecraft as
   a means of capturing the historically conditioned interdependence of race and
   racism. These authors define it as a term that does not attempt to replace racism
   but rather to provide "a kind of fingerprint evidence that racism has been on the
   scene." They use it to mark the types of cultural, political and social positioning
   that necessitate the production of race.

9 W. E. B. Du Bois, *The Souls of Black Folk* (Mineola, NY: Dover Publications, 1994),
   p. 1; Paul Gilroy, *There Ain't No Black in the Union Jack: The Cultural Politics of Race
   and Nation* (Chicago: University of Chicago Press, 1991), 11.

10 Gilroy, *There Ain't No Black in the Union Jack*, 11–12.

11 Gilroy, *There Ain't No Black in the Union Jack*, chs. 2 and 5.

12 Michel-Rolph Trouillout, *Silencing the Past: Power and the Production of History*
    (New York: Beacon, 1997); see also Dipesh Chakrabarty, "Postcoloniality and the
    Artifice of History: Who Speaks for the 'Indian' Past," *Representations* 37 (winter,
    1992): 1–26.

13 Fields and Fields, *Racecraft*, chs. 1 and 2. My thinking about the term "disavowal"
    here is informed by Stuart Hall. See Stuart Hall with Bill Schwarz, *Familiar Stranger:
    A Life Between Two Islands* (Durham, NC: Duke University Press, 2017), 100.

14 Royal Historical Society, *Race, Ethnicity and Equality: A Report and Resource for
    Change* (London: Royal Historical Society, 2018), 23. In pursuing this work, the
    RHS explored issues of diversity and inclusion that had long been on the agenda

of organizations including the Black and Asian Studies Association. Hereafter referred to as RHS Report.

15 RHS Report, 83. See also Meleisa Ono-George's important essay addressing the parallel conversations that need to be had about the absence of Black British history and the lack of Black historians in UK universities. Ono-George notes that it is highly unlikely that an undergraduate student "studying the history of Britain will encounter a Black historian, in print or in person, in UK universities," an issue that she notes is indicative of "a larger and more pernicious issue of inequalities within the study of history in UK higher education." Meleisa Ono-George, "'Power in the Telling': Community-Engaged Histories of Black Britain," *History Workshop Online*, November 18, 2019, www.historyworkshop.org.uk/power-in-the-telling/ (accessed December 5, 2019).

16 It should be noted that the argument here is about the wider institutionalization of this field rather than the existence of a robust historiography that clearly establishes its contours. Key texts include Folarin Shyllon, *Black People in Britain, 1555–1833* (Oxford: Oxford University Press, 1977); Peter Fryer, *Staying Power* (London: Pluto Press, 1984); Ron Ramdin, *The Making of the Black Working Class in Britain* (London: Gower, 1987); Gretchin Gerzina, *Black London: Life Before Emancipation* (New Brunswick, NJ: Rutgers University Press, 1995); Norma Myers, *Reconstructing the Black Past: Blacks in Britain, 1780–1830* (London: Frank Cass, 1996); Jeffrey Green, *Black Edwardians Black People in Britain, 1901–1914* (London: Routledge, 1998); Hakim Adi, *West Africans in Britain, 1900–1960* (London: Lawrence and Wishart, 1998); Caroline Bressey and Hakim Adi, *Belonging in Europe: The African Diaspora and Work* (London: Routledge, 2013); Marc Matera, *Black London* (Berkeley, CA: University of California Press, 2015); Kennetta Hammond Perry, *London is the Place for Me: Black Britons, Citizenship and the Politics of Race* (New York: Oxford University Press, 2016); David Olusoga, *Black and British* (London: Macmillan, 2016); Miranda Kaufmann, *Black Tudors* (London: One World, 2017); Rob Waters, *Thinking Black: Britain, 1964–1985* (Oakland, CA: University of California Press, 2019); Onyeka Nubia, *England's Other Countrymen: Black Tudor Society* (London: Zed Books, 2019); Hakim Adi (ed.), *Black British History: New Perspectives from Roman Times to the Present Day* (London: Zed Books, 2019). Additionally it should be noted that at the time of this writing, there exists an MRes course in the History of Africa and the African Diaspora at Chichester University and there are plans to develop an MA course in Black British history at Goldsmiths University to begin in 2020.

17 On this framing of the relationship between Britain as empire and Britain as nation I borrow from Gary Wilder, *The French Imperial Nation-State: Negritude and*

Colonial Humanism Between the Two World Wars (Chicago: University of Chicago Press, 2005).

18 Catherine Hall, "Britain's Massive Debt to Slavery," *Guardian*, February 27, 2013, www.theguardian.com/commentisfree/2013/feb/27/britain-debt-slavery-made-public (accessed May 2, 2020), and Catherine Hall, "Troubling Memories: Nineteenth Century Histories of the Slave Trade and Slavery," *Transactions of the Royal Historical Society* 21 (2011): 147–69. It is important to note that Hall and her colleagues make a distinction between their project's attention to integrating the history of slave ownership into modern British history and the larger agenda of integrating slavery as a type of antidote to triumphant narratives of abolition. See also Catherine Hall et al. *Legacies of British Slave Ownership: Colonial Slavery and the Formation of Victorian Britain* (Cambridge: Cambridge University Press, 2014), 5. William Pettigrew makes a similar point about interrogating the history of the politics of the slave trade. See William Pettigrew, *Freedom's Debt: The Royal Africa Company and Politics of the Atlantic Slave Trade, 1672–1752* (Chapel Hill, NC: University of North Carolina Press, 2013), 8. However, here I am trying to explicitly think about what it would mean to expand the connections between slavery and modern British history to account for experiences of enslavement.

19 Barnor Hesse, "Forgotten Like a Bad Dream: Atlantic Slavery and the Ethic of Postcolonial Memory," in David Theo Goldberg and Ato Quayson (eds.), *Relocating Postcolonialism* (New York: Oxford University Press, 2002), 143–73, On the afterlives of slavery, see Saidiya Hartman, *Lose Your Mother: A Journey Along the Atlantic Slave Route* (New York: Farrar, Straus, and Giroux, 2008); Brian Connolly and Marisa Fuentes, "Introduction: From Archives of Slavery to Liberated Futures," *History of the Present* 6.2 (2016): 105–16.

20 Geoffrey Cubitt, "Museums and Slavery in Britain: The Bicentenary of 1807," in Ana Lucia Araujo (ed.), *Politics of Memory: Making Slavery Visible in the Public Space* (New York: Routledge, 2012), 159–77.

21 DCMS, "Reflecting on the Past and Looking to the Future: The 2007 Bicentenary of the Abolition of the Slave Trade in the British Empire," 2007.

22 Key works in this vein include but are not limited to Eric Williams, *Capitalism and Slavery* (Chapel Hill, NC: University of North Carolina Press, 1944); Roger Anstey, *The Atlantic Slave Trade and British Abolition, 1760–1810* (London: Humanities Press, 1975); Seymour Drescher, *Capitalism and Anti-Slavery: British Mobilization in Comparative Perspective* (New York: Oxford University Press, 1987); David Turley, *The Culture of English Anti-Slavery, 1780–1860* (London: Routledge, 1991); J. R. Oldfield, *Popular Politics and British Anti-Slavery: The Mobilisation of Public Opinion Against the Slave Trade, 1787–1807* (Manchester: Manchester University

Press, 1995); Claire Midgley, *Women Against Slavery: The British Campaigns, 1780–1870* (London: Routledge, 1995); Christopher Leslie Brown, *Moral Capital: The Foundations of British Abolitionism* (Chapel Hill, NC: University of North Carolina Press, 2006); David Brion Davis, *Inhuman Bondage: The Rise and Fall of Slavery in the New World* (New York: Oxford University Press, 2006); Robin Blackburn, *The Overthrow of Colonial Slavery, 1776–1848* (London: Verso, 2011); Nicholas Draper, *The Price of Emancipation: Slave-Ownership, Compensation and British Society at the End of Slavery* (Cambridge: Cambridge University Press, 2010); Manisha Sinha, *The Slave's Cause: A History of Abolition* (New Haven, CT: Yale University Press, 2016).

23 The best-known rebuke of aspects of the Williams thesis is captured in Seymour Drescher's *Econocide: British Slavery in the Era of Abolition* (Pittsburgh, PA: University of Pittsburgh Press, 1977). However, work by Selwyn Carrington and David Beck Ryden's more recent study offer evidence in support of Williams's thesis regarding the economic viability of slavery during the era of abolition. See Selwyn Carrington, *The Sugar Industry and the Abolition of the Slave Trade* (Gainesville, FL: University of Florida Press, 2002); David Beck Ryden, *West Indian Slavery and British Abolition, 1783–1807* (Cambridge: Cambridge University Press, 2010).

24 Joseph Inikori, *Africans and the Industrial Revolution in England: A Study in International Trade and Economic Development* (Cambridge: Cambridge University Press, 2002). More recent studies which draw upon the Williams thesis focusing on economic development in the U.S. include Sven Beckhart, *Empire of Cotton: A Global History* (New York: Vintage, 2015); Edward Baptist, *The Half Has Never Been Told: Slavery and the Making of American Capitalism* (New York: Basic Books, 2016).

25 Williams, *Capitalism and Slavery*, ch. 11. On the relationship between the historical co-production of racism and systems of capitalist exploitation past and present, see Gargi Bhattacharyya, *Rethinking Racial Capitalism: Questions of Reproduction and Survival* (London: Rowman and Littlefield International, 2018).

26 Some examples include Catherine Hall, "Afterward: Britain 2007: Problematising History," in Cora Kaplan and John Oldfield (eds.), *Imagining Transatlantic Slavery* (Basingstoke: Palgrave, 2010), 191–201; Anthony Tibbles, "Facing Slavery's Past: The Bicentenary of the Abolition of the British Slave Trade," *Slavery and Abolition* 30.2 (2009): 277–89. Tibbles's article is part of special issue of *Slavery and Abolition* devoted to this topic.

27 Diana Paton, "Interpreting the Bicentenary in Britain," *Slavery and Abolition* 30.2 (2009), 285.

28 For a critical discussion of the relationship between the demarcation of time and conceptions of race, see Crystal Marie Fleming, *Resurrecting Slavery: Racial Legacies and White Supremacy in France* (Philadelphia, PA: Temple University Press), 16–17.

29 Thomas Holt, *The Problem of Freedom* (Baltimore, MD: Johns Hopkins University Press, 1992).

30 This problematic is powerfully constructed in Hesse, "Forgotten Like a Bad Dream."

31 Salamishah Tillet, *Sites of Slavery: Citizenship and Racial Democracy in the Post-Civil Rights Imagination* (Durham, NC: Duke University Press, 2012), 3–9.

32 Here I'm also thinking about questions raised by Saidiya Hartman and Marisa Fuentes. Hartman asks how we tell stories about an unfinished abolition, "an elusive emancipation and a travestied freedom?" Saidiya Hartman, *Scenes of Subjection* (New York: Oxford University Press, 1997), 10. See also Marisa Fuentes, *Dispossessed Lives* (Philadelphia, PA: University of Pennsylvania Press, 2016).

33 Mary Prince, *The History of Mary Prince*, ed. Sara Salih (Harmondsworth: Penguin, 2000).

34 Here I am borrowing Alison Donnell's notion of a heterodox Black British literary canon that functions as an "agent of cultural interrogation and dialogue rather than an authority and closure." See Alison Donnell, "Afterward: In Praise of a Black British Canon and the Possibilities of Representing the Nation 'Otherwise,'" in G. Low et al. (eds.), *A Black British Canon?* (Basingstoke: Palgrave, 2006).

35 Sara Wajid, "'They Bought Me as a Butcher Would a Calf or a Lamb,'" *Guardian*, October 19, 2007, www.theguardian.com/uk/2007/oct/19/race.historybooks (accessed April 15, 2020).

36 Sandra Pouchet Paquet, "The Heartbeat of a West Indian Slave: The History of Mary Prince," *African American Review* 26.1 (1992): 131–46; Jenny Sharpe, "'Something Akin to Freedom': The Case of Mary Prince," *Differences* 8.1 (1996): 31–57; Mary Jeanne Larabee, "'I Know What a Slave Knows': Mary Prince's Epistemology of Resistance," *Women's Studies* 35 (2006): 453–76; Dwight McBride, *Impossible Witness: Truth, Abolition and Slave Testimony* (New York: New York University Press, 2001), ch. 3.

37 Prince, *The History of Mary Prince*, 31–3.

38 Ibid.

39 Susan Amussen, *Caribbean Exchanges: Slavery and the Transformation of English Society, 1640–1700* (Chapel Hill, NC: University of North Carolina Press, 2007); Catherine Molineux, *Faces of Perfect Ebony: Encountering Atlantic Slavery in Imperial Britain* (Cambridge, MA: Harvard University Press, 2012); Molly Corlett,

"Between Colony and Metropole: Empire, Race and Power in Eighteenth Century Britain," in Hakim Adi (ed.), *Black British History: New Perspectives from Roman Times to the Present Day* (London: Zed Books, 2019), 37–51.

40 This point is also critical to arguments presented in Gilroy, *There Ain't No Black in the Union Jack*.

41 Haroon Siddique, "Sadiq Khan Backs London Slavery Museum to Challenge Racism," *Guardian*, August 11, 2019, www.theguardian.com/world/2019/aug/11/sadiq-khan-backs-british-slavery-museum-to-challenge-racism (accessed April 15, 2020).

42 Omar Khan, "Opportunity For All: A Diverse and Thriving City," in Kate Murray and Vanessa Singh (eds.), *Capital Gains: A Global City in a Changing World* (London: Fabian Society, 2019), 51–62.

43 For example, see Kehinde Andrews, "A New Slavery Museum Will Have No Impact on Racism in Britain," *Guardian*, August 13, 2019, www.theguardian.com/commentisfree/2019/aug/13/museum-slavery-not-solve-problem-racism-britain (accessed April 15, 2020).

44 Amit Chaudhuri, "The Real Meaning of Rhodes Must Fall," *Guardian*, March 16, 2016, www.theguardian.com/uk-news/2016/mar/16/the-real-meaning-of-rhodes-must-fall (accessed April 15, 2020).

45 For a discussion of the distortions associated with Rhodes's legacy in response to the Rhodes Must Fall campaign, see John Newsinger, "Why Rhodes Must Fall," *Race and Class* 58.2 (2016): 70–8.

46 Roseanne Chantiluke, Brian Kwoba and Athninangamso Nkopo (eds.), *Rhodes Must Fall: The Struggle to Decolonise the Racist Heart of Empire* (London: Zed Books, 2018).

47 Dalia Gebrial, "Rhodes Must Fall: Oxford and Movements for Change," in Gurminder K. Bhambra, Dalia Gebrial and Keren Nişancıoğlu (eds.), *Decolonising the University* (London: Pluto Press, 2018), 25–6; Mariya Hussain, "Why Is My Curriculum White?," March 11, 2015, www.nus.org.uk/en/news/why-is-my-curriculum-white/ (accessed April 15, 2020); Michael A. Peters, "Why is My Curriculum White?," *Educational Philosophy and Theory* 47.7 (2015): 641–6. As a corollary, there were also a series of discussions including a public panel discussion hosted by UCL featuring leading Black scholars including Nathan Richards, Deborah Gabriel, Nathaniel Adam Tobias Coleman, Lisa Amanda Palmer, William Ackah, and Shirley Anne Tate raising the question, "Why Isn't My Professor Black?" See Jamilah Jahi, "Why Isn't My Professor Black?," *UCL Blog*, March 21, 2014, https://blogs.ucl.ac.uk/events/2014/03/21/whyisntmyprofessorblack/ (accessed December 5, 2019).

2

"Regular White man": reveries of reverse colonization[1]

Stuart Ward

O N 15 MARCH 2019, a 28-year-old white nationalist from Grafton, New South Wales, entered a mosque in Christchurch, New Zealand, to carry out an unprovoked armed assault on countless Muslim men, women and children at prayer. By the time he was finally apprehended, he had assailed a second mosque and murdered a staggering fifty-one people. Immediately prior to the attack, a copy of his 73-page personal "manifesto" arrived at the office of New Zealand Prime Minister Jacinda Ardern, which he also posted online. "The Great Replacement" was inspired by the right-wing French nationalist Renaud Camus's 2012 credo, *Le Grand Remplacement*, positing a global liberal conspiracy to substitute white populations around the world with non-European peoples, especially Muslims.

Although the killer's credo has now been outlawed in New Zealand and direct references to its contents are discouraged, there is one aspect that demands scrutiny: the historical optics that framed its warped logic. Railing against "an invasion on a level never seen before in history", the author invoked the threat of extinction by reverse colonization, the high stakes calling for the most drastic measures. By slaughtering innocents he was merely doing his bit for white civilization. Besides, he assured himself, there were "no innocents in an invasion, all those who colonize other peoples [*sic*] land share guilt". Styling himself as "a regular White man, from a regular family", he laid claim to a special status conferred by his very ordinariness. It was his whiteness that rendered him "regular", imposing a duty to resist irregular incursions from abroad with all the force he could muster.

The mere mention of colonization and displacement carries heavily freighted connotations in Australia and New Zealand; the cumulative weight of decades of public rancour over the legal and moral legacies of Indigenous dispossession. For an unhinged Australian to refashion these terms as totems of white civilization under siege is clearly a minority persuasion. But it does shed light on the galvanizing properties of collective historical awareness in a society still grappling with its settler origins. For all the everyday markers of a migrant society and the lingering sentimentalization of Britain as "home", white Australians have a long history of pushing memories of their own disruptive arrival to one side, as though their physical presence were the upshot of innate historical forces untouched by human agency.

This is partly a matter of scale. So comprehensive was the colonization of Australia – and so uncompromising in its claims – that it became that much easier to screen out memories of prior habitation. But it is also about security of tenure. For the best part of two centuries, reconciling violent histories of invasion and wholesale massacres with an idealized myth of sturdy pioneers taming virgin territory posed a moral conundrum, the burden of which could only be brushed aside by the settlers themselves "appropriating the status of the native".[2] By such intricate procedures the Australian settler colonies became thoroughly naturalized as white men's countries, marked out for eternal habitation by peoples whose authority and staying power were beyond question.

In recent years, the logic of Australia's imminent colonization-in-reverse has gained a particularly corrosive new purchase in the public sphere. In August 2018, the conservative columnist Andrew Bolt sparked a momentary media storm with a nationwide syndicated piece called "The Foreign Invasion", registering an impassioned protest against the levels of immigration into Australia. "Immigration is becoming colonisation", he averred, "turning this country from a home into a hotel." Two weeks later, the far right cross-bencher Fraser Anning used his maiden speech in the Senate to advocate a "final solution" for the immigrant problem, harking back to "the days of Menzies" – Australia's longest-serving conservative prime minister who persisted with a racially selective migrant intake into the 1950s and 1960s. Both interventions echoed the 2005 injunction of legal academic Andrew Fraser, who warned that "white Australians now face a life-or-death struggle to preserve their homeland. Whether effective resistance to their displacement and dispossession can be mounted is another question." Central to Fraser's charge was a dim view of the fortitude of Australia's ruling elites, many of whom "actually take pride in their active collaboration with the Third World colonisation of Australia".[3]

Back in 2005, such sentiments earned Fraser a summary suspension from university teaching and an early retirement.[4] Thirteen years later, however, they had become distinctly more marketable. Bolt's full-page feature article was accompanied by a cartoon depicting assorted ethnic caricatures poised to devour an Australia-shaped meat pie. Although both he and Fraser Anning inevitably met trenchant criticism, they nevertheless tapped a vein of popular anxiety highly receptive to their inverted colonial analogies. The absence of any trace of irony was fully consistent with older traditions of hard-wired disavowal of modern Australia's beginnings as a settler colony. By no yardstick could "immigration" credibly be cast in the same category as "invasion" or indeed "colonization", but as rousing metaphors they were bound to elicit a ready response – serving at once both as a reminder and a repudiation of the fate of Australia's Aborigines.

Sounding the alarm of impending colonization taps into a deeper seam of anxiety about the turning tide of settler colonialism that echoes similar twists of logic in other parts of the world over the past half century or more. The spectre of a "home" defiled by peoples once kept in their colonial place was remarkably reminiscent of the global upheavals of the 1960s, with the Powellite moment in England, the rebellion of Rhodesian whites against the principle of majority rule, and the wider dislocations of an unravelling empire among the scattered remnants of "Greater Britain". It was equally consistent with the very earliest invocations of "decolonization" – a term originally coined in Germany in the 1920s to describe the sudden loss of the German colonial empire. From the very moment of its inception, the idea became bracketed with the spectre of "the colonized becoming colonizers".[5]

Just as setter colonialism relied on the racial and cultural affinities of globally dispersed whites to instil confidence in its high-risk commercial stakes, so too the existential challenge of empire's end would elicit global convulsions of white reaction that continue to resonate into the present. Taken to extremes, the ironic detachment of a colonizing people, seemingly unaware of their direct line of descent from the original colonizers, can bring catastrophic consequences. The tragic events in Christchurch of March 2019 were but an extremist's take on a persistent theme with wider implications for an Australia still steeped in the legacies of white privilege.

* * *

Australia's earliest white settlers had no difficulty seeing themselves in the light of colonizers – indeed, their everyday speech was saturated with reminders of their intruder status. The original nineteen counties that comprised the Colony of New South Wales were known collectively as "the limits of location", signalling the dangers that lurked in the uncharted wilderness beyond. Those who first ventured out to seek their fortunes needed a licence from the Crown to "depasture" their livestock in "vacant" land, all the while acutely aware of the Indigenous presence virtually everywhere they went. Their rapid expansion into new colonial hinterlands was governed by the logic of resource extraction, seeking quick rewards from the grasslands, forests, and the earth itself – anywhere that could yield tradable commodities. These were not self-sufficient yeoman farmers in the mould of the American frontier myth but the vanguard of a collective drive for the spoils of conquest.[6]

Indeed, for these early colonists, itinerant striving for material gain framed their entire self-understanding – labelling themselves variously as "diggers", "squatters", "whalers", and "cedar getters". The latter term went to the very heart of the enterprise – they were "getters", their every effort geared to securing whatever items of value they could carry off with them. Early place names flagged their material ambitions: the Port of Newcastle was originally "Coal River", the first NSW goldfield evoked the biblical legend of gilt-clad "Ophir", while "Silverton" in the far west announced the discovery of the Colony's first major silver lode.

The Christchurch gunman's home town of Grafton on the Clarence River, some 600 km north of Sydney, furnishes a prime early example of this single-minded ethos. Originally dubbed "The Settlement", there could be no question that its earliest arrivals were indeed "settlers" bent on exploiting local resources for whatever they were worth. The first wave consisted of pardoned convicts scouring the northern river system for the "red gold" of the cedar forests in the 1830s. Shortly afterwards came the pastoralists, led by the legendary squatter Edward Ogilvie, who famously appealed to the initially hostile Bundjalung people that he "only wanted the grass" to fatten his flocks (leaving all manner of material and spiritual rights to the original owners, in theory at least).[7] Gold miners would later arrive in droves, their claims exhausted within a few short years to leave a legacy of ghost towns such as Solferino and Lionsville; abandoned monuments to an extractive colonial economy.

In these early years the Settlement comprised a brittle network of remote, isolated, rag-tag encampments of displaced souls, precariously cut off from their place of origin (two of the early pastoral properties were dubbed *Purgatory* and *Pandemonium*).[8] Their sense of alienation came palpably to the fore in their fear and loathing of the local Aboriginal people. One team of cedar getters in the late 1830s was described as "an unruly lot whose fondness for rum and violence towards local women caused serious trouble".[9] Convinced as they were of their vulnerability to attack, they did not hesitate to take the law into their own hands as they plied the river with guns at the ready. Aborigines were reportedly "terrified at the sight of firearms" from the earliest days of contact – a sure sign that they were accustomed to their frequent use.

Indeed, armed reprisals for Aboriginal theft of flour and livestock became commonplace – to the point where the Settlement squatters could become "homicidal maniacs" when they found their sheep butchered.[10]

In 1841, only a few miles to the west where the Orara River meets the Clarence, a reprisal party of local pastoralists and mounted police indiscriminately slaughtered a large gathering of Aboriginal men, women, and children. According to one local witness "their dead bodies subsequently floated down past the Settlement".[11]

A few years later an even greater number were devastated by poisoned flour that had been distributed as "payment" for work carried out at the property of Thomas Coutts (his name preserved for posterity in the nearby township of Coutts Crossing).[12] Such crimes were regarded by whites as a necessary evil in a frontier setting beyond the reach of legal redress for Indigenous "outrages". Or in the casual verdict of the *Sydney Morning Herald*, the unchecked violence at the Settlement arose from the exposed flank of a community "plagued by the blacks" and "the unprotected manner in which the whole population had been left to fight their own battles".[13]

But the perils of exile fail to take in the full scale of the settlers' motivations or their longer-term repercussions. The earliest arrivals may have felt like vulnerable outcasts, cut off from the comforts of the familiar world they left behind. But their frame of reference was avowedly global. The dogged pursuit of colonial commodities would have been futile without the rapid expansion of transoceanic networks and metropolitan markets that invested these goods with such alluring value. In an age when "people's horizons of desire changed", success came first to those who understood the laws of a fledgling global economy and how to bend them to their material advantage.[14]

What wool, gold, and cedar shared in common was their relative ease of extraction, storage, refinement, and above all transportation across untold distances, fuelling the cloth mills of Lancashire, lining the coffers of British capitalism, and furnishing the elegant interiors of high society around the world. The 1850s saw a sudden spike in international demand for another colonial commodity – Australian tallow – spurred by the needs of fighting the Crimean War. The Settlement squatters promptly switched from sheep grazing to cattle, amassing huge fortunes "on the profits from grease for the guns".[15] The shots that rang out at Inkerman and Sevastopol would reverberate in unanticipated ways in an undeclared warzone at the opposite end of the earth.

Such long-distance deployments of capital and labour could not have been carried off purely on the strength of market forces or improvements in shipping and infrastructure. The whole enterprise of shifting huge quantities of staples over vast oceans (and over extended lines of credit) was an exercise fraught with risk, which could only be overcome by devising networks of implied fealty and trust.[16] Raising the requisite manpower and money required a minimum of reassurance that the effort involved would not be dashed by the tyranny of distance; and that property investments with slow-maturing returns would be protected by shared legal and social custom.

Crucial in this regard was the enabling factor of white kinship networks. As James Belich maintains, "shared language, assumptions, habits, tastes and experience lowered what economists now call 'transaction costs'" in an extended circle of transoceanic trust that "lubricated and buttressed economic interaction".[17] Investor and immigrant confidence in the unprecedented scale of their ambition was the crucial constitutive element of an ever-expanding frontier of Greater British settlement.[18] Magee and Thompson similarly emphasize the determining influence of "co-ethnic networks" in de-risking an otherwise precarious undertaking, thereby breaking down barriers to long-distance trade. Their evidence from colonial lines of credit, contracts, and remittances clearly suggests a tendency among early colonial entrepreneurs to favour their own complexion in their speculative dealings overseas.[19]

This point is crucial to understanding the racial underpinnings of early settler colonialism. Ethnic chauvinism and visceral racial prejudice were not just the incidental by-products of settler intrusions, flaring up at the forward zone of violent contact with Indigenous peoples. These qualities were the very precondition of the invasive practices of colonial occupation, not merely in terms of discounting the prior claims of "lower races", but more crucially in forging an imagined world of reliable white kinsfolk that rendered the whole project commercially viable. For all the ongoing debate about the scale of genocidal intent in the settlement of the Australian colonies, one point remains clear: the perception that the country had been cleared for unimpeded white occupation was good for business.[20]

The earliest occupants of the Settlement may have felt isolated, but they were by no means cut off. Far more so than their counterparts back in England, their material circumstances fostered a keen sense of connectivity to a globally dispersed communion of the British race.

* * *

More than half a century has passed since W. E. H. Stanner invoked the "great Australian silence" to explain the extraordinary capacity of Australians to obliterate the memory of their violent intrusion into the Aborigines' domain. In his 1968 Boyer Lectures, Stanner surmised that the disappearance of Indigenous people from popular historical awareness was no mere mental lapse or casual oversight, but a "cult of forgetfulness practiced on a national scale". Though his aphorism has now passed into general usage, routinely cited in classrooms, lecture halls, and public debate, the underlying properties of "forgetfulness" – its origins, motivations, and practical manifestations – remain largely misunderstood. It was not simply that Aboriginal people became subject to a mass conspiracy of studied reticence (on the contrary, abundant accounts of their presence, bearing, customs, and presumed destiny pervade the historical record). It was more about expunging traces of their dynamic interactions with the early colonists themselves – the everyday reminders of the latter's intruder status. It was about shoring up the moral and emotional foundations of wholesale territorial dispossession, thus rendering the occupation of the continent more palatable and hence complete.[21]

These were subtle processes that evolved only very gradually, from the time of the settlers' earliest aspirations for something more permanent and enduring. Edward Ogilvie may have initially "only wanted the grass", but it wasn't long before he constructed an elaborate "squatter's castle" on the upper Clarence, recasting the landscape in the familiar contours of an old-world country estate.[22] When the Settlement was renamed

"Grafton" in 1851 (after Governor FitzRoy's grandfather), there could no longer be any doubt that the settlers had come to stay. Tales of massacres and the Aboriginal "menace" did not fade overnight, but in time they shed the matter-of-fact justifications of earlier accounts and became shrouded in scepticism and disquiet. One 1914 retelling of the Orara River Massacre in the *Clarence and Richmond Examiner* openly condemned the "sickening story" as "a disgrace to Christianity", yet concluded on an incredulous note: "'History must be lies', once wrote someone of note. No doubt he was partly right. No doubt he was partly wrong. But the details of many old-time Australian stories 'gang aft aglee' ... the Orara story, as told in the foregoing ... is surely a wild exaggeration."[23]

It would be more than thirty years before the story emerged again in the *Examiner*, this time prefaced with the rider: "The tale has been told by father and mother to son and daughter for over 100 years, and those who now hear one of its many variations, are apt to inquire whether there is any truth in it."[24] This was not simply about forgetfulness. Nor was it fuelled solely by a sense of moral repugnance. What predisposed later generations to disbelief was an instinctive reluctance to view their forebears as a colonizing people, cast in the guise of trespassers. "Pioneers" was their preferred collective noun – having long since dropped the appellation "settler" along with the original name of the Settlement itself.

But this in no sense obliterated the influence of "co-ethnic networks" in ordering their world and orienting their place in a wider scheme of dispersed kinship. Australia's earliest settlers would bequeath an outlook that was highly parochial, perceiving their lot from a far-flung vantage point, but they were also unusually worldly in their social formation, identifying loosely but readily with racialized counterparts at vast removes from themselves. As a consequence, attitudes towards immigration were never wholly exclusionary (in a society where demand for imported labour was typically strong), but rather highly selective according to the same ethnic affinities and fealties that had underwritten the early pattern of occupation.

The "White Australia Policy" of 1901 enshrined these principles as the newly federated nation's founding legal instrument. Determining the

61

right of entry into the physical expanse of an entire continent also doubled as an audacious instrument of conquest – at a time when the original occupants were widely written off as a "doomed race", consigned to the margins by the dictates of natural law.[25] But it was also adopted at a time of acute racial anxiety about Australia's northern neighbours, with a boom in invasion scare novels bearing titles such as *The Coloured Conquest* (1903), *The Commonwealth Crisis* (1908), and *Reaping the Whirlwind* (1909). These avidly devoured fictions betrayed deeper apprehensions about a wholesale *Asiatic Invasion of Australia* (1895), and it is here we find the first intimations of colonization in reverse – with Northern Australia deemed particularly vulnerable to the incursions of an "Asiatic settlement" comprised of "Fair Lily Colonies". With an astounding absence of overt self-reflection, these authors drew implicitly on fading memories of their own colonizing intrusions, elaborately conjuring an Australia "stealthily" overwhelmed by "a thriving little colony" of non-whites.[26]

* * *

These susceptibilities have made a dramatic comeback in the twenty-first century, from the time of Pauline Hanson's emergence at the helm of the populist "One Nation" Party in the late 1990s. The gradual rightward shift of the mainstream parties since that time was prompted largely by the need to outflank Hanson's racially exclusive stance on immigration and refugee policy – a process already evident in August 2001 when the Howard government refused permission for the Norwegian freighter MV *Tampa* to land 433 asylum seekers. The subsequent repercussions overlapped with the 9/11 terrorist attack on New York only weeks later, culminating in the divisive 2001 federal election and Howard's highly effective politicization of Australia's northern reaches with the electoral slogan: "We decide who comes into this country". The era of "border protection" and "stopping the boats" had begun, fused with a newly energized vigilance against the threat posed by Islamic fundamentalism.

What had changed, however, was the terms of reference, with frequent resort to euphemism to avoid discomfort with the older, unapologetically racial demarcation lines of the White Australia era. Religion subsumed race in the vocabulary of exclusion, together with vaguely defined principles of cultural assimilability. In his clarion call to resist the current wave of "colonization", Andrew Bolt referred in passing to his own parents who had emigrated from Holland in the 1950s and who had successfully assimilated "into the wider 'us'". "Wider" is the operative term, evoking the unusual bandwidth of settler-colonial sympathies that could fashion a self-contained and indeed highly parochial "us" out of the broader international sweep of admissible whites.

For all the emphasis on the threat posed by inward migration, these decades of reaction were also pre-empted by developments in the politics of Indigenous rights – particularly in the 1990s when a series of High Court cases recognized the principle of Native Title and the prospect of Aborigines reclaiming ownership of Crown Land and joint management of major mining and pastoral leases.[27] The 1997 Royal Commission into the practice of forced removal of Aboriginal children from their families brought additional focus to historic wrongs perpetrated against Australia's first peoples. Although voices were raised in protest against the iniquity of "special rights" accorded only to Aborigines, these objections lacked a political centre of gravity at the time and failed to secure any immediate electoral purchase – the resultant void setting the scene for the decades to come.[28]

It is remarkable in retrospect how long it took for the backlash to occur in an Australian context. Bill Schwarz's chapter in this volume triangulates the forces of white reaction in the 1960s from England to Rhodesia to the US South – personified respectively by Enoch Powell, Ian Smith, and George Wallace, all railing against a perceived assault on white privilege worldwide. Although Australia was confronted with similar challenges to its traditional racially defined social composition during these years (best symbolized by the retrenchment of the White Australia Policy in the latter part of the decade), no single figure or movement embodied popular resistance to the tide of change. Ironically, at the very moment that W. E. H. Stanner declared an end to the white blinkers of the "great Australian silence" in 1968, Enoch Powell was promoting Australia as one of the last bastions of the white man; a place to which his constituents increasingly looked to escape the scourge of immigration at home.[29]

Curiously, no counterpart to Powell, Smith, or Wallace ever emerged in Australia during these years of profound transition; no political embodiment of white resentment who might resist the prevailing liberal trends. The most likely candidates would have been drawn from the Country Party, with its heavily rural constituency and deeply conservative social ethos. And indeed, there was abundant sympathy and empathy in the party's ranks for the plight of white Rhodesians in particular, with periodic demands on the party leadership to lend stronger support to Smith's cause. Although State Premiers such as Queensland's Joh Bjelke-Petersen occasionally tapped into white resentments, the response of the Federal Country Party leader, Jack McEwen, suggests a deep reluctance to antagonize Australia's newly decolonized neighbours at a time of unprecedented regional turmoil and military escalation in Indonesia and Vietnam. McEwen's natural predisposition to side with white Rhodesian farmers was thus offset by equally ingrained fears of becoming embroiled in a racial war to Australia's north. As he explained to his disgruntled membership in January 1967: "To act on the argument which many here have used would amount to taking the side of the white man against the black. However deep our personal sympathies may be for Rhodesian settlers, this course would be one of deadly national danger for Australia."[30]

It would only be decades later, when the full implications of Stanner's aphorism emerged clearly into view, that a white backlash against the Indigenous rights movement began to take hold. Debates over Indigenous land tenure dovetailed with the so-called "history wars" of the early 2000s, when chroniclers of frontier violence and Indigenous massacres were charged with exaggeration and outright "fabrication". Every aspect of the historical wrongs perpetrated against Aborigines seemed ripe for contestation, from the suitability of 26 January as a national holiday to the need for a national apology to the "Stolen Generation" of Aboriginal children. Symbolic gestures that might have raised fewer objections decades earlier (like the 1967 referendum granting Indigenous people citizenship rights) now became the object of deep divisions between left-of-centre progressives and a newly galvanized and better-organized groundswell of ethnic populism.

At Coutts Crossing outside Grafton – scene of the mass poisoning referred to earlier – these pressures culminated in a move to devise a new name for the town to erase the stigma of Thomas Coutts's 1848 crime. The proposal was put to a public vote in June 2018, resulting in a paltry 13 residents in favour against 183 vehemently against.[31]

* * *

Grafton today is a tranquil northern rivers country town, prized for its Jacaranda-lined avenues and bearing few obvious markers of the hardship and depravity of the "Settlement" era. There can be no suggestion that the community bears any responsibility for the carnage visited upon Christchurch in March 2019, and the distress caused by their association with such an appalling tragedy is entirely regrettable. But the town's origins nevertheless underline the hysteria and hypocrisy at the heart of the killer's doctrine. Although Brenton Tarrant had a history of supporting "alt-right" causes in Australia, his "manifesto" was strangely silent on his own national origins, seemingly preoccupied with the more urgent plight of fellow whites in France, Germany, Sweden, and even Serbia.

But as Dirk Moses points out, his use of the language of colonization, occupation, and extinction is no idle coincidence, evoking the telltale signs of a form of colonialism much closer to home – a colonialism marked, not primarily by the exploitation of native labour, "but through its elimination and replacement by immigrant-settlers: one society displaces another".[32] The exterminatory logic that once shaped the contours of the archetypal settlement of northern New South Wales lurked conspicuously, if subconsciously, beneath the surface of Tarrant's manifesto in its radical prescription to save the white man's world.

Similarly, the assailant's identification with a wider global constituency of disenfranchised whites is consistent with the sliding affective scales of settler-colonial selfhood. Tellingly, his manifesto is more certain about the identity of the invaders than the invaded – the latter depicted in the vaguest terms as "us", "our people", "our lands", "our borders", or more generally as "Europeans". This blanket term served as a belated form of symbolic repatriation, enabling all whites (not least himself) to don the designated garb of "native Europeans" displaced by non-white intruders.[33] Such brazen conceit was amplified by the fact that he himself had migrated to New Zealand a mere eighteen months prior to the attack, thus requiring a double displacement – spatially as well as historically – to frame his purpose in terms of indigenous resistance to foreign invasion.

The invocation of "an assault on the European people that, if not combated, will ultimately result in … complete racial and cultural replacement" is in no sense a new or original idea. As a system of logic, it stems from the conditions of settler colonialism itself, anticipating the very structures of physical and discursive erasure that had attended many a prior incursion by commodity-seeking whites into Indigenous homelands. Its echoes stretch from the Asian invasion scares of a century ago to the more recent clamour of white supremacists in the streets of Charlottesville chanting: "You will not replace us." The fundamental stakes are no different from Andrew Fraser's "life-or-death struggle" or Andrew Bolt's entreaty to his fellow Australians to "resist this colonising of Australia while there is still an 'us' that can".[34]

Where the extremist parts company with the polemicist is in his literal rendering of "resistance", "struggle", or Tarrant's preferred term: "combat". His conviction that "radical, explosive action is the only desired, and required, response to an attempted genocide" is self-evidently a demented viewpoint, in no way desired or endorsed by those advocating purely political measures who happen to share his fundamental diagnostics. It is therefore unnerving to read the equivocal responses of leading right-wing figures as they strove to disentangle the upshot of Christchurch from their own unflinching cause.

Fraser Anning issued the most ambivalent of tweets in the immediate aftermath of Christchurch: "Does anyone still dispute the link between Muslim immigration and violence?" (followed by further statements citing the immigration of "Muslim fanatics" to New Zealand as the "real cause of bloodshed").[35] Renaud Camus also resorted to Twitter to register his "worry … for our Muslim friends" before seizing the opportunity to double down on his worldview: "I think that for [their own] security they should gather in a vast fortress, the 'land of Islam' … and live in peace according to their tastes and according to their faith, well protected against the unhinged."[36] Neither evidenced the slightest awareness of the dangers inherent in literal readings of their own rhetoric, with Camus claiming that the attacks were more obviously inspired by ISIS than anything he might have said himself. In virtually the same breath, however, he complained of Tarrant's "blatant plagiarism" in the title of his Christchurch manifesto.

Andrew Bolt was quicker to condemn the atrocity outright as the work of a "sick bastard" and a "nutter looking for a cause greater than himself to excuse his murderous evil".[37] This seems incontestable, but Bolt was apparently content to leave it at that, as though the killer's core grievance bore no discernible likeness to his own widely publicised resentment that "our sense of an 'us' is now being shattered". Conspicuous by its absence was any reflection on the duty of care to weigh one's words in proportion to their likely – or even unlikely – consequences. Given the all-too-frequent occurrence of mass shootings and lone-wolf massacres, it should have taken no great mental effort to contemplate an armed "nutter" responding to the existential scaremongering that increasingly passes for mainstream journalism.

Even among liberal and progressive opinion, there was an inclination to disown a "regular white man" on a shooting rampage as an unrepresentative aberration – "unAustralian" in the words of the Labor Party's Penny Wong.[38] Others pointed to his long absence from Australia's shores and his "cosmopolitan" attachment to eclectic causes elsewhere in the world. As one well-meaning Melbourne columnist assured readers: "To call him Australian, in any meaningful sense, is misleading; he'd passed into a dark, borderless, alt-right fraternity."[39] A laudable sentiment, but it overlooks too much, not least Australia's historically wide arc of ethnic identification and racial affinities that provided ready access to such a shifting, "borderless" landscape. There are reasons why the "cult of forgetfulness" continues to obscure the legacies of systemic racial violence, and why settler colonies provide such fertile ground for reveries of reverse colonization.

Notes

1 Sincere thanks to Mark McKenna, Ewan Morris, Dirk Moses, Bill Schwarz, and the editors of this volume for comments on an earlier draft.

2 Bain Attwood, "Denial in a Settler Society: the Australian Case", *History Workshop Journal* 84 (autumn 2017): 24–43 (31); revelations about the scale and persistence of frontier massacres in Australia have proliferated since the publication of Henry Reynolds's pathbreaking *The Other Side of the Frontier* (Townsville: James Cook University, 1981). In 2017 a team at the University of Newcastle launched a comprehensive interactive website mapping "Colonial Frontier Massacres in Australia, 1788-1930": https://c21ch.newcastle.edu.au/colonialmassacres/ (accessed 7 July 2020).

3 Andrew Bolt, "The Invasion of Australia", *Herald Sun*, 2 August 2018; Andrew Fraser, "Rethinking the White Australia Policy", September 2005, www.ironbarkre sources.com/articles/fraser2005rethinkingwap.htm (accessed 15 April 2020). An extract also appeared in *The Australian Higher Education Supplement*, 21 September 2005, after the *Deakin Law Review* refused to publish his inflammatory remarks.

4 See, for example, "University Speaks Out on Professor's Racist Comments", *Sydney Morning Herald*, 27 July 2005.

5 See Stuart Ward, "The European Provenance of Decolonization", *Past & Present* 230.1 (2016): 227–60.

6 As Russel Ward observed more than sixty years ago, albeit for different purposes, in *The Australian Legend* (Oxford, 1958).

7 Martha Rutledge, "Ogilvie, Edward David (1814–1896)", *Australian Dictionary of Biography*, National Centre of Biography, Australian National University, http:// adb.anu.edu.au/biography/ogilvie-edward-david-777/text7017, first published 1974 (accessed 16 April 2019).

8 *Daily Examiner* (Grafton), 5 June 1937.

9 Australian Museum Consulting (2014), *Clarence Valley Aboriginal Heritage Study*, report to Clarence Valley Council, 38–39, www.clarence.nsw.gov.au/page. asp?f=RES-CAM-60-43-25 (accessed 15 April 2020).

10 C. D. Rowley, *The Destruction of Aboriginal Society, Volume 1: Aboriginal Policy and Practice* (Canberra: Australian National University Press, 1970), 110–12.

11 Rowley, *Destruction of Aboriginal Society*, p. 113. The numbers – as is often the case with Indigenous massacres – are disputed. See Newcastle project, note 2 above

12 "Coutts Crossing Named after "Mass Murderer" Property Owner", *Daily Examiner*, 30 May 2018.

13 31 January 1948, cited in Rowley, *Destruction of Aboriginal Society*, 111, 113.

14 C. A. Bailey, *The Birth of the Modern World: 1780–1914* (Oxford: Blackwell, 2004), 6.

15 Rowley, *Destruction of Aboriginal Society*, 109.

16 Gary B. Magee and Andrew S. Thompson, *Empire and Globalisation: Networks of People, Goods and Capital in the British World, c. 1850–1914* (Cambridge: Cambridge University Press, 2010), 117–18.

17 James Belich, *Replenishing the Earth: The Settler Revolution and the Rise of the Anglo-World, 1783–1939* (Oxford: Oxford University Press, 2009), 179, 208.

18 Magee and Thompson, *Empire and Globalisation*, 167.

19 Magee and Thompson, *Empire and Globalisation*, 134, 167.

20 See especially A. Dirk Moses (ed.), *Genocide and Settler Society: Frontier Violence and Stolen Indigenous Children in Australian History* (New York: Berghahn Books, 2005); see also Patrick Wolfe's argument that "settler colonialism is inherently eliminatory but not invariably genocidal" in "Settler Colonialism and the Elimination of the Native", *Journal of Genocide Research* 8.4 (2006): 387–409.

21 W. E. H. Stanner, *After the Dreaming: Black and White Australians—An Anthropologist's View* (Sydney: ABC, 1969), 24–5; Mark McKenna, "Moment of Truth: History and Australia's Future", *Quarterly Essay* 69 (2018): 13.

22 See George Farwell, *Squatter's Castle: The Saga of a Pastoral Dynasty* (Sydney: Angus and Robertson, 1983).

23 "The Crime at the Orara", *Clarence and Richmond Examiner*, 4 July 1914. "Gang aft aglee" is a misspelling of a line from Robert Burns's celebrated 1785 poem "To a Mouse" (meaning "often go askew").

24 The piece by R. C. Law nevertheless vouched for the accuracy of the story and other local massacres. See "Fact Always at Root of Tradition", *Daily Examiner*, 29 May 1948.

25 See, for example, Russell McGregor, *Imagined Destinies: Aboriginal Australia and the Doomed Race Theory, 1880–1939* (Melbourne: Melbourne University Press, 1997).

26 See David Walker, *Anxious Nation: Australia and the Rise of Asia, 1850–1939* (St Lucia: University of Queensland Press, 1999), 98–140, esp. 118–20, 129.

27 The literature is extensive but the foundational work is Henry Reynolds, *The Law of the Land* (Ringwood, Vic.: Penguin, 1992).

28 With the notable exception of Pauline Hanson's minor breakthrough in the 1998 Queensland State election – an early portent of political developments more generally in the decades ahead.

29 See Bill Schwarz, *The White Man's World* (Oxford: Oxford University Press, 2011).

30 National Archives of Australia, M58/113, press release by Deputy Prime Minister John McEwen, "Rhodesia", January 1967.

31 See *Daily Examiner*, 28 June 2018.

32 A. Dirk Moses, "'White Genocide' and the Ethics of Public Analysis", *Journal of Genocide Research* 21.2 (2019): 201–13 (208–9), DOI: 10.1080/14623528.2019.1599493.

33 Moses, "White Genocide", 10.

34 Bolt, "The Invasion of Australia"; Fraser, "Rethinking the White Australia Policy".

35 *Sydney Morning Herald*, 15 March 2019.

36 https://twitter.com/RenaudCamus/status/1106860147375308801 (accessed 15 April 2020).

37 Andrew Bolt, blog post, *Herald Sun*, 15 March 2019, www.heraldsun.com.au/blogs/andrew-bolt/mosque-shooting-in-new-zealand-many-dead/news-story/ceac4doc5f92a32d2c62754c74d4ca30 (accessed 15 April 2020).

38 Quoted in Binoy Kampmark, "NZ Shooter: The Myth of Australian Values", *Eureka Street* 29.5 (2019), www.eurekastreet.com.au/article/nz-shooter--the-myth-of-australian-values (accessed 15 April 2020).

39 Julie Szego, "Christchurch Shooter Confounds Our Assumptions", *Age*, 23 March 2019.

3

Wild power:
the aftershocks of decolonization
and Black Power

Bill Schwarz

The revolution is now on the inside of the house.

Malcolm X, 1964[1]

"… every state that claims sovereign power" carries inside it the potential for the makings of an "unlimited, unmonitored wild zone of power".

Susan Buck-Morss, *Thinking Past Terror*[2]

ON 12 NOVEMBER 2016 photos of Nigel Farage schmoozing with Donald Trump sped through the ether. In the glitz of Trump Tower the calculated vulgarity of the *faux* selfies signified an integral component of the occasion, a sublimely narcissistic announcement of the incoming order. The unbridled ostentation and self-satisfaction weren't a sideshow. Trump & Co. are projected as contemporary icons. In the high-voltage buzz of Trumpian triumphalism, the susceptibilities of the ousted political class don't stand a chance. Usually these outlandish domestic interiors only enter the public eye at the moment when tyrants are deposed, their palaces ransacked. Not so on this occasion.

The Trump audience conceded pride of place, for the day, to Farage. It signalled his ascension. He wasn't, however, alone. He was accompanied by his *über*-blokeish prankster crew: Arron Banks, Gerry Gunster, Andy Wigmore, and Raheem Kassam, staking their claim to have been the progenitors of Brexit and lords of disorder, all.[3] Neither Trump in the US, nor those charged with making Brexit happen in the UK, had a clue how they should proceed. How is it possible to forget the stupefaction on the part of Boris Johnson and Michael Gove, on the morrow of the referendum just a little while earlier, realizing in the very instant the cameras were thrust under their noses that they were emperors undressed? In the shock of victory all they could do was to double-down, recycle their erstwhile fabrications, and prolong the charade that had beamed them up into the political limelight in the first place.

Subsequently Trump's allies from England have found themselves edged out of the Washington razzmatazz, even if covert, dodgy alliances persist below the line of public vision. But the triumphalism of Farage and Trump wasn't misconstrued. They were right about the scale of their victory. The new world, they boasted, would arrive in a blink of the eye. Promises about the imminent realization of "The Wall" in the US and of "Independence Day" in the UK – more prosaically, Brexit – abounded.[4] Once the reality principle reasserted itself, the fate of these projects began to look less accommodating.

What though does this mean historically? How do we explain the mind-bending rendezvous of Trump and Farage, in the shadow of Roosevelt and Churchill, not as aberration – derived, perhaps, from a lingering hope that when we recover our senses we will return to politics as once they were – but as history? Or to put this another way: how do we understand the "wildness" of the wild political order we now confront?

The simultaneity of Brexit and Trump invites transatlantic analysis.[5] These locate globalization at the conceptual core of their interpretations, taking us back to 9/11, the "war on terror", the international banking collapse of 2008, and the long years of austerity when electorates had to pay the cost for high-rolling financial recklessness. These conjunctural analyses are vital, illuminating the inner forms of the current situation. However, I'm going to follow an alternative tack by drawing attention to a single – a longer, deeper, less visible – historical duration: that of race during and after the break-up of the European colonial empires. I seek to introduce depth-of-field to the *longue durée*, re-envisioning the gravity with which the past operates in the present.

Race radicals and their enemies

I suggest two working propositions. My arguments are formed in an attempt to clarify the interconnections between Britain, its overseas colonies, and the United States. I've sought to indicate more specific lines of development in the endnotes.

First, we should acknowledge the scale of the breaking of European colonialism and acknowledge, also, alongside this, the significance of its historical correlate: the contemporaneous movements in the US for civil rights and Black Power, which sought to break the racial imperative through which the American republic has reproduced itself.

Today we seldom encounter historical interpretations which highlight the destruction of Europe's colonial world-systems as a tale of human beneficence and self-realization. This is no longer a narrative which incites confidence. It's clear why. The societies that emerged from colonial rule found themselves enmeshed in new modes of authoritarianism, in which the state turned its guns on its own people, and barbarous ethnic wars followed one after the other. Colonialism, far from being consigned to the *oubliette* of history, resurfaced in a myriad of unanticipated guises.[6] However, what this preoccupation with the depredations of the postcolonial situation obscures is the bare historical fact that the dark-skinned dispossessed subverted a racial order which had held for four or more centuries. In this respect Frantz Fanon's vision in *The Wretched of the Earth*, unpersuasive from our own historical perspective, nonetheless represents a luminous voice of its time.[7] Generations of men, women, and children devoted their lives to emancipation; for an interlude they created a time when it was feasible to imagine that the liquidation of the old empires would generate benevolent historical outcomes, and in which the logic of race would fracture.

In order to understand the scale of decolonization we need also add the US to the frame.[8] The anti-colonial movements which broke the European overseas empires identified their enemy as the social systems – that which sustained the white man's world – in which race functioned as the animating current.[9] This was less a matter of identifying the locus of racial power as a particular institutional arrangement (colonial or non-colonial), than as an epistemic system in which race worked as the principle through which every social relation was imagined and articulated. Aimé Césaire's 1950 broadside, *Discourse on Colonialism*, is a lucid, uncompromising exemplar of this manner of thinking.[10] In the decades that followed, for the *groupuscules* strewn across the globe endeavouring to destroy the given racial order, these precepts turned into a new common sense.[11] The circulation of ideas and personnel traversed distinct theatres of racial struggle.[12] The deeper the global engagement of the race militants, the further they were inclined to identify the shared affinities of those who subscribed to the protocols of white dominion, whether in the colonies or in the US.[13] The destruction of Europe's colonial empire and the destruction of the racial hierarchies of the United States came to be viewed as common objectives in the larger struggle.[14] The borders separating anti-colonialism in Africa, Asia, and the Caribbean (and indeed in the European metropoles) from the anti-race politics of the US melted. Notwithstanding formal distinctions between colonial and non-colonial, after the Second Wold War the global order that sanctioned white power was under attack from haphazard, mobile, and transnational networks of race rebels.[15]

The convergence of (first) the movements pursuing independence in the colonies, (second) those groups within the metropoles of Europe which, while advocating the end of colonial rule overseas, also struggled against the race hierarchies at home, and (third) the black freedom struggles in the US, *in their combination* created the promise of a global revolution.[16] During the time of decolonization and Black Power, exhortations to revolution zipped from one locale to another, in a cacophony of dissident voices. After Watts in August 1965, Detroit and Newark in July 1967, and the succession of localized uprisings across the US in the wake of the assassination of Martin Luther King in April 1968, this sensibility reached deep into everyday life.[17]

To highlight these affiliations to revolution goes against the grain of current political good sense. Even to think along lines premised on the invocation of revolution appears unduly programmatic, evident of a nostalgia for another far-off age. We know that there never arrived a juncture of transcendent, radical rupture. Despite the dreams of a generation, the revolutions never took off. In their place we have been faced by a complex, entangled, and unresolved dialectic of victories-in-defeat and defeats-in-victory. This is the legacy we are required to inhabit. More generally it's how history works. Alongside the advances – the everyday multicultural urban worlds of new generations – the amplification of race, as a binding social determinant, continues apace.[18]

All this is true. But contemporary scepticism concerning the idea of revolution should not lead us to suppose that in the wake of the Second World War social insurgency on the part of the race militants never occurred. There were countless manifestations of localized rebellions against the founding logics of the white man's world. They operated according to particular local times and circumstances; they were driven by distinct clusters of social determinations; some persisted for decades (Vietnam), while others flared more briefly; they all resulted in contrary, and contradictory, outcomes. Yet when this plurality of experiences are situated together, and placed in the single frame, whether under the banner of anti-colonialism, or of the US freedom struggles, common properties move into focus. A discernible *longue durée* takes shape.

In some sectors of the former anglophone colonial world the processes identified by Richard Drayton as "secondary decolonization" – by which he refers to the continuing struggle for social liberation in the aftermath of formal independence – transmuted into a phenomenon with the attributes of a specifically postcolonial variant of Black Power.[19] A comparable trajectory holds for the experience of race radicals in the European metropoles.[20] The founding categories (decolonization, civil rights, Black Power), combined with the predominating geopolitical locations (colony, metropole, the US), defy any simple classification. It's the unruly, subterranean connections which prove most intriguing.

I don't say this in order to retrieve older revolutionary reveries. If they wish, readers can call this global concatenation of rebelliousness a revolution. My purpose is to attest only to the political scale of the aspirations of the historical agents of decolonization and of the North American struggles for racial emancipation. It's not that these bids for liberation never occurred. They did. Their historic scale is the issue. But they were – in part, or largely – *defeated*, pitched against batteries of state violence.

Today, I suggest, we witness a late instalment of a profound historic reaction to the bid for emancipation by the racially oppressed of a generation ago. Moreover this was a defeat whose historic significance has dropped out of the public memory, even as its hold on the present remains material.[21] This takes us back to Walter Benjamin's "Theses on the Philosophy of History". He ponders the properties of political defeat. He argued that: "The only historian capable of fanning the spark of hope in the past is the one who is firmly convinced that even the dead will not be safe from the enemy if he is victorious. And this enemy has never ceased to be victorious."[22]

Second, in the crucible of European decolonization and its North American correlates, racial whiteness was reanimated as a political force. A collective mentality arose among those whites who, facing assaults on white privilege, came to experience themselves as a defeated race.[23] *The scale of the challenge to white power generated, in turn, the scale of the reaction. To draw from an incendiary intervention of the period – Régis Debray's* Revolution in the Revolution?, *written shortly before his imprisonment in Bolivia in 1967 – the revolution revolutionized the counter-revolution. Out of the ruins of colonial supremacy in Europe, and out of the ruins of a racially segregated United States, emerged cells of whites determined to avenge the racial defeat which they convinced themselves they had suffered. The figure of the white man experienced a historically consequent resurrection. For devotees of white rule, out of calamity there arose a dream of salvation.*

An initial impetus for this volume lay in a conviction that, as a result of the defeat of the colonial empires, the reflexes of white nationalism were globalized. But this requires analytical precision. In Africa and Asia, as the flags of Europe came down, the existential disorientation of the defeated cadres of the white world inspired a new counter-politics which stretched long into the future. From the outset, this politics, its populism accentuated, was psychically charged, generated by unappeased racial panic.

A collective apprehension arose from whites believing that they were facing extinction *as whites*.[24] This structure of feeling assumed a new currency, based on a conviction that across the globe the "black man", and assorted configurations of non-white peoples, were gaining "the whip hand".[25] The race hierarchies of the slave plantation were, it seemed, being inverted, whites becoming the newly enslaved. From our own history it takes an effort of intellectual will to recall the scale of the racial fears which underwrote the emergent postcolonial world. The prolonged arc of political reaction, turning on the valorization of racial whiteness, recast the political life of the West.

Yet white fears that racial privilege was in jeopardy were not unfounded. Denunciations of white authority pulsated across the airwaves as never before, a potent element in the brew which made the sixties "the sixties". The extravagance of the language employed by the avatars of the white race must not lead us to assume that the assault on white supremacy existed only as a troubled fantasy. The confrontation was for real.

It's valuable to return to Ronald Segal, a white, exiled South African journalist, a man of admirable democratic instincts. In 1967 he published an alarming audit of what he identified as the global "race war", which he believed lay just around the corner. Whites, he proposed, on account solely of their perceived racial affiliation, were everyday drawing closer together as black militancy became increasingly strident.[26] His argument captures the temper of the times, working to illuminate the lines of connection between the fact of race in the overseas empires and the racialized antagonisms that were seizing the metropolitan nations, the USA included. Segal was a talented thinker. He was a man of sober temperament. Careful not to inflate what he discerned lying in wait, he nonetheless harboured deep fears of a racial Armageddon. Nothing, quite, was realized in the manner he had sketched. His book was not prediction, but a warning.

For us it remains a troubled reminder of the dangers carried in the spectre of race a generation ago.

It is, however, a paradox that in the very moment of decolonization the historic bid to break the power of race had the unintended effect of intensifying investments in the magical properties of racial whiteness. Whiteness, newly clothed, came to function as a panacea for the disorder all around. Or to view this more comprehensively: the stalled bid for racial emancipation unleashed the re-racialization of the politics of the old metropoles.[27]

From whiteness "defeated" to state power

We need to track the movement from the spontaneous, highly strung, and on occasion pathological manifestations of white panic, in the immediacy of their formation – unprocessed and ungrounded, crystallized in the perception of a global defeat of the white race and driven by an existential dread – to the coalescing of deeper mentalities, bearing their appointed "philosophies" and arriving at the point where they acted *as politics*, crossing the line and entering the field of state power.[28]

For "politics" I remain close to Antonio Gramsci, who provides the means to think the relations between popular life, the symbolic dimensions of thought, and the larger field of state power. The movement from inchoate popular sensibilities, on the ground, to an orchestrated "historic bloc" he understood to represent the bedrock of political practice. He was drawn to the idea that anything could, in the appropriate circumstances, *become* politics.[29] This suggests that politics is itself contingent, shifting from conjuncture to conjuncture. What counts "as politics" is itself the consequence of political struggle. Each conjuncture carries with it a new configuration of the means by which politics works. This allows us to understand how the fraught pathologies, arising from the forms in which militant whiteness was lived in the moment of decolonization, possessed the potential to "become" – to be *translated* into – a formal politics. Gramsci deduced from his reading of Machiavelli that what he called "political passions" mark the ground from which a codified politics is elaborated. Political ideologies become, in effect, determinate ideologies "by a creation of concrete phantasy, which acts on a dispersed and shattered people to arouse and organize its collective will".[30] "Concrete phantasies" work here as a species of "mentality".

During the 1960s and 1970s the self-appointed tribunes of the white race addressed their plural constituents *as if* they were a "dispersed and shattered people": *as if* they were a defeated people. The stories they wove were lurid, their "passions" unconcealed. It may seem incomprehensible that the "concrete phantasies" underwriting the sensibility of whiteness-defeated came, a generation later, to be transmogrified – by means of an occult alchemy – into a set of governing practices inhabiting sectors of the historical democracies. That the whites of the early twenty-first century are a defeated people doesn't, on the face of it, make sense. But that is what I'm arguing has occurred. In this way, we can approach the ethnic populisms in the historical Atlantic democracies that have crossed the threshold and entered the field of state power.

The symbolic means that allowed this to happen was paradoxical. What historically signalled the defeat of black liberation, or the forestalled realization of black liberation, *came to be restaged as the defeat of whites*, in which the hopes for universal emancipation were not only driven out from the political world. They were expelled, too, from social memory.

The USA: the corrupt north, the redemptive south

If the twentieth century was the century of the colour-line, May 1954 represents a significant turning point. On 7 May, after a siege of eight weeks, the French in Vietnam were vanquished at Dien Bien Phu. After nearly ten years a guerrilla army defeated a European colonial power, expelling it from its land. It made possible the Bandung Conference of the following year and made plausible its rhetoric, proclaiming the end of the epoch of the white man.[31] The defeat also did much, particularly, to induce in the French army a psychotic vengefulness against "their" colonized, which later underwrote the prosecution of the war against the National Liberation Front in Algeria: and indeed in the metropole, evident through October 1961 in the systematic police murders of scores of Algerians in the centre of France's capital.[32] In the aftermath of the collapse of French authority in Vietnam, the USA was drawn into the vacuum. In 1954, on five separate occasions, the president, Dwight Eisenhower, was advised by his National Security Council, abetted by secretary of state John Foster Dulles and vice president Richard Nixon, once more to unleash atomic bombs on what they determined to be a hostile Asian power.[33]

Ten days after Dien Bien Phu the US Supreme Court, in its ruling on *Brown* v. *the Board of Education*, declared unconstitutional segregation in the nation's schools, a decision that created momentary jubilation among blacks in every corner of the nation.

These events, one domestic to the USA, the other more obviously international in its ramifications, repositioned the frontlines of race in the US, triggering a tectonic shift that reordered the foundations of the colour-line.[34] This transformation, slowly in its early moments in the fifties but accelerating in the sixties, polarized America. By the time of Black Power in the middle of the decade, "Vietnam" and "race" – or "decolonization" and "race" – no longer appeared as separate issues. Increasingly they marked a frontline that cut through both public and private life, dividing the official nation from its myriad of malcontents.

Yet the extent and depth of the struggle against racial injustice kept on slipping out of the collective memory of the political nation, notwithstanding the contemporary archive of materials – the profusion of movies, novels, histories, musics – working to commemorate the integrity of black mobilization. Commensurately, as this occurred, the very fact of the white backlash evaporated from social consciousness, as if there had never been such a thing.

The case of Martin Luther King is instructive. Memorialization, even in the moment that it is designed to cultivate remembrance, simultaneously imposes new regimes of forgetfulness. The further King is remembered, the further he's forgotten. There is barely any extant memory in the dominant political institutions of the United States of the vilification that King experienced during his lifetime. Nor is it easily recalled the degree to which denunciation emanated from the heartlands of the white republic: from the White House (not only of Lyndon Johnson, but of the Kennedy brothers), from the institutions of the federal state, and from the bulk of the nation's informed press.[35] For long there has been the conviction, among the remnants of the radical left, that towards the end of his life King's condemnation of the war in Vietnam was increasingly insistent and that, as this happened, his commitment to social struggles – to the (class) injustices of the oppressed in Chicago, Memphis, and elsewhere – deepened. Although King never chose to identify as a socialist this is, nonetheless, true. The more he struggled on the colour-line, the more he appreciated that the enemy was not only racial. Yet the forgetfulness regarding *this* King runs deep.

In April 1963 the Christian leaders of the civil rights movement pressed for the battle against segregation to move to Birmingham, Alabama.[36] The reasoning was luminous. If segregation were to be broken in a citadel of white supremacy, then its widespread destruction would follow. At the end of the year King collected his writings and speeches from the campaign, including his "Letter from Birmingham Jail", under the title *Why We Can't Wait*. King was explicit in drawing out the lines of connection between the racial struggles in the US and the movements for national liberation in Africa and Asia. Yet arresting is that the opening chapter is headed "The Negro Revolution". King, like a multitude of his allies in the black struggles of 1963, believed he was in the midst of making a revolution. This was a common perception. King's use of the term, in particular, was precise. The race struggles constituted what he specified as "The Third American Revolution". First there was the revolution of the late eighteenth century, which forged the independent nation; the second comprised the Civil War, leading in 1863 to the abolition of slavery; and – in a direct lineage – the "Third Revolution" was happening in 1963, a hundred years later. King's wasn't the unencumbered commitment to revolution of a figure such as Stokely Carmichael, who had emerged from the voter-registration backlands of Lowndes County, Alabama. The concept of America's "Third Revolution" came out of the pacifist, Christian, reputedly moderate strand of civil rights. It stipulated its own forms of militancy, conspicuously so in the strategic decision that the black children of Birmingham should march themselves into the underworld of the penitentiaries and improvised stockades of Alabama. Yet while all this is so, the idea of a "Third American Revolution" has been excised from contemporary memory. Who recalls it now? An entire continent of history has been cauterized from the nation's consciousness.

In part the narrowing of the horizons of black struggles, on the public agenda, can be explained by the mobilizations of disaffected whites, as whites *and* as the newly disinherited, which served to resist the incursions made by insurgent blackness. In the person of George Wallace we can see the irregular, crazed journeys that created a new political constituency by carrying the sensibilities of white disaffection into the field of state power.[37] This was a fraught process, marked by many false starts and occasions to double-back. In the process Wallace destroyed himself as an electoral figure in the nation's politics. But by the time his public life was cut short, much of what he had fashioned as the white "silent majority" had none too silently *become politics*. The racial core of Wallace's populist sensibilities migrated to Nixon's dreams for the future. With Nixon this was spoken in a different voice from Wallace's. Even though Nixon's populist instincts were more equivocal, he and Wallace shared a common enemy. They recognized radical blackness as the principal agent seeking to bind together all the varied manifestations of disorder which flashed across the TV screens.

In the autumn of 1963, Wallace toured the Ivy League universities, joking with his audiences, while simultaneously, with his inimitable brio, taunting them.[38] He wove together his opposition to civil rights with a new emphasis on low taxes and on rolling back the state. In the new year, he opened his presidential campaign in Wisconsin. The breakthrough occurred on 1 April. Booked by an ex-marine, Bronko Gruber, to speak at the Serb Memorial Hall in Milwaukee, Wallace faced an audience of "ethnics", to employ the psephological jargon of the time, consisting of Serbs, Poles, and Hungarians. As he entered the hall the audience, in an unanticipated moment of congregation, sang "Dixie" both in English and in their native tongues. Wallace's defence of a God-fearing America, in conjunction with his frenzied condemnation of civil rights – meaning, in this instance, nothing other than *blacks* – proved an intoxicating success. Southern populism had been smuggled across the Mason–Dixon Line, producing an explosive new element in the nation's politics. Shortly after, in the Indiana and Maryland primaries, Wallace stormed ahead.

He was a true son of a remembered Confederate past, born and bred a regular white supremacist in the Alabama mode. What he knew from his lived experience, however, did not spontaneously translate into formal politics. As a young adult, he had been an instinctive New Deal Democrat.[39] When in the late 1940s he first became active in politics he had only hesitantly allied himself to white supremacy, *as politics*. However, he was to discover that his backwoods white Methodist South was on the point of dislocation, and that the white citizens of Alabama were not reticent in turning race into a commanding political axiom. In the immediate aftermath of *Brown* v. *Board of Education* the racial backlash began to assume an organized political form, spreading from Mississippi across the southern states and cohering around a variety of well-funded White Citizens' Councils.

Wallace delivered his inaugural speech as governor of Alabama in Montgomery on 14 January 1963. He took the oath of office standing on the gold star marking the spot where, a century earlier, Jefferson Davis had been sworn in as provisional president of the Confederate States of America. Those listening donned white flowers to signify their allegiance to Anglo-Saxon supremacy. Wallace's speech had been drafted by the former Klansman Asa Carter. It played on memories of the Civil War *as* the present. He understood a new politics was required, driven by the will of the poor and of the neglected, in order to repair the ills perpetrated by the Washington elite and to ensure that the world was turned the right side up again. In this Alabama could call upon a providential history, for in Montgomery was to be found "this very heart of the Great Anglo-Saxon Southland".[40]

On four occasions he was to mount a campaign for the presidency: in 1964, 1968, 1972, and – after he was crippled following Arthur Bremer's attempt on his life on 15 May 1972 – again in 1976. His was a wildcat populism, which he embraced even while he couldn't bring himself to jettison the established party institutions.[41] He could never be sure where in national politics his allegiances would take him. In the fire and brimstone, each campaign burnt him up, every victory bringing his political destruction nearer. This "alchemist" of the new conservatism proved an active agent in the making of the racialized, populist conservatism of later decades.[42]

What made his entry on to the national stage possible were precisely the legislative advances of the civil rights movement, engineered particularly by President Johnson. A startling moment, a rare public occasion that induced King to tears, occurred in the wake of the bloody Selma confrontation of March 1965. The previous year the Civil Rights Act had been passed which outlawed discrimination on grounds of race, colour, religion, gender, or national origin. Although ambitious, the powers to enforce the provisions of the Act were weak. Johnson, who had spent the first decades of his political life as a segregationist, concluded on grounds of strategic calculation that it was necessary to force through a second Act. In the Capitol he announced that within the week Congress would have a new civil rights bill, with Selma as his justification. "Their cause must be our cause too. Because it is not just Negroes, but really it is all of us who must overcome the crippling legacy of bigotry and injustice." He paused, and continued: "And we shall overcome."[43] At this point, rhetorically at least, the civil rights fight for racial justice crossed the line and entered the state. No wonder King wept. At this juncture symbolism was all. For the moment it seemed as if the political world had been turned upside-down. Simultaneously, however, it served to resonate among those who believed the given racial order was in jeopardy, giving credence to the fear that the federal government had, all along, been in cahoots with the black militants. Wallace was in his element.

The main beneficiary of Wallace's arrival on the national stage was Nixon. In 1968 Republican strategists fell upon the tactic of "Who hates whom?", and organized electoral politics accordingly. In North and South alike, fear of what blacks had achieved became definitive, while the continuing authority of white southern Democrats deepened. The radicalism of the new politics didn't derive, innocently, from the realization that it would polarize the nation. It was, on the contrary, that social polarization was pursued as a virtue in itself. It marked the political line that divided the economically independent from the hapless, a frontline driven by unadorned racial fear.

It was these events that led Nixon, on 3 November 1969, to address the nation and call upon the "silent majority" to support him on Vietnam.[44] The invocation of the silent majority proved "the administration's masterstroke".[45] In the very act of its naming, the silent majority ceased to be silent. Nixon, sensing the political tide was turning his way, was well pleased: "We got those liberal bastards on the run now!"[46]

Nixon gave this a southern spin, the legacy of Wallace and the Serb Memorial Hall indelibly present. Nixon came to be deeply attached to the strategic idea of the South. His chief of staff, Bob Haldeman, recorded a classic Nixonite nocturnal monologue, delivered on the eve of his second presidential election, its hallucinogenic properties telling:

> He then got into his feeling for the South … Makes the point that union leaders are like the South. They want to abide by the law and they respect the Presidency … Our New American Majority appeals across the board for the same reasons to people. The basic American values. A strong United States patriotism, strong moral and spiritual values. Anti-permissiveness. They are turned off on welfare because it's wrong and because they are anti-elitist, plus they have selfish motives. They are American to the core. The Southerners are more so than the rest of the United States, because they are not poisoned by the elite universities and the media, but we're also high in Polish, Italian, mountain areas, farm states. Weak in the suburbia/big cities because here people are soft … That square America is coming back and that we didn't just gather a bunch of haters. The real issue is patriotism, morality, religion.[47]

Race, clearly, still had much work to do.

In our own times, what had once been articulated in Nixon's nocturnal monologues Trump has carried into the light of day: unapologetically spoken out loud at the hustings, addressing an America he *calls* his own in a bid to *make* America his own.

The defeat of the British world; the destruction of England

Like any number of other populists with race in their sights, Wallace's location in the political world was ambiguous. Rhetorically he aligned himself with downtrodden whites in opposition both to the state and to the social elites who made state power work. At the same time he was governor of Alabama and sought to cross the threshold and gain a grip on the executive authority of the federal state. Despite his protestations, and despite his personal reveries, he was never only "of the people". He operated, if waywardly, from inside the institutions of the state.

Nor did there ever exist a clear point when the psychic life of the imagined defeat of the white race freed itself from its founding passions and settled into a recognizably institutionalized politics. In Nixon the spontaneous mentalities that drove the initial experience of racial defeat were disciplined. But politics had turned. Populist properties assumed a greater gravity. The "gradations" of racial populisms intensified, entering the field of state power.

When we switch attention to the British world, to Britain and its "white" colonies, we encounter similar ambiguities, notwithstanding the profound differences in the respective configurations of race. There are three trajectories, each propelled by the apprehension that a defeat of historic dimensions had been suffered. First, there was the fallout from the challenges to colonial authority overseas, and the consequent reverberations that broke into the domestic polity. Second, there occurred the emergence of home-grown race tribunes, of whom Enoch Powell was supreme. And third, seemingly at a tangent, there emerged the constellations of the feminine and domestic moral crusaders who, while always hesitant in their approaches to race, believed that the (white) family in England had become prey to forces intent on the destruction of the nation. They sought, in reaction, to activate a popular politics able to recover the virtues of private life, free from the state. As Malcolm X observed, the revolution had come home: it was operating "inside the house".

The defeat of the white man's world

We can begin with Rhodesia. After Ian Smith's Unilateral Declaration of Independence for Rhodesia in 1965, the ties between the white militants of Rhodesia and those of the metropole deepened; each lived within the other. In the process, the domestic political field was reconfigured, the "defeat" of kith and kin overseas speaking to those whites who were sure they were living a defeat in England. It was commonplace to hear that the fate that had befallen Rhodesia, abandoned by Britain's ruling caste and left as the plaything for black revolutionaries, was but a premonition of what was heading England's way.

Smith was finally dispatched from office in June 1979, the *coup de grâce* delivered by Margaret Thatcher. He was convinced that he and his nation had been betrayed by erstwhile friends, now subject to unspeakably malevolent forces. He believed it his duty to speak for his own "dispersed and shattered people", searching for virtue in a world overrun by dark anarchy. His memoir, *The Great Betrayal*, published in 1997, is a mind-bending testament to whiteness unhinged. On every page it enacts the psychology of defeat. Smith presents himself as an abandoned soul condemned to stumble through the darkness, holding fast to that which was most elemental: the prospect of whiteness redeemed. Smith's telling of the story of the destruction of whiteness is driven by the ubiquity of betrayal, where allies turn themselves into enemies. He had been "stabbed in the back".[48] "Treason and corruption ... quietly and insidiously" penetrated "underground". "By the time one becomes aware of the destruction which has taken place, it is too late."[49]

It seemed at the time that Smith's was a conception of the world informed exclusively by the past, insistent on defying history. In retrospect, this seems not to have been so. It carried with it more of the future than those who disparaged Smith were able to acknowledge. What were once perceived as eccentric intoxications now pass, in some quarters, as the ruling common sense.

The defeat of England

On the face of it there is little that unites Powell and Wallace.[50] Yet despite the different historical circumstances, the identities between the British and the US experiences are, if partial, nonetheless compelling. Indeed it is precisely the difference in respective circumstances that makes their conjunction extraordinary: in historical formations so *unlike* a common process of neo-conservative recomposition can be identified. Powell was not Wallace, Wolverhampton was not Montgomery, nor the Race Relations Acts equivalent to the civil rights legislation. Yet in their respective bids to reorder the relations between people and state, given form by their insistence on placing race at the centre of things, equivalents emerge.

I won't discuss here Powell's notorious speech of 20 April 1968, invoking "Rivers of Blood".[51] Admittedly, it has the virtue of dramatizing the passage from unprocessed and ungrounded racial sensibilities, heavy with apprehension that an unnamed defeat has taken hold, to the more recognizable domain of "politics". The vast archive of letters from distraught citizens, which in the weeks following the speech were sent to Powell, represents a constitutive element of the larger phenomenon of *Powellism*, in which the figure of Powell himself – eccentric, narcissistic, intractable in his compulsion to attract scandal – is of lesser consequence than the following he had engendered. The day after Powell delivered the speech Edward Heath sacked him from his shadow cabinet, not wishing his party to be identified with Powell's views on race. This was a principled act on Heath's part. Yet in this very moment, for the many who came to support Powell, it worked to position him as the pre-eminent figure who had been shabbily treated by the powers-that-be, amplifying his populist credentials.

For my argument the crucial moment occurred shortly after, on 13 June 1970. Powell returned to Northfield, his childhood home, and reflected on the imminent danger to England presented by the hidden presence of man-ifold "Enemies Within". Its extravagant derangements are breathtaking.

"When the *Prince of Wales* and the *Repulse* disappeared beneath the waters of the Gulf of Siam", he declared, "at least we knew that Britain had suffered a defeat." Here, in the old labour heartlands of Northfield, Powell revived the memory of the disasters that presaged the collapse of Britain's Pacific empire, spelling out the connections between the defeat of Singapore in 1942 and of England in 1970:

> Britain at this moment is under attack. It is not surprising if many people still find that difficult to realize. A nation like our own, which has twice in this century had to defend itself by desperate sacrifice against an external enemy, instinctively continues to expect that danger will take the same form in the future. When we think of an enemy, we still visualize him in the shape of armoured divisions, or squadrons of aircraft, or packs of submarines. But a nation's exist-ence is not always threatened in the same way. The future of Britain is as much at risk now as in the years when Imperial Germany was building dreadnoughts, or Nazism rearming. Indeed the danger is greater today, just because the enemy is invisible or disguised, so that his preparations and advances go hardly observed.

There was, he announced, an enemy inside the nation, invisible to and, wilfully or unwilfully, ignored by those whose task it was to govern. This was an enemy depicted in the third person singular, and in the masculine form, in the idiom of antique military manuals: "he" was determined to destroy here, to outflank there, all the while seeking to secure ascendancy over "his" victims. The tale told was lurid and wild in its appeal to a homely reasonableness. The enemy, plague-like, was all around, winning victories when nobody was looking. It had become, quintessentially, the enemy of the everyday.

The speech rehearsed the convictions that Powell had long been practising: that madness was reason and reason madness, that truth was lies and lies truth: "The public are literally made to say that black is white." This terminology – black and white – was not coincidental. For Powell, race lay at the heart of the matter. He expressed outrage that there were those who could deny that "the English are a white nation". This he condemned as "heresy", the product of "a sinister and deadly weapon" which entailed "brainwashing by repetition of manifest absurdities". In his overarching scenario of decline and anarchy, black immigration constituted the decisive factor.

> 'Race' is billed to play a major, perhaps a decisive, part in the battle of Britain, whose enemies must have been unable to believe their good fortune as they watched the numbers of West Indians, Africans and Asians concentrated in her major cities mount towards the two million mark, and no diminution of the increase yet in sight.

Race signified more than immigration. It was, in Powell's imagination, the issue that bound together all the arenas of disorder, the single principle with the capacity to articulate all that threatened "the peaceable citizen". "The exploitation of what is called 'race'", he said, "is a common factor which links the operations of the enemy on several different fronts." Race, in this sense, became the means for signifying ethics itself. "[T]he battle of Britain" was to be "fought and won in the moral sphere".[52]

The destruction of England's families: a fallen world

In these years, "the moral sphere" boasted its own tribunes. On 27 January 1964, Mary Whitehouse launched in Birmingham the Clean Up TV Campaign (CUTV), which the following year turned into the National Viewers' and Listeners' Association (NVALA). The organization circulated a pamphlet that explained why she and her colleagues felt compelled to intervene in public life:

> Nothing seemed left but for the ordinary women of Britain to take matters into their own hands and to make it quite clear to the B.B.C. that we were prepared to fight for the right to bring up our children

in the truths of the Christian faith, and to protect our homes from exhibitions of violence.[53]

The event was reported in the local press, in turn generating stories nationally. Similar meetings spontaneously took place across the country. Within forty-eight hours, the mail began to arrive in bulk at the Whitehouse home.

This catalogue of condemnation derived from the belief that television was transmitting, and *making speakable* or normalizing, the ills of society. They were, it seems, everywhere – contagious, rampant, closing in – while the state had lost its authority. The weakening of Christianity, "drinking and foul language", the collapse of law and order, homosexuality, abortion, sterilization, ridiculing the armed forces: all fell within the remit of Whitehouse and her campaigners. Television was taken as the privileged medium by which social degeneration entered the lives of the nation, colonizing home after home. But, in truth, TV was never the real issue. It served principally to make tangible and nameable the anarchy that loomed. Through vigilant monitoring, what otherwise was frighteningly out of reach could be *located*; those responsible could be named and held to account.

The following May, a giant public meeting was organized at Birmingham Town Hall. Patricia Duce, the wife of a motor engineer, was charged with demonstrating how the CUTV was to operate. She opened by reminding her audience that her family had personified "a Britain that was worthwhile, clean and strong". But she quickly moved to the business in hand. Over the previous weeks she had led a small group who monitored 217 BBC television programmes in terms of "the overall impact on the viewer and whether this impact was in fact negative, destructive or offending against moral standards". As Duce insisted, the offending programmes worked to validate "freedom from the restraining influence of any decent instinct".[54]

Whitehouse herself took the larger view, dwelling on the role of the BBC as a governing institution, which she found grievously wanting. "The immediate object of this campaign is to restore the BBC to its real position of respected leadership of this country. We are NOT against the BBC, we are FOR the BBC." Even so, the BBC's readiness to ally itself with the forces of moral disorder presented itself to her as symptomatic of a deeper crisis *of the state*. The Ministry of Health she condemned for its lack of vigilance over the rise of venereal disease; the Home Office, the government office charged with the policing of British domestic life, she found lacking in moral energy; while the Ministry of Education refused to follow its own guidelines on inculcating schoolchildren with proper views on sexual matters. Whitehouse's emphasis on the BBC derived from her conviction that the Corporation possessed the greatest responsibility owing precisely to its proximity to the formal institutions of the state. Notwithstanding her roster of malefactors, it was the BBC that worked most to unnerve her. "We find it difficult to understand that those who weald [*sic*] power at Broadcasting House do not take account of the lesson of history – that a nation going soft at the centre is ripe for fall and take over."

But all was not lost. If the British people had "abdicated [their] wider responsibilities in the tired years after the war", the fight was now on. "It is to do what we may to right this wrong that we have thrown overboard our anonymity and come out to fight!"[55] At this point Whitehouse was enjoining the English *people* to mobilize against those who governed *the state* and who were proving too weak-willed to vanquish the enemies within.

It was exactly her very "ordinariness" that supplied her political cachet. Although her sympathies were undoubtedly to the right, her conception of the world was one that had little time for formal politics. Her utopian imaginary was peopled by those who were just like her – a manic politics of radical *sameness* – ethically civic and feminine, normatively heterosexual, English, and immovably white. Television could be part of this world, but only if it were programmed to looped showings of *Songs of Praise* and *The Black and White Minstrels* (showcasing minstrelsy as light entertainment for twentieth-century Britain), which stood out to the NVALA as "clean, wholesome and entertaining".[56] Whitehouse worked hard to be seen to operate in a moral cosmos untouched by political interest. In 1970 she wrote to the Revd Michael Seward, the information officer at the Church of England, to explain that she was neither of left or right: the struggle which exercised her was that "between right and wrong". "We live", she concluded, "in a fallen world."[57]

Yet working to mobilize the feminine and the domestic inevitably required accommodation with the business of politics. Even as Whitehouse espoused the chimera of non-politics, or anti-politics, she exuded a core of Jacobin intransigence. The force of her public interventions depended on her conviction that it was the duty of the citizen to be eternally vigilant. She took her citizenly duties to be paramount, sure that public institutions should be accountable to those whom they served. Her succession of authored books functioned as handbooks for social activism, carrying the necessary telephone numbers and addresses that every fledgling moral agitator would require. In October 1964 she abandoned her career as a schoolteacher to become a full-time CUTV cadre, forsaking what she publicly held most dear: her ordinariness. Whitehouse was becoming an exponent of what Michelle Nickerson has termed for the US "housewife populism".[58] When she announced her new-found role as a professional activist she expressed the hope that this would bring about the return of Britain to the nation it had once been, "strong and clean".[59] It was time for the privileges of anonymity to be "thrown overboard" and the struggle to be enjoined.

When Whitehouse called for a "strong and clean" nation, or depicted certain TV programmes as "clean", or even when they sought to "clean up" TV, they were drawing from an older imperial lexicon in which "cleanliness" signified an ethnic identification of unremitting rectitude. Whitehouse herself was possessed by the overpowering notion that she lived in corrupt times and that there had once existed a disciplined, virtuous moral order. Mostly this was articulated in theological categories, in which she fashioned herself as a resurrected Pilgrim. *We live in a fallen world*. But fantasized perceptions of lost times are always encoded in complex ways. Confronted by an anarchy that threatened to undo all the work of past generations, the idea of a nation that had once been great, and in which order had prevailed, took hold. In the fifties, Whitehouse observed, "we watched our empire slipping away".[60]

Despite her posture that neither left nor right held meaning for her, to imagine the nation once to have been "strong and clean" prescribed a politics of authoritarian temper, where older colonial and racial investments reverberate. If vigilance were relaxed, then even good folk could be turned. In a draft article in 1963, just at the time when her public persona was first taking off, she addressed "parents and teachers everywhere in the country": "How can we give [children] what it takes to face the onslaught of dirty, materialistic atheism which attacks them on every side? [This is] part of a deliberate plan to soften up the characters of men and women that they will become 'useable' and 'traitors'."[61] On such grounds, she identified those quislings in the state who were selling ordinary folk down the river. Treachery was all around. On such grounds she, too, took it to be her mission to arouse her "dispersed and shattered" constituencies.

"Wild power"

And Covenants, without the Sword, are but Words, and of no strength to secure man at all.

Thomas Hobbes, *Leviathan*[62]

Susan Buck-Morss writes that "every state that claims sovereign power" carries with it the potential to unleash an "unlimited, unmonitored wild zone of power". In the historic Atlantic democracies these "wild" zones of power, unmonitored, have become brutally evident. The arrival of Trump in office in the United States and of Boris Johnson and his cohorts in the UK indicate the degree to which "wildness" has begun to colonize the political mainstream. They are far from alone. Many such phenomena are perilously proximate. Axiomatic is not simply the presence of variants of ethnic populism, which even in traditionally stable democracies have persistent if chequered histories. Telling is their gradual incursion into the field of state power.

A new structure of politics emerges which, paradoxically, feeds off species of anti-politics.[63] Violence, real and symbolic, is more securely embedded in the everyday practices of governance. In Bonapartist mode, the executive habitually runs roughshod over the legislature, with government-by-tweet setting new precedents, by-passing the inherited "checks and balances" that historically mediated the relations between citizen and state. The differentiation between media celebrities and those delegated to take responsibility for public matters, or the distinction between a "fictive" world and a "real" world, get dizzyingly confused. The customary prohibitions on unashamed mendacity evaporate. The very business of government appears alarmingly receptive to the incursions of emotive and unprocessed reflexes, justified (if justified at all) by calculated appeals to the popular will. It is this which (in the UK at any rate) is indiscriminately, repetitively, condemned as "populism".

Overbearing is the matter of race. This isn't a question only of the *persistence* of race but more of its amplification. The imbrication of racial power and state power draws ever tighter. The legitimacy of invoking the virtues of race represents a sharp break with the recent historical past. The "wildness" of contemporary public life is, I suspect, to be located in the varied allegiances to the dream of a revived racial order.

It's for this reason – in a bid to explain the "wildness" of wild power – that I'm compelled to return to the global racial panics generated in the reaction to decolonization and civil rights/Black Power. Powell admitted that race had become the principle of articulation through which, *in the metropoles*, all social relations accrued meaning. Of course, there are other vantage points to adopt. But race alerts us to a crucial nerve-point of the contemporary political world. At the time of decolonization, the reactions I allude to here were testament to a collective psychic mentality, raw and unprocessed. Yet these tones can be heard again, although now emanating from inside the state, from inside "the house".

The relations connecting *those* pasts to *this* present are not unmediated. Yet I'm persuaded that the mid-twentieth-century drama of insurgent blackness now functions in public life as the "vanishing mediator" in the contemporary, unbridled reassertions of right populisms.[64] As the experiences of decolonization and civil rights/Black Power move deeper into the past, their visible historical gravity diminishes. Yet in the haphazard, irregular zones of *memory* these pasts are still material, continuing to operate in the present. Even if "vanished" from the conscious mind, they work to orchestrate the present. It may be that this represents less a new "structure of politics" than the *incipient erosion, or the incipient destruction, of politics* as a field of social action.

This brings us to Hannah Arendt. In *The Origins of Totalitarianism* she advanced the counterintuitive argument that totalitarianism represented, not the occasion when every corner of the social world was politicized, but exactly the contrary. What she learned from Hitler's Germany and Stalin's Soviet Union was that these were regimes in which the political field itself was disassembled. Paradoxically, *the state* engineered a situation of comprehensive de-politicization, in which there could be no bargaining with adversaries. Those deemed as political antagonists had to be eliminated.[65] Totalitarianism, for Arendt, is predicated on the relegation of politics to a deep-freeze. It represents the antidote to politics, as we have known it.

In this, too, Benjamin is close. "A storm is blowing in from Paradise …", he wrote early in 1940, in response to the figure of the angel in Paul Klee's painting *Angelus Novus*. The angel's face is turned to the past, his eyes wide and his mouth open. This is, Benjamin explains, the angel of history:

> Where a chain of events appears before *us*, *he* sees one single catastrophe, which keeps piling wreckage upon wreckage and hurls it at his feet … This storm drives him irresistibly into the future to which his back is turned, while the pile of debris before him grows toward the sky. What we call progress is *this* storm.[66]

In our times the fallout from unregulated power all around us accumulates. The chaos deepens as the future appears ever darker. Benjamin's vision is ever more urgent. The words are familiar. But their resonance deepens.

Notes

1 Malcolm X, cited in Saladin Ambar, *Malcolm X at Oxford Union: Racial Politics in a Global Era* (New York: Oxford University Press, 2014), 35. With thanks to

my co-authors, particularly Camilla Schofield, Jennie Sutton, Stuart Ward, Clive Webb, and Dan Geary; thanks as well to John Munro (especially), Rob Waters, and Richard Drayton.

2   Susan Buck-Morss, *Thinking Past Terror: Islamism and Critical Theory on the Left* (London: Verso, 2006), 31.

3   For Farage's posse, see Arron Banks, *The Bad Boys of Brexit: Tales of Mischief, Mayhem and Guerrilla Warfare in the EU Referendum Campaign* (London: Biteback, 2016).

4   www.independent.co.uk/news/uk/politics/eu-referendum-nigel-farage-4am-victory-speech-the-text-in-full-a7099156.html (accessed 15 April 2020).

5   Anthony Barnett, *The Lure of Greatness: England's Brexit and America's Trump* (London: Unbound, 2017).

6   Bill Schwarz, "Decolonization as Tragedy?", in John H. Arnold, Matthew Hilton, and Jan Rüger (eds), *History after Hobsbawm: Writing the Past for the Twenty-First Century* (Oxford: Oxford University Press, 2018), 96–117.

7   Frantz Fanon, *The Wretched of the Earth* (Harmondsworth: Penguin, 1967); Frantz Fanon, *Alienation and Freedom* (London: Bloomsbury, 2018).

8   In the historiography, see Wm. Roger Louis, "The Dissolution of the British Empire in the Era of Vietnam", *American Historical Review* 107.1 (2002): 1–25; A. G. Hopkins, "Rethinking Decolonization", *Past and Present* 200 (2008): 211–47.

9   Bill Schwarz, *The White Man's World* (Oxford: Oxford University Press, 2011).

10 Aimé Césaire, *Discourse on Colonialism* (New York: Monthly Review, 1972); Gary Wilder, *Freedom Time: Negritude, Decolonization, and the Future of the World* (Durham, NC: Duke University Press, 2015).

11 Richard H. King, *Civil Rights and the Idea of Freedom* (New York: Oxford University Press, 1992); Richard H. King, *Race, Culture and the Intellectuals* (Baltimore, MD: Johns Hopkins University Press, 2004).

12 Bill Schwarz, "Black America and the Overthrow of the European Colonial Order: The Tragic Voice of Richard Wright", in Ruth Craggs and Claire Wintle (eds), *Cultures of Decolonisation: Transnational Productions and Practices* (Manchester: Manchester University Press, 2016), 29–50.

13 To stay with Carmichael: Stokely Carmichael and Charles V. Hamilton, *Black Power: The Politics of Liberation in America* (Harmondsworth: Penguin, 1969); *Ready for Revolution: The Life and Struggles of Stokely Carmichael* (New York: Scribner, 2005); *Stokely Speaks: From Black Power to Pan-Africanism* (New York: Random House, 1971); Peniel Joseph, *Stokely: A Life* (New York: Basic Civitas, 2014).

14 In contemporary political science this view occurs in Ira Katznelson's magisterial *Fear Itself: The New Deal and the Origins of Our Time* (New York: Liveright, 2013), 39; Aziz Rana, *The Two Faces of American Freedom* (Cambridge, MA: Harvard University Press, 2014), tracks the nation's historical evolution from its settler origins.

15 The literature on the interactions between the US and the UK is growing; it is too large to cite here. But see John Munro, "Imperial Anticommunism and the African American Freedom Movement in the Early Cold War", *History Workshop Journal* 79 (2015): 52–75.

16 Elaine Mokhtefi, *Algiers, Third World Capital: Freedom Fighters, Revolutionaries, Black Panthers* (London: Verso, 2018).

17 Joel Stone (ed.), *Detroit 1967: Origins, Impacts, and Legacies* (Detroit, MI: Wayne State University Press, 2017); Mark Binelli, *The Last Days of Detroit: Motor Cars, Motown and the Collapse of an Industrial Giant* (New York: Vintage, 2014). For an insightful account of how the insurgency travelled through popular life, see Stuart Cosgrove, *Detroit 67: The Year That Changed Soul* (Edinburgh: Polygon, 2016), the opening volume of his Soul Trilogy. See also Kathryn Bigelow's 2017 movie, *Detroit*.

18 Paul Gilroy, *After Empire: Melancholia or Convivial Culture?* (Abingdon: Routledge, 2004).

19 Richard Drayton, "Secondary Decolonization: The Black Power Movement in Barbados, c. 1970", in Kate Quinn (ed.), *Black Power in the Caribbean* (Gainesville, FL: University Press of Florida, 2014), 117–35. For the case of South Africa, see Gail M. Gerhart, *Black Power in South Africa: The Evolution of an Ideology* (Berkeley, CA: University of California Press, 1978).

20 Robert Waters, *Thinking Black: Britain 1964–1985* (Berkeley, CA: University of California Press, 2018); Kennetta Hammond Perry, *London is the Place for Me: Black Britons, Citizenship and the Politics of Race* (New York: Oxford University Press, 2015); Marc Matera, *Black London: The Imperial Metropolis and Decolonization in the Twentieth Century* (Berkeley, CA: University of California Press, 2015).

21 Jordan Camp, *Incarcerating the Crisis: Freedom Struggles and the Neoliberal State* (Berkeley, CA: University of California Press, 2016). In 2016 Zadie Smith said of the evolution of her writing: "If the clouds have rolled over my fiction it is not because what was perfect has been proved empty but because what was becoming possible – and is still experienced as possible by millions – is now denied as if it never did and never could exist." *Free Fall: Essays* (Harmondsworth: Penguin, 2018), 39.

22 Walter Benjamin, "Theses on the Philosophy of History", in his *Selected Writings, Vol. IV: 1938–1940*, ed. Howard Eiland and Michael W. Jennings (Cambridge, MA: Belknap Press of Harvard University Press, 2006), 391.

23 Wolfgang Schivelbusch, *The Culture of Defeat: On National Trauma, Mourning, and Recovery* (London: Granta, 2003), particularly his emphasis on the "dreamworlds" generated by historic defeats.

24 Following the defeat of Japan in 1945, Christopher Bayly and Tim Harper think in terms of the reimposition of European rule in South-East Asia as a form of *recolonization*: *Forgotten Armies: Britain's Asian Empire and War with Japan* (Harmondsworth: Penguin, 2005), and *Forgotten Wars: The End of Britain's Asian Empire* (Harmondsworth: Penguin, 2008). A defining element was the lingering memory of white Allied prisoners of war, after the capture of Hong Kong and Singapore, condemned to unmediated racial subordination, becoming *natives*: Gerald Horne, *End of Empire: African-Americans and India* (Philadelphia, PA: Temple University Press, 2008).

25 These were the words that Enoch Powell quoted from a constituent in his speech of 20 April 1968; see Bill Smithies and Peter Fiddick (eds), *Enoch Powell on Immigration* (London: Sphere, 1969), 35.

26 Ronald Segal, *The Race War* (New York: Bantam, 1967), viii.

27 Bill Schwarz, "'The Only White Man in There': The Re-Racialisation of England, 1956–1968", *Race and Class* 38.1 (1996): 65–78.

28 See, for my purposes, Michel Vovelle, *Ideologies and Mentalities* (Cambridge: Polity, 1990), ch. 7, "The *Longue Durée*", emphasizing the genealogical duration of symbolic systems. See also Bill Schwarz, "Forgetfulness. England's Discontinuous Histories", in Astrid Rasch and Stuart Ward (eds), *Embers of Empire in Brexit Britain* (London: Bloomsbury, 2019), 49–58. Close to my theme is Lefebvre's classic *The Great Fear*. "It was characteristic of the Great Fear that these alarms [of marauding brigands] spread far and wide with the most astonishing speed instead of staying purely local … people believed that they were coming because they were expecting them." Georges Lefebvre, *The Great Fear of 1789: Rural Panic in Revolutionary France* (London: New Left Books, 1973), 137.

29 Sally Davison, David Featherstone, and Bill Schwarz, "Introduction: Redefining the Political", in Stuart Hall, *Selected Political Writings: 'The Great Moving Right Show' and Other Essays*, ed. Sally Davison, David Featherstone, Michael Rustin, and Bill Schwarz (London: Lawrence and Wishart, 2017), 1–15.

30 Antonio Gramsci, *Selections from the Prison Notebooks* (London: Lawrence and Wishart, 1971), 125–6.

31 Dipesh Chakrabarty, "The Legacies of Bandung: Decolonization and the Politics of Culture", in C. J. Lee (ed.), *Making a World After Empire: The Bandung Moment and its Political Afterlives* (Athens, OH: Ohio University Center for International Studies, 2010), 45–68.

32 Jim House and Neil MacMaster, *Paris 1961: Algerians, State Terror, and Memory* (Oxford: Oxford University Press, 2006).

33 Stephen E. Ambrose, *Eisenhower. Vol. II: The President, 1952–69* (London: Allen and Unwin, 1984), 229.

34 This can be read through the prism of popular music: Brian Ward, *Just My Soul Responding: Rhythm and Blues, Black Consciousness and Race Relations* (London: UCL Press, 1998).

35 Richard Lentz, *Symbols, The News Magazines, and Martin Luther King* (Baton Rouge, LA: Louisiana State University Press, 1990).

36 Bill Schwarz, "'Our Unadmitted Sorrow': The Rhetorics of Civil Rights Photography", *History Workshop Journal* 72 (2011): 138–55.

37 For the difficulties in integrating Wallace in the historiography, see Alan Brinkley, *Liberalism and Its Discontents* (Cambridge, MA: Harvard University Press, 1998), ch. 16, "The Problem of American Conservatism".

38 Dan T. Carter, *The Politics of Rage: George Wallace, the Origins of the New Conservatism, and the Transformation of American Politics* (New York: Simon and Schuster, 1995). I rely on this fine account in Bill Schwarz, "The Silent Majority: How the Private Becomes Political", in Anna Von Der Goltz and Britta Walsdscmidt-Nelson (eds), *Inventing the Silent Majority in Western Europe and the United States: Conservatism in the 1960s and 1970s* (New York: Cambridge University Press, 2017), 147–71; and "'Segregation Tomorrow'", *New Formations* 33 (1998): 112–24. For the longer duration, see Dan T. Carter, *From George Wallace to Newt Gringrich: Race in the Conservative Counterrevolution* (Baton Rouge, LA: Louisiana State University Press, 1999); Thomas J. Sugrue, *Not Even Past: Barack Obama and the Burden of Race* (Princeton, NJ: Princeton University Press, 2010).

39 Katznelson, *Fear Itself*, details the alliance between Roosevelt and the southern Democrats. His discussion of "fear" is of the first importance.

40 Cited in Carter, *Politics of Rage*, 11.

41 Michael Kazin, "The Grass-Roots Right: New Histories of US Conservatism in the Twentieth Century", *American Historical Review* 77.1 (1992): 136–55.

42 Carter, *Politics of Rage*, 12.

43 I follow Robert A. Caro's account which opens his *The Years of Lyndon Johnson. Vol. II: Means of Ascent* (London: Pimlico, 1992), xiii–xxi.

44 Richard Nixon, "The Silent Majority", 3 November 1969, http://watergate.info/1969/11/03/nixons-silent-majority-speech.html (accessed 15 April 2020).

45 Jeremy Varon, *Bringing the War Home: The Weather Underground, the Red Army Faction, and Revolutionary Violence in the Sixties and Seventies* (Berkeley, CA: University of California Press, 2004), 134.

46 Richard Reeves, *President Nixon: Alone in the White House* (New York: Simon and Schuster, 2001), 145.

47 Reeves, *President Nixon*, 631–2.

48 Ian Smith, *The Great Betrayal: The Memoirs of Ian Douglas Smith* (London: Blake, 1997), 186.

49 Smith, *Great Betrayal*, 319–20.

50 With thanks to Michael Kazin for sharing with me his unpublished paper, co-written with Stéphane Porion, "George Wallace and Enoch Powell: Comparing the Politics of Populist Conservatism in the US and the UK".

51 Enoch Powell, "Rivers of Blood", in Lord Howard (ed.), *Enoch at 100: A Re-evaluation of the Life, Politics and Philosophy of Enoch Powell* (London: Biteback, 2014). See Akala, *Natives: Race and Class in the Ruins of Empire* (London: Two Roads, 2018); and Camilla Schofield, *Enoch Powell and the Making of Postcolonial Britain* (Cambridge: Cambridge University Press, 2013).

52 Enoch Powell, "The Enemies Within", in John Wood (ed.), *Powell and the 1970 Election* (Kingswood, Surrey: Elliot Right Way Books, 1970), 106–9.

53 Ben Thompson, *Ban This Filth! Letters from the Mary Whitehouse Archive* (London: Faber, 2012), 34.

54 Thompson, *Ban This Filth!*, 68–9.

55 Thompson, *Ban This Filth!*, 69–71.

56 Thompson, *Ban This Filth!*, 375, citing an NVALA verdict.

57 Whitehouse, cited in Thompson, *Ban This Filth!*, 327.

58 Michelle Nickerson, *Mothers of Conservatism: Women and the Postwar Right* (Princeton, NJ: Princeton University Press, 2012).

59 Thompson, *Ban This Filth!*, 73.

60 Mary Whitehouse, *Whatever Happened to Sex?* (Hove: Wayland, 1977), 8.

61 Thompson, *Ban This Filth!*, 27. Or alternatively, before the Nazis took over Poland they flooded the bookstalls with pornography – "This is a fact", Whitehouse, *Whatever Happened to Sex?*, 176.

62 Thomas Hobbes, *Leviathan* (1651), ed. Richard Tuck (Cambridge: Cambridge University Press, 1996), 117.

63 For an early assessment, see Jane Caplan, "Donald Trump: Between Election and Inauguration", *History Workshop Journal* 83 (2017), 3–9.

64 Fredric Jameson, "The Vanishing Mediator: Narrative Structure in Max Weber", *Working Papers in Cultural Studies* 5 (1974): 111–49.

65 Hannah Arendt, *The Origins of Totalitarianism* (London: Allen and Unwin, 1958); and her manuscript, "On the Nature of Totalitarianism. An Essay in Understanding", The Hannah Arendt Papers at the Library of Congress, https://memory.loc.gov/cgi-bin/ampage?collId=mharendt&fileName=05/051930/051930page.db&recNum=0 (accessed 15 April 2020).

66 Benjamin, "Theses on the Philosophy of History", 392.

Opposing civil rights

4

Enoch Powell's America / America's Enoch Powell

Clive Webb

O N SATURDAY 20 April 1968, J. Enoch Powell delivered what is arguably the most controversial speech in post-war British history.
The Conservative MP and Shadow Secretary of Defence addressed an
audience of party activists at the Midland Hotel in Birmingham. In what
soon became known as the "Rivers of Blood" speech, Powell warned that
Britain faced imminent disaster because of mass immigration from the
Commonwealth nations of Asia, Africa, and the Caribbean.[1] His intervention in the migration debate provoked a heated public reaction that exposed
and exacerbated political cleavages in British society.

This chapter uses a transatlantic lens through which to reassess the
origins and impact of Powell's "Rivers of Blood" speech. In so doing, it
contributes to recent scholarship that evaluates the mutual influence of
Britain and the United States in shaping diasporic racial politics.[2] That
literature has focused largely on the adoption and adaptation of American
civil rights activism by campaigners for racial equality in Britain and, to
a lesser extent, the reverse transmission of political tactics. Scholars have
concentrated on both grassroots tactics and governmental reform, particularly the influence of American federal legislation and its enforcement
at state and local level on the race relations laws enacted in Britain during
the 1960s.[3] However, the political reactionaries who fought to protect

white racial privilege have received far less attention. Situating "Rivers of Blood" in a transatlantic context provides further insight into the interpenetration of British and American race relations.

The racial conflict that afflicted the United States in the late 1960s was a potent stimulus to the tone and content of Powell's speech. "Rivers of Blood" in turn had an important impact on the opposing forces in the American civil rights struggle. For African Americans who saw their domestic struggle for racial reform as one front in a larger global fight against white hegemony, there was a strong sense of revulsion at the speech and expressions of solidarity with Britain's racial and ethnic minorities. Powell also attracted the attention of white racists who were waging an increasingly desperate defence of Jim Crow. Despite the many dissimilarities between the immigration issue in Britain and the race politics of the American South, segregationists perceived Powell as a politically powerful champion of white supremacy who could revitalize their own dwindling fortunes.

* * *

Powell's motivations for making his speech were complex. His desire to overthrow Edward Heath as leader of the Conservative Party, his opposition to a Race Relations Bill that would outlaw racial discrimination in housing and employment, and his recent success in campaigning for restrictions on the number of Kenyan Asians expelled from their own country being admitted to Britain were all contributory factors.

Yet Powell's perception of the United States was also profound. Powell's caustic criticism of American race relations formed one front of a broader intellectual assault on the United States. He made his disdain for the country clear in "The Great Dilemma", a reflection on his first transatlantic trip published by the *Sunday Telegraph* a month before the Birmingham speech. Powell opened with the observation that the short tour he had undertaken did not qualify him "to pontificate with assurance on all aspects of American life, history and politics", before proceeding to do precisely that. The Conservative MP subscribed to a condescending attitude common on the British political right that American culture was an oxymoron. "All the wealth, all the success, all the accumulation of treasure and learning in the United States", he asserted, "has not availed to make it metropolitan." Far from producing any distinctive culture of its own, he continued, the United States owed much of the artistic and intellectual distinction it had achieved to European émigrés. Powell also demonstrated a disdain for American foreign policy that appealed to the prejudices of both the political left and right in Britain. He cited the ongoing Vietnam War, of which he was a long-standing opponent, as evidence of the naivety of American policymakers who believed that with the appropriate resources they could remould the rest of the world in their own image.[4] In a later speech he similarly disparaged this "technological optimism", which he believed had created unrealistic expectations about the capacity of the state to create what President Lyndon Johnson had described as "the Great Society".[5]

While the tenor of his attitude towards the United States was typically one of disdain, when it came to the country's race relations Powell reacted with fearful apprehension. Specifically, he saw in the American urban disorders of the late 1960s a warning of Britain's own possible fate. Powell initially refuted any comparison between the racial dynamics of Britain and the United States. He stressed what he considered "the far-reaching difference between the American and the British phenomena and the almost total falsification which results from seeing and describing the British phenomenon in American terms". Specifically, Powell contrasted the "negro minority" of the United States with an immigrant population in Britain that was "preponderantly of Asian origin" and growing in such numbers as to constitute "an Oriental colonisation" of his own country.[6]

The parallels between race relations in Britain and the United States were in truth far from precise, in terms of history, demographics, and law. Nonetheless, the *perception* that the Atlantic divide between the two countries had become ever narrower during the course of the twentieth century had an important influence on the ideas and actions of Britons and Americans, both blacks and whites, reformists as well as reactionaries. Despite his protestations, Powell's ominous warning of imminent racial catastrophe in Britain owed much to the example of the United States. The racial conflict in American inner cities during the late 1960s sounded a warning bell that resounded across the Atlantic. American race relations influenced not only the tone and content of "Rivers of Blood", but also its critical reception in Britain and the United States.

Powell's ominous predictions stemmed from a conviction that America's present racial troubles provided a portent of Britain's possible future. Unless the British government imposed tight controls on the number of foreign nationals entering the country, he prophesied, the "tragic and intractable phenomenon" of racial disorder "is coming upon here by our volition and our own neglect". The threat of Britain succumbing to the same urban disorder that blighted the United States had, he believed, become increasingly acute because of the transatlantic dissemination of Black Power. In July 1967, the African American radical Stokely Carmichael had visited Britain in pursuit of his mission to connect the African American struggle for racial equality with other liberation movements and thereby forge a global movement against Western imperialism and capitalism. The large urban riots of African Americans in Newark and Detroit – both of which were triggered by police violence and harassment – received front-page coverage in the British press, and coincided almost precisely with Carmichael's arrival. With Black Power seen by many commentators as having fanned the flames of ghetto rioting in the United States, anxieties grew that his entry to Britain would act as the catalyst for imitative acts of violence. "Has a revolution started?" asked a *Times* advertisement for an interview with Carmichael. "Will England go the way of America?"[7]

Carmichael remained in the country for less than two weeks, but his presence had a galvanic impact on the nascent Black Power movement in Britain as well as civil rights radicals in Northern Ireland. Establishment fears led Home Secretary Roy Jenkins to issue an order banning the African American activist from returning to Britain on the grounds that he had incited racial hatred, which the government had outlawed under the Race Relations Act of 1965.[8] Carmichael did not have to be in the country to be perceived as a continuing threat. In December 1967, the BBC ran a radio interview with him while he was in Paris. The organization was forced to apologize for the broadcast following pressure from a politician who claimed that the interview contravened the incitement clause of the Race Relations Act. That politician was Enoch Powell.[9]

In response to Carmichael and burgeoning black militancy in Britain, the Conservative MP undertook a tour of the United States during which he studied the recent urban disorders. While there he also established a contact who sent him what eventually amounted to hundreds of newspaper cuttings about the rioting. The evidence Powell accumulated at first hand and through the press informed the analysis provided in the "Rivers of Blood" speech.[10] He now revised his earlier claim that race and ethnic relations in Britain and the United States were dissimilar. As historian Camilla Schofield observes, he explicitly equated the impact of a rapid influx of black southern migrants to cities such as Detroit during and after the Second World War and the future prospects for British urban centres whose populations were swollen by New Commonwealth immigrants. As he asserted in a speech to the Southall Chamber of Commerce in November 1971:

> An almost precise arithmetical parallel is afforded by the trans-formation of the cities of the northern and north-eastern States of America which has taken place since World War II, a process which is an immigration in all but name ... At an interval of twenty or thirty years you can leave out "Detroit" and insert "Birmingham."[11]

The American experience informed not only the content of "Rivers of Blood", but also its popular reception in Britain. Powell's warning that Britain was at risk of emulating American racial conflict resonated with a public that had already been exposed for months to scenes of urban rioting on the other side of the Atlantic. Recent developments in communications satellites enabled the media to narrow the oceanic distance between Britain and the United States, transmitting near simultaneous reports on the long hot summers that afflicted American inner cities in the late 1960s. Images of rioting and violence broadcast into the homes of British audiences collapsed their comfortable sense of distance from events on the other side of the Atlantic, feeding fears of similar conflict erupting in their own country. Writing in the early 1970s, sociologists Paul Hartmann and Charles Husband observed how "the image of black–white confrontation derived from the media coverage of the American disorders becomes the model for thinking about the British situation, both because it is known to be familiar to the audience, and because it fulfils expectations of how race relations situations develop".[12] In delivering the "Rivers of Blood" speech, Powell therefore gave voice to social anxieties already swirling in the British public's collective imagination. In September 1967, the BBC had broadcast a documentary titled *The Colour War* that attempted to address three questions arising from American urban unrest: "Why is it happening? Will it get worse? Will it happen here?"[13] Powell provided emphatic answers to concerns that had plagued the public for more than six months, answers that confirmed their worst fears. Yes, he affirmed, it could happen here. And soon.

* * *

Given how important American race relations were in shaping "Rivers of Blood", it is surprising that scholars have not considered its critical reception in the United States. Powell, a prominent and outspoken politician, had already attracted considerable press interest on the other side of the Atlantic. His comments about immigration therefore generated enormous American media attention, reversing the usual transatlantic trend of British newspapers devoting front-page coverage to the United States.

Powell had many admirers in the United States, especially conservatives attracted by his advocacy of restricting the social and economic role of the state. The excitement he generated is conveyed by an advertisement for a lecture Powell gave in Milwaukee during May 1969 on the need for an unfettered free market that proclaimed "A GROWING NUMBER OF AMERICAN CONSERVATIVES BELIEVE HE MAY WELL BE BRITAIN'S 'MAN OF THE HOUR'".[14] Powell's transatlantic appeal was evident from his participation in public events such as the Rational Debate Series, convened by the American Enterprise Institute for Public

Policy Research, a conservative think tank in Washington, DC. The debate brought together Powell and former Illinois senator Paul H. Douglas, a strong advocate of African American civil rights who had served as the architect of several of President Johnson's Great Society programmes. Powell added intellectual weight and international prestige to a conservative backlash against federal government reforms that had purportedly cost much but delivered little. His speech disparaged Johnson's attempt to harness the power of the state to improve the material conditions of American citizens, contending that a free market system was "itself a form of government, a method of regulating the economic relations between citizens which is enormously superior in efficiency to the alternative".[15] This critique of liberal interventionism offered a resonant transatlantic harmony to the swelling voices of American conservatism and anticipated the reaction against big government under the administrations of Richard Nixon and especially Ronald Reagan.

Powell continued to undertake numerous speaking engagements in the United States over the next few years. He capitalized on his status as former minister for health in Harold Macmillan's government to deliver a series of lectures in September and October 1971 on "the failures of socialized medicine and why America should not adopt a National Health Insurance system".[16] Two years later, he shared a stage with such conservative luminaries as Irving Kristol and William F. Buckley at a Center for Constructive Alternatives symposium in Michigan.[17] Powell's association with Buckley, founder of the influential magazine *New Review*, also included his making several appearances on the conservative publisher's public affairs television show *Firing Line*.[18] The Conservative MP's populist instincts even led to an appearance on the *Dick Cavett Show*, sharing an unlikely billing with actor Roger Moore.[19]

It was nonetheless "Rivers of Blood" that gained Powell his greatest notoriety in the United States. He could not avoid the issue even when he sought to focus on other matters. During a tour of American university campuses to discuss the importance of the free market, for instance, he found himself constantly having to defend himself against accusations of racism.[20]

The US press drew on its own country's civil rights struggle to interpret Powell, drawing analogies between the maverick British politician and American opponents of black civil rights. Some journalists compared Powell with reactionary Arizona senator Barry Goldwater, whose failed presidential campaign of 1964 had included a pledge to defend southern states' rights against federal civil rights reform. Powell's representation of himself as a fearless advocate of free speech who opened up public debate on a controversial social issue that other politicians avoided drew comparison with Goldwater's infamous statement that "extremism in the defense of liberty is no vice".[21] Other likenesses included Vice President Spiro Agnew and Senator Joseph McCarthy, neither of which withstood close scrutiny but which nonetheless captured the spirit of Powell as a reactionary bête noire of the liberal left.[22]

More commonly though, reporters saw Powell as the transatlantic counterpart of George Wallace, the former Alabama governor who launched a third-party candidacy for the presidency in the same year as the "Rivers of Blood" speech.[23] Wallace had first attracted notoriety following his inaugural gubernatorial address in January 1963, in which he pledged to defend "segregation now … segregation tomorrow … segregation forever". Although the personalities of the erudite classical scholar and the plain-spoken southern politician appeared to be poles apart, Powell and Wallace both espoused a reactionary form of populism that exploited white working-class resentment towards black people and the liberal elites who supposedly accorded them preferential treatment. As the *New York Times* asserted, for all of his intellectual sophistication, Powell was little more than "George C. Wallace with an Oxford accent".[24]

Powell himself had a strong aversion to being labelled the British George Wallace because of his determination to promote the intellectual respectability of his position on race and immigration. He made a concerted effort to rid himself of his reputation as a racist demagogue in an address delivered at Tulane University in April 1971. Powell informed his audience that, far from being a racist, his actions in opposing unrestricted immigration were comparable to statesmen such as Winston Churchill who in response to the rise of Nazism during the 1930s had advocated Britain's rapid rearmament. According to Powell, in both instances popular misunderstanding had resulted in "an inversion of reality". The politicians who called for rearmament had at the time been branded warmongers when their actual intention was to forestall military conflict. Likewise, his own purpose in warning of what he foresaw as the consequences of mass immigration was to prevent rather than provoke violence. "Those who wanted to avert war, and pointed to the means of avoiding it, were represented as desiring it", Powell asserted. "Those who wanted to prevent internecine strife by the simplest means while those means were still available, were represented as imbued with hatred." In drawing this analogy Powell evidently intended to demonstrate that, like the politicians of the interwar era, history would also later redeem him. Whether he succeeded in cleansing his stained reputation is nonetheless open to speculation. Powell might have intended his speech to bolster himself rather than to belittle people of colour, but by suggesting that Commonwealth migrants were as much of a hostile threat to Britain as the Wehrmacht, he did little to demonstrate his racial pluralism.[25]

The American press was not persuaded by Powell's efforts to distance himself from accusations of racism. Indeed, emphasizing his bigotry presented a welcome opportunity to deflect long-standing British criticism of race relations in their own country. Throughout the 1950s and 1960s, the British media had offered strong moral and political support for the African American freedom struggle. According to a survey of western European nations conducted by the United States Information Agency in 1956, Britain was, along with the Netherlands, the harshest critic of American racial politics.[26] The tone of this criticism was often condescending. British political commentators used American racial conflict as a counterpoint to their own country's supposedly more progressive treatment of peoples of colour, both at home and in its colonies.[27]

During the 1960s, the forward advance of civil rights reform in the United States nonetheless appeared to narrow the Atlantic divide. With federal legislation having, if not routed white supremacy, then at least forced it into retreat, Britain, by contrast, seemed to be slow to facilitate the integration of its racial and ethnic minority population. The election in 1964 of Conservative candidate Peter Griffiths as MP for the West Midlands town of Smethwick following a campaign that manipulated the racial anxieties of white voters provided evidence of this complacency, as did the ineffectual Race Relations Act, itself modelled on American civil rights legislation, passed by the Labour government the following year. As the *Guardian* concluded, Britain had started to surrender the moral high ground that it had occupied for so long. "From our island, where multiracialism is still a word and not a reality, we are not in a position to condemn or to offer guide-lines for the future."[28]

Powell's dramatic intervention in the immigration debate rapidly accelerated a process already in motion, resulting in the conclusion of many American political observers that while the United States was progressing towards a more perfect union, Britain was degenerating into a society resembling the Jim Crow South. "In some respects Britain is the mirror image of the United States in the 1950s, particularly in the rhetoric that is used in discussing racial matters", observed American political scientist Richard Longaker, who was at the time of Powell's speech based at London's Institute of Race Relations. "One feels that one has heard it all before."[29] If Longaker's tone was forlorn, then for other political commentators there was a certain schadenfreude in seeing a Britain that had for so long sanctimoniously disparaged American race relations now succumbing to prejudice and intolerance. Responding to "Rivers of Blood", the *Philadelphia Inquirer* ridiculed Powell and other Britons for their overreaction to what was by American standards a very small and therefore far more easily assimilable non-white population. "Some self-righteous fingers have been pointed at America's racial troubles by the British", the paper reminded readers. "Instead of criticizing the shortcomings of others, they ought to try setting a good example themselves."[30]

* * *

It was not only the mainstream press whose attention Powell attracted. Hs position on race and immigration also drew the interest of American racists who at a time of increasing political retreat in the fight against black civil rights drew renewed inspiration from his mobilization of grassroots support and impact on electoral politics. Powell attracted accolades from segregationists who saw him as an uncompromising champion of the white race. This led in 1971 to Powell undertaking a trip to the American South where he addressed members of the Citizens' Council, the region's pre-eminent segregationist organization.

Southern segregationists' support for Powell reveals that the transatlantic relationship between British and American racists was more reciprocal than is usually understood. Yet as the civil rights reforms of the 1960s forced American segregationists into retreat, so their dominance over the British far right yielded to a more equal partnership. By the time Powell came to international prominence, two landmark federal laws had revolutionized southern race relations: the Civil Rights Act of 1964, which demolished the legal foundation of racial segregation, and the Voting Rights Act of 1965, which secured greater political representation for African Americans. Most white southerners had come to accept that at least minimum compliance with federal court orders to desegregate public facilities was preferable to the continued destabilization of their communities by recalcitrant resistance. The openly racist defence of Jim Crow ceded to a coded language emphasizing individual rights and freedom of choice.[31]

Yet a recalcitrant hardcore of southern segregationists continued to resist any racial reform. As historian Zoe Hyman has demonstrated, during the 1960s international politics assumed growing importance to these white supremacists. With massive resistance under increasing pressure from political forces not only outside but also increasingly within the South, segregationists looked beyond regional and national borders in search of new alliances to sustain their cause. They drew particular inspiration from South Africa and later Rhodesia, states where, in contrast to the American South, white rule was ascendant. In building alliances with these regimes, southern segregationists broadened their political standpoint beyond the parochial interests of their own region to embrace a global ideology of white racial supremacy. As the old racial order in their own region collapsed, so southern white supremacists endowed South Africa and Rhodesia with ever greater significance as the unassailable strongholds of an otherwise defeated cause.[32] As Roy Wilkins, the executive secretary of the National Association for the Advancement of Colored People (NAACP), asserted, white extremists might be in the minority within their own region but they regained a sense of strength in numbers by seeing themselves as members of an "imagined community of white men".[33]

The rise of Powellism made Britain a similar source of hope to segregationists. It helped offset their own losses by seeing the American South as only one front in a larger global conflict, the outcome of which remained undecided. Through Powell they experienced a sense of vicarious power that compensated for their own political weakness. For a waning massive resistance movement, Powell provided inspirational evidence that the global fight to preserve white racial integrity was not lost. A Gallup poll of British public opinion in late April 1968, for instance, revealed that 74 per cent of respondents sympathized with the sentiments of "Rivers of Blood".[34]

Powell was by this time already moving in the same intellectual circles as southern segregationists. For example, he penned an article for the racial science journal *Mankind Quarterly*, which also published contributions from southern white supremacists such as Carleton Putnam and Wesley Critz George.[35] Powell's essay, "Population Figures in the United Kingdom", attempted to demonstrate that official figures undercounted the number of non-white immigrants in Britain.[36]

In October 1971, Powell accepted an invitation to deliver lectures in Mississippi and Louisiana. The tour's organizer was Roger Pearson, a British anthropologist based at the University of Southern Mississippi who had strong ties with the American far right.[37] Powell's itinerary included talks to college faculty in Hattiesburg, Mississippi, and New Orleans and a private luncheon in Jackson, Mississippi, hosted by the Citizens' Council.[38] There were no invitations to the media because Powell wanted to avoid adverse publicity back in Britain. Having strategically dissociated himself from far right organizations in his own country, this collusion with the Council is revealing of how Powell operated in a less constraining political environment.[39] Powell vehemently denied that he was a racist. As he asserted, "If by a racist you mean a man who despises a human being because he belongs to another race, or a man who believes that one race is inherently superior to another in civilisation or capability, then the answer is emphatically no." Yet his readiness to associate privately with organized racists in the Deep South undermines his public assertions.[40]

There was no immediate similarity between the political contexts in which Powell and the Council operated. While Powell opposed a mass immigration to Britain that had only occurred during the previous two decades, white southerners had interacted with African Americans for centuries. Powell shared what Josiah Brownell describes in his chapter as a "racial population panic", the fear that whites would be demographically overwhelmed by people of colour. By contrast, the South had historically attracted fewer immigrants than any other region of the United States. Although there were some foreign settlers, they constituted only a fraction of the larger population.[41] Nor did Powell frame his racial politics in a way that fitted the traditional black/white binary of the South. His concern was as much, if not more, with Asian immigrants as with those from the Caribbean. Powell's resistance to immigration was nonetheless rooted in a notion of distinct and incompatible cultures that resonated with white southerners who feared the societal collapse that they believed racial integration would bring about.

Powell had developed this idea during his posting to India in the Second World War. According to Powell, India was unfit for political democracy because of "communalism", by which he meant that its people identified themselves more in terms of caste than nation. This absence of any unified sense of belonging rendered it impossible to create and sustain a system of political democracy. Powell applied this concept to Britain, arguing that immigrants lacked the same sense of identification with their adopted nation as did the indigenous population. As the number of immigrants increased, so too did the threat to unity and order. The racial homogeneity of a nation was therefore the very foundation of political democracy.[42] This line of reasoning would have resonated with segregationists fearful of the impact of black enfranchisement, especially in a state such as Mississippi where African Americans constituted around half the population. The analogy between Britain and the American South was, however, far from precise. Powell himself saw Caribbean immigrants as less of a challenge to British democracy than those who came from South-East Asia because they shared a certain common identity with the native population in terms of language and religion. However, the nuances of Powell's argument were probably of less importance to southern segregationists than the broader point about the dangers posed by racial heterogeneity.

Powell appealed to the Council for a number of other reasons. His criticisms of race relations in cities such as Newark and Detroit resonated with southern segregationists who claimed that white northern liberals should concentrate on discrimination against African Americans in their own communities rather than criticize conditions south of the Mason–Dixon line. Powell's opposition to the imposition of economic sanctions on the white minority government in Rhodesia also chimed with white southerners who saw the status of that regime as analogous to their own. Above all, however, it was his warning of the disaster that would come from misguided attempts to create a multiracial society that resonated with his audience.[43]

There are no transcripts of the addresses that Powell gave on his trip to the American South, but his subject was race relations. The timing of the tour was important since it came only a year after Mississippi had belatedly desegregated its public school system. According to Roger Pearson, Powell's lectures "would greatly raise their [segregationists'] own morale, and would be of definite value, as they are influential in their own part of the world". The Council drew particular inspiration from Powell's criticism of the British establishment's efforts to foster racial integration, which the organization compared with its own federal government's promotion of busing to enforce school desegregation.[44] As an expression of his gratitude to Powell for rekindling the flame of Council members' political faith, Pearson later sent him a one-year subscription to the white South African publication *Behind the News*, further evidence of how racists perceived the global interconnectedness of their cause.[45]

Revealing as this episode is of the increasing significance of international politics to southern segregationists, it also tells us much about the way in which Powell negotiated a fine line between political extremism and mainstream respectability. The attraction of addressing the Council was presumably that it provided him with an international platform to articulate his opinions on immigration. Representatives from the local and state establishment attended the Jackson luncheon, creating something of the ceremonial aspect of a visit by a foreign dignitary. At the same time, Powell's decision to eschew publicity suggests a concern not to alienate the conservatives who were attracted to his ideas about free trade and private enterprise but disavowed racism. William F. Buckley, who on several occasions hosted Powell on his *Firing Line* television programme, had by the late 1960s abandoned his opposition to federal civil rights reform and sought to purge racial demagogues from the renascent conservative movement. This included his disavowal of the American politician most commonly compared with Powell, George Wallace.[46] Buckley admitted that he remained "undecided" about Powell. The British politician's fraternization with the Citizens' Council therefore risked his rather precarious relationship with the more respectable luminaries of American conservatism. Significantly, it was a risk he was willing to take.[47]

* * *

While Powell attracted white segregationists, he repelled African Americans. The black press in the United States provided extensive coverage of Powell's role in fomenting the rise of organized racism in Britain. African American newspapers had long taken an active interest in race relations on the other side of the Atlantic, particularly from the late 1940s with the arrival of the Windrush generation of migrants. The rise of Powellism should not have come as a surprise to African Americans. Over the course of the twentieth century, the black press in the United States had charted Britain's failure to come to terms with transformations to the global racial order, both in terms of its reluctance to surrender an empire that suppressed the democratic aspirations of millions of people of colour, and the unwelcoming reception of the unprecedented number of Caribbean and Asian migrants who came to the country in the wake of the Second World War. Although unprecedented in terms of the outspokenness of his racism, Powell was therefore seen not as an aberration but rather as symptomatic of Britain's decline over many decades.

Race relations in Britain had earlier attracted the attention of African Americans searching for inspirational models on which to base their vision of a more egalitarian United States. Some African Americans had in the late nineteenth and early twentieth centuries favourably compared what they saw as benevolent white British colonial rule with the endemic racial violence and discrimination of their own country.[48] Whether they entirely believed their representation of the British Empire is unclear. Exaggerating the supposed contrast between Britain and the United States also served as a rhetorical strategy to shame their own country into improving the state of its race relations.[49]

However, as African Americans developed an increasingly global political consciousness during the interwar era, their criticism of the British sharpened. By the First World War, African American leaders had come to recognize the interconnectedness of their own struggle for liberation with the nationalist insurgencies against colonial domination in Africa, Asia, and the Caribbean. Britain therefore became seen as an enemy rather than an ally in the world uprising against white supremacy. At the same time as they became increasingly critical of white Britons, African Americans developed ties with pioneering black activists in Britain that formed part of what Paul Gilroy described as the Black Atlantic, the diasporic network that spanned across national boundaries and oceanic space. The NAACP, for example, featured Dr Harold Moody's League of Coloured People, founded in 1931, in the pages of its *Crisis* magazine.[50] African American solidarity with nationalist movements in countries including Burma and especially India also led them to oppose a post-war American financial loan to Britain unless decolonization was made an explicit condition.[51]

The rise of Enoch Powell did not therefore represent a sudden moment of historical rupture for African Americans but, rather, the culmination of a longer-term process of political regression. African American newspapers had once hoped that the United States would reach a point of convergence with Britain in terms of the treatment of racial and ethnic minorities. The rise of Powellism suggested that while the racial politics of the two countries had become more analogous, this owed less to progressive reform in the United States than to the increasingly reactionary nature of Britain. Having once used an idealized notion of Britain as a political foil to the Jim Crowism of their own country, the African American press concluded that race relations in the United States had, if anything, now surpassed conditions on the other side of the Atlantic.[52]

African American newspapers were unequivocal in their denunciation of the "Rivers of Blood" speech. *Jet* magazine branded Powell "England's Top Racist".[53] The *Chicago Defender* accused the MP of having spewed "a venom that may well poison the well of public opinion" on race and immigration. The paper concluded that Powell's incendiary rhetoric threatened to create the "bloody clashes on the American style" against which he claimed to be warning. The *Defender* also shared with other black newspapers the conviction that the British government must move fast to contain the damage Powell had done by passing the new Race Relations Bill introduced by Labour Home Secretary Roy Jenkins the previous year.[54]

African Americans drew on conditions in their own country to interpret Powell. Black editorialists made the same comparison as the mainstream media between Powell's demagoguery and George Wallace's reactionary populism.[55] The *Pittsburgh Courier* additionally compared the failure of England and Wales Attorney General Elwyn Jones to prosecute Powell for contravening the incitement to racial hatred clause of the 1965 Race Relations Act with the United States Supreme Court decision in *Brandenburg* v. *Ohio* upholding the Ku Klux Klan's First Amendment right to freedom of speech. In both instances, the state had failed to protect racial minorities from the danger posed by hate speech.[56]

This extensive critical coverage of Powell demonstrates how African Americans continued to contextualize their own struggle against racism as one front in a larger global insurgency against white supremacy. A syndicated opinion piece on Powell by Whitney Young of the National Urban League evoked W. E. B. Du Bois's dictum that "The problem of the twentieth century is the problem of the color line" in explaining the relevance of British race relations to African American readers.

According to Young, "the future of the globe is tied closely to the success of international efforts" to facilitate relations between all races and thereby avert "the ultimate disaster of race war". The diasporic identity that united black people around the world meant that the struggle against racism in one nation was shared by all. This was especially true of Britain because the rise of racism in that country had broader diplomatic implications. Powell's importance in securing a surprise Conservative victory in the general election of 1970 had encouraged the party to shift rightwards on race and immigration. Young feared that this could include an easing of diplomatic pressure on the white supremacist regimes in South Africa and Rhodesia. "America's attempt to win greater influence among African states will suffer a setback", he warned, "if our government does nothing to keep the British to their previous policy of support of the UN's position."[57]

* * *

Back home in Britain, newspaper coverage of Powell also demonstrates how American race relations provided a framework within which the media tried to analyse the rise of racism in the country. Recent events in the United States, specifically the murder of Martin Luther King and the resultant African American unrest that swept through urban areas across the country, informed the critical reception of Powell's speech.

An array of historical and current influences informed British responses to mass immigration from the Commonwealth. Foremost among them were the experiences first of empire, and more contemporaneously, of decolonization. The imperial past and its aftermath shaped the opinions of advocates as well as opponents of immigration. As both Jordanna Bailkin and Wendy Webster have argued, Britain sought to retain close ties with its former colonies by promoting the Commonwealth as a multiracial fraternity. The need to retain strong diplomatic and trade relations encouraged public concern for the welfare of migrants from decolonized nations who came to Britain.[58] Conversely, the mass immigration of people of colour also led some Britons to adopt a frontier mentality similar to that of colonial settlers who sought to defend what Webster describes as their "embattled Englishness" against a huge and hostile force.[59]

The experience of fighting a war against the forces of fascism further informed British attitudes not only to mass immigration but also the racist reaction epitomized by Powell. During the post-war era, the horrors of the Holocaust had redefined public discourse on race. Although the political establishment enacted discriminatory measures against immigrants, it did so without overt reference to race. As also became true of their American counterparts, British politicians instead coded their language through the use of synonyms for race such as law and order and public health. This differentiated them from more blatant racists whose agitation against immigrants political commentators commonly compared with the rise of fascism in the 1930s.[60] By exceeding the boundaries of what was deemed legitimate public discourse on the immigration issue, Powell therefore exposed himself to accusations of Nazism. Home Secretary Roy Jenkins responded to "Rivers of Blood" by alerting the public to the "dreadful danger" of a "Nazi Britain". Edward Heath, who had expelled Powell from the shadow cabinet, also evoked the spectre of Nazism in a speech calling on Young Conservatives to resist his nemesis. Tyranny, he proclaimed, "had to be fought in Germany in the thirties, in America in the fifties, and wherever it happens today it must be fought".[61]

The American experience was also integral to the way that the British press interpreted Powell. In one publication after another, cartoonists satirized the Conservative MP by portraying him as an aspirant Imperial Wizard of the Ku Klux Klan. These editorial cartoons used the Klan figuratively rather than literally. While there was no suggestion that Powell actually sought to mobilize a British Klan, his incendiary rhetoric demonstrated the susceptibility of the British electorate to southern-style demagoguery. A cartoon in the *New Statesman*, for instance, depicted Powell manipulating a shadow puppet (a visual play on his position within the Conservative shadow cabinet) of an armed Klansman taking aim at immigrants. The *Sunday Mirror* similarly featured a cartoon in which Powell had ignited a fire, the white flames of which assumed the form of Klansmen. The *Telegraph* also portrayed Powell as planting seeds of hatred in British soil that germinated into Klansmen. Although the Klan served only as a visual metaphor, these satirical images show how a Britain struggling with the transition to a multiracial society used events on the other side of the Atlantic as an interpretative lens through which to understand the causes and potentially dire consequences of anti-immigrant intolerance.[62]

The apparent deepening of America's racial divisions further informed political reaction to the "Rivers of Blood" speech. Martin Luther King's assassination in Memphis, Tennessee, little more than two weeks earlier on 4 April 1968 had burst the swelling banks of black anger in the United States. A wave of civil disorders erupted across the country. For British commentators across the political spectrum, the riots were a potent warning of what could befall their own country if political leaders failed to find legislative solutions to the increasingly fractious race issue. According to the chairman of the Institute of Race Relations, Lord Walston, King's death and the violent civil unrest that it precipitated were "dreadful reminders of what can happen in a civilized and liberal country if the problems associated with race relations remain unsolved".[63] Walston was not alone in urging the immediate enactment of a new Race Relations Bill to facilitate the integration of a black population that was becoming more and more alienated from mainstream society, as evidenced by the rise of Black Power politics in Britain. Even the *Daily Mail*, while uncertain about the proposed law, urged Parliament to "learn from the American experience just how racial problems fester if neglected" and push forward with a close reading of its provisions. The price of failure, it concluded, was too terrible to contemplate.[64]

The unrest that followed King's death informed political reaction to Powell's speech. To many observers, Powell threatened to precipitate the very conflict against which he was warning. A *Times* editorial that denounced what it described as "An Evil Speech" concluded that coming within weeks of King's assassination and its destructive aftermath, "It is almost unbelievable that any man should be so irresponsible as to promote hatred in the face of these examples of the results that can follow."[65] Anthony Goodman, formerly of the Campaign Against Racial

Discrimination, went so far as to denounce "Rivers of Blood" as "the type of speech made in the United States by many white people who, not only by their words, but also by their actions ... have provided the background for the bullet which ended the life of Martin Luther King". The eventual enactment of the Race Relations Bill in October 1968 therefore served in some respects as a means of honouring King's legacy. As Labour MP David Ennals asserted, the implosion of the non-violent movement in the United States demonstrated that "Those who suggest that we ought to delay before bringing in our legislation are playing with fire and danger."[66]

Conclusion

Situating Powellism in a transatlantic context demonstrates its impact far beyond British domestic politics. While this essay has focused on the critical reception of "Rivers of Blood" in the United States, further research will reveal the global reach of Powell's influence. In particular, more work needs to be done on the political effect that the maverick politician had on the public discussion of race and migration in the Commonwealth, including those countries from whence the new settlers to Britain came, and predominantly white nations such as Australia where immigration was a source of heated public debate.

Ultimately, for all the parallels drawn between Britain and the United States, there were as many differences as there were similarities. Enoch Powell was not only a very different personality than George Wallace, but so too were the racial conditions in their respective countries and the solutions they proposed to address them. Powell's proposed repatriation of racial minorities was not, for example, a shared aim of Wallace. In both instances, however, these maverick politicians mobilized a discontented white population that believed it had been marginalized by an unaccountable political elite that prioritized the interests of racial minorities. The populist appeal of Powell and Wallace had an important influence on party politics in their respective countries, the former helping to secure an electoral swing to the Conservatives and the latter encouraging the Republicans' successful pursuit of their southern strategy. Although

Powell and Wallace fell as rapidly as they rose, they demonstrated how politicians could manipulate white nationalist sensibilities to electoral advantage on both sides of the Atlantic, a legacy bequeathed to Brexiteers and Donald Trump. The rise of reactionary populism not only in Britain and the United States but around the world suggests that Powell has finally achieved mainstream respectability for the political opinions espoused in "Rivers of Blood" that eluded him in his own lifetime.

Notes

1 The best of the many analyses of Powell and the "Rivers of Blood" speech include Bill Schwarz, *The White Man's World* (Oxford: Oxford University Press, 2011), and Camilla Schofield, *Enoch Powell and the Making of Postcolonial Britain* (Cambridge: Cambridge University Press, 2013).

2 A good starting point for this is Robin D. G. Kelley and Stephen Tuck (eds), *The Other Special Relationship: Race, Rights, and Riots in Britain and the United States* (New York: Palgrave Macmillan, 2015).

3 Brett M. Bebber, "'Standard Transatlantic Practice': Race Relations and Antidiscrimination Law across the Atlantic", *Journal of Civil and Human Rights* 4.1 (2018): 5–36. For the transnational history of "race relations" as a field of British sociology and colonial expertise, see Paul Rich, "End of Empire and the Rise of 'Race Relations'", in *Race and Empire in British Politics* (Cambridge: Cambridge University Press, 1986), 169–204.

4 Enoch Powell, "The Great American Dilemma", *Sunday Telegraph*, 17 March 1968, 7. For more information on Powell's opposition to the Vietnam War, see Robert Shepherd, *Enoch Powell* (London: Hutchinson, 1996), 306–7.

5 John Roberts, "Buckley Heard by Tulane Unit", *Times-Picayune*, 22 April 1971, 22.

6 Undated and untitled speech, the papers of Enoch Powell, Churchill Archives Centre, Cambridge, POLL 10/7.

7 *The Times*, 10 March 1968.

8 "Racial Incidents Plaguing British", *New York Times*, 26 July 1967, 22.

9 "BBC Admit Interview 'Error'", *Guardian*, 23 December 1967, 14.

10 Shepherd, *Enoch Powell*, 338.

11 Schofield, *Enoch Powell and the Making of Postcolonial Britain*, 214; J. Enoch Powell, speech delivered at Longford, Middlesex, Southall Chamber of Commerce, 4 November 1971, POLL 3.2.1.20. Powell's collection of press clippings is in POLL 8.1.5.

12 Paul Hartmann and Charles Husband, "The Mass Media and Racial Conflict", *Race & Class* 12.3 (1971): 275.

13 David Hendy, *Life on Air: A History of Radio Four* (Oxford: Oxford University Press, 2007), 20.

14 "Economic Expediency – Road to Chaos", advertisement for event hosted by the Milwaukee Society, 7 May 1969, POLL 10/6B.

15 Paul H. Douglas and J. Enoch Powell, *How Big Should Government Be?* (Washington, DC: American Enterprise Institute for Public Policy Research, 1968), 61.

16 M. R. Saxon to Leonard Read, Foundation for Economic Education, 14 May 1971; Enoch Powell to Leonard Reed, 18 May 1971, POLL 10/6B.

17 Center for Constructive Alternatives symposia programme, February 1973, POLL 10/7.

18 Television listings, *Times-Picayune*, 31 January 1971, 44. Powell was advertised as "England's Most Controversial M.P."

19 "Television Highlights", *Oregonian*, 14 May 1971, 71.

20 *San Francisco Chronicle*, 23 May 1969, newspaper clipping, POLL 10/6B.

21 See, for example, *San Francisco Sunday Examiner & Chronicle*, 25 May 1969, newspaper clipping, POLL 10/6B.

22 John P. Leacacos, "Britain Strives to Solve Racial Unrest in Decade", *Plain Dealer* (Cleveland, OH), 10 October 1970, 1.

23 See, for example, "Racial Issue in Britain", *Philadelphia Inquirer*, 23 April 1968, 22; Roger Ricklefs, "Britain's Tories and Their Racist Image", *Wall Street Journal*, 26 April 1968, 15; and "Britain's 'Wallace' Has His Own Party Edgy", *Washington Post*, 4 November 1968, A2.

24 "Racism in Britain's Election", *New York Times*, 6 June 1970, 30. See also Frank Melville's extended article in the 15 December 1968 edition of the paper, "One Visit to America and Britain's Enoch Powell Began Sounding Like George Wallace". Powell was actually educated at Cambridge. His accent was also that of the city where he was born and raised, Birmingham, something that set him apart from many other leading Conservatives and strengthened his populist appeal.

25 J. Enoch Powell, "Government and Nations Errors: Rearmament and Immigration", speech delivered at Tulane University, 21 April 1971, POLL 4/1/7 File 3.

26 Hazel Erskine, "The Polls: World Opinion of U.S. Racial Problems", in Michael L. Krenn (ed.), *Race and the U.S. Foreign Policy from the Colonial Period to the Present: A Collection of Essays* (New York: Garland, 1998), 275–88.

27 Kennetta Hammond Perry, "'Little Rock' in Britain: Jim Crow's Transatlantic Topographies", *Journal of British Studies* 51 (2012): 155–77.

28 Editorial, "On the Road to Montgomery", *Guardian*, 11 March 1965, 10. For more on the Griffiths campaign, see Joe Street, "Malcolm X, Smethwick, and the Influence of the African American Freedom Struggle on British Race Relations in the 1960s", *Journal of Black Studies* 38.6 (2008): 932–50.

29 Richard P. Longaker, "Britain's Color Problem Deepens", *Los Angeles Times*, 14 May 1968, A5.

30 "Racial Issue in Britain", *Philadelphia Inquirer*, 23 April 1968, 22.

31 Kevin M. Kruse, *White Flight: Atlanta and the Making of Modern Conservatism* (Princeton, NJ: Princeton University Press, 2005).

32 Zoe L. Hyman, "American Segregationist Ideology and White Southern Africa, 1948–1975", PhD thesis, University of Sussex, 2011.

33 Roy Wilkins, "Britain's George Wallace", *Baltimore Afro-American*, 15 October 1968.

34 Amy Whipple, "Revisiting the 'Rivers of Blood' Controversy: Letters to Enoch Powell", *Journal of British Studies* 48.3 (2009): 717–18.

35 William H. Tucker, *The Cattell Controversy: Race, Science, and Ideology* (Urbana, IL: University of Illinois Press, 2009), 120–4.

36 J. Enoch Powell, "Population Figures in the United Kingdom", *Mankind Quarterly*, October 1970, 87–95.

37 For more information on Pearson, see Russ Bellant, *Old Nazis, the New Right, and the Republican Party: Domestic Fascist Networks and their Effect on U.S. Cold War Politics*, 2nd edn (Cambridge, MA: Political Research Associates, 1989), 60; and Sara Diamond, *Roads to Dominion: Right-Wing Movements and Political Power in the United States* (New York; Guilford Press, 1995), 87.

38 Arrangements for the tour discussed in Roger Pearson to Enoch Powell, 20 June 1971; Powell to Pearson, 29 June 1971; Pearson to Powell, 12 July 1971; Pearson to Powell, 21 August 1971; Powell to Pearson, 31 August 1971; Powell, 10 September 1971; Curtis W. Caine to A. F. Summer, 25 October 1971, POLL 10/6. See also George Shannon, "Enoch Powell in Jackson", *Citizen*, November 1971, 16–23. Powell certainly addressed faculty at the University of Southern Mississippi but it is unclear from this correspondence at which institution in New Orleans he spoke. On his USM visit, which also included an elaborate reception, see Monte Piliawsky, *Exit 13: Oppression & Racism in Academia* (Boston: South End Press, 1982), 105, 113, 223, n. 1.

39 Paul Foot, *The Rise of Enoch Powell* (Harmondsworth: Penguin, 1969), 56–7.

40 Peter Alexander, *Racism, Resistance and Revolution* (London: Bookmarks, 1987), 45.

41 Rowland T. Berthoff, "Southern Attitudes Toward Immigration, 1865–1914", *Journal of Southern History* 17.3 (1951): 328–60. On more contemporary immigration trends, see Mary E. Odem and Elaine Lacy (eds), *Latino Immigrants and the Transformation of the U.S. South* (Athens, GA: University of Georgia Press, 2009).

42 Peter Brooke, "India, Post-Imperialism and the Origins of Enoch Powell's 'Rivers of Blood' Speech", *Historical Journal* 50.3 (2007): 669–87.

43 Daniel McNeil, "'The rivers of Zimbabwe will run red with blood': Enoch Powell and the Post-Imperial Nostalgia of the Monday Club", *Journal of South African Studies* 37.4 (2011): 731–45.

44 Pearson to Powell, 15 May 1971, POLL 10/6. For further analysis of Powell's relationship with the Citizens' Council, see Daniel Geary and Jennifer Sutton, "Resisting the 'Wind of Change': The White Citizens' Councils and European Decolonization", in Manfred Berg and Cornelius Van Minnen (eds), *The U.S. South and Europe* (Lexington, KY: University Press of Kentucky, 2013), 265–79.

45 Schofield, *Enoch Powell and the Making of Postcolonial Britain*, 318.

46 Alvin Felzenberg, "How William F. Buckley, Jr., Changed His Mind on Civil Rights", *Politico*, 13 May 2017, www.politico.com/magazine/story/2017/05/13/william-f-buckley-civil-rights-215129 (accessed 23 July 2018).

47 Unidentified newspaper clipping, William F. Buckley, Jr, "Understanding Powell", POLL 10/6B.

48 See, for example, James Weldon Johnson, "The Practice of Lynching: A Picture, the Problem and What Shall Be Done About It", *Century Magazine*, November 1927, 65–70; and cartoon, "Darkest India—Whitest America", *Chicago Defender*, 17 December 1927, 1.

49 There were also those who dissented from the notion of British imperialism as a progressive force. See, for example, the observations about W. E. B. Du Bois's visit to Britain in 1921 in Walter White, *A Man Called White: The Autobiography of Walter White* (Athens, GA: University of Georgia Press, 1995), 60–2.

50 Harold Moody and W. B. Mumford, "The League of Colored Peoples", *The Crisis* 40.1 (1933), 13–14; "Colored Peoples in the British Empire", *The Crisis* 47.6 (1940), 174, 186.

51 "'No Loan to Britain for Imperialism'—NAACP", *Pittsburgh Courier*, 22 December 1945, 34. See also Horace R. Cayton, "England's Greed", *Pittsburgh Courier*, 9 March 1946, 7.

52 "Britain Backing Racism", *Pittsburgh Courier*, 18 May 1968, 3; "English Get More Racist", *Pittsburgh Courier*, 16 November 1968.

53 "England's Top Racist Wants No Blacks There", *Jet*, 18 March 1971, 46.

54　"Racism in Britain", *Chicago Defender*, 4 May 1968, 10; "Britain Faces Racism", *Chicago Defender*, 13 July 1968, 10.

55　Powell was "the George Wallace of Britain", according to the *Pittsburgh Courier*. "A Dangerous Racist", *Pittsburgh Courier*, 14 May 1977, 6. See also "Racist Says Daughter Can Wed Who They Like", *Jet*, 23 January 1969, 29.

56　"Racial Taunts To Be Allowed", *Pittsburgh Courier*, 7 December 1968, 2.

57　Whitney M. Young, Jr, "To Be Equal", *Soul City Times* (Milwaukee, WI), 9 July 1970, 4.

58　Jordanna Bailkin, *The Afterlife of Empire* (Berkeley, CA: University of California Press, 2012), 24, 50; Wendy Webster, *Englishness and Empire 1939–1965* (Oxford: Oxford University Press, 2005), 159.

59　Webster, *Englishness and Empire*, 152.

60　Andy R. Brown, *Political Languages of Race and the Politics of Exclusion* (Aldershot: Ashgate, 1999), xix–xxi; Christopher Hilliard, "Words That Disturb the State: Hate Speech and the Lessons of Fascism in Britain, 1930s–1960s", *Journal of Modern History* 88 (December 2016): 787.

61　"Roy Jenkins Sees "Dreadful Danger" of a Nazi Britain", *Observer*, 5 May 1962, 2; "Heath Tells Powell 'I'll Fight Tyranny'", *Daily Mail*, 18 November 1968, 1.

62　Arthur Horner, cartoon, "Shadow Cabinet", *New Statesman*, 26 April 1968; Edward McLachlan, cartoon, "McLachlan's View", *Sunday Mirror*, 28 April 1968; Nicholas Garland, cartoon, "Where the seeds of the whirlwind have been sown", *Daily Telegraph*, 19 January 1970, 2.

63　Lord Walston, "Lessons from America", letter to the editor, *The Times*, 10 April 1968, 11.

64　"The Two Battles", *Daily Mail*, 8 April 1968, 1.

65　"An Evil Speech", *The Times*, 22 April 1968, 11.

66　HC Deb. 23 April 1968 vol. 763, col. 163.

5

From Belfast to Bob Jones: Ian Paisley, Protestant fundamentalism, and the transatlantic right

Daniel Geary

O N A SEPTEMBER Friday in 1969, students and faculty at the fundamentalist Bob Jones University in Greenville, South Carolina, gathered to hear a lecture about the "real situation" in Northern Ireland. The speaker was the burly and charismatic Ian Paisley, a Belfast minister who had become the leading political voice opposing the Catholic civil rights movement in Ulster. Paisley was well known at the university: he was close with its president, Bob Jones, Jr., who in 1966 had awarded Paisley an honorary doctorate. "Just say that you believe in civil rights," Paisley told his audience, "and you can do what you like: you can stone a policeman, hurl a petrol bomb, burn down a Protestant church, or smear a Protestant preacher." Paisley urged his audience to see their struggle as connected to his own. The Northern Ireland civil rights movement, he claimed, was part of an "international conspiracy ... a deliberate association of attacks against law and order and for revolution and anarchy and Marxism." "What is happening in Ulster today," he prophesied, "will happen in America tomorrow."[1]

Paisley's audience already perceived many manifestations of the "international conspiracy" of which he spoke. Bob Jones University was established in 1927 with the belief that a rising theological modernism challenged the nation's godly character. In the 1960s, its leaders felt similarly besieged by the advancement of the American civil rights movement. The school's founder, Bob Jones, Sr., had in 1960 published a pamphlet, *Is Segregation Scriptural?* Answering in the affirmative, he opined that African Americans were lucky their ancestors had been enslaved because otherwise they "might still be over in the jungles of Africa today, unconverted." In 1969, the racially segregated university was on the verge of a thirteen-year battle with the federal government to retain its status as a tax-free charitable organization while continuing to exclude black students.[2]

Paisley spoke at a moment when the U.S. was becoming a key battleground in international opinion about Northern Ireland. Analogies between the civil rights movement there and the African American freedom struggle were commonplace. Indeed, the Northern Irish civil rights movement consciously drew iconography, tactics, and inspiration from the U.S., including the "civil rights" name.[3] Paisley's visit to Greeneville came at the conclusion of his impromptu American trip in which he retraced the steps of Bernadette Devlin, the Northern Irish civil rights activist and recently elected U.K. Member of Parliament. Devlin's speaking tour, in which she frequently compared the position of Catholics in Northern Ireland to that of African Americans, won widespread sympathy for her cause.[4] As a young Marxist woman, Devlin embodied many trends Paisley found threatening. At Bob Jones, he sneered that Devlin had invented claims of Catholic oppression in Northern Ireland: "You could see the crocodile tears flowing down to the bottom of her mini skirt."[5] But on one point Paisley agreed with Devlin: the civil rights movement in Northern Ireland was analogous to that of radical African Americans. Yet to Paisley both movements represented not social justice but social disorder.

Visiting Bob Jones University, Paisley sought to cement an anti-civil rights internationalism that drew on his existing links with Americans based on shared theological and political commitments. Paisley's tour was sponsored by his long-time American ally, Carl McIntire, the militant fundamentalist and right-wing radio host. Speaking in Belfast in August, 1969, McIntire argued that "the Catholic civil rights movement was similar to the work of black revolutionaries in the United States who burned

American cities."[6] When he returned to the U.S., McIntire was disturbed by Devlin's ability to draw positive press coverage and quickly organized Paisley's tour to counter her claims.

Ian Paisley makes a particularly fascinating case for the study of the transatlantic right. Though religion trumped race as the dominant source of identity in Northern Ireland, Paisley was an ethnonationalist who asserted the fundamentally Protestant nature of Northern Ireland. Paisley's militant version of Ulster nationalism had a clear affinity with the American far right in which white nationalist views predominated. Like American white nationalists, Paisley defended the white supremacist regimes of Rhodesia and South Africa. Paisley's attacks on civil rights and liberal internationalism also won him allies on the British right such as Enoch Powell.

Paisley shared with his transatlantic allies not simply a cause but a mindset concerned with a "conspiracy" of sinister forces and the "treachery" of national elites. Protestant fundamentalists' concern that growing secularism, liberalism, and ecumenicism threatened the true faith infused the right's sense of besiegement and victimization. Paisley and his interlocutors tapped into the same emotional register of ethnic populism that saw the "true" citizens of the nation betrayed by their liberal governments and supranational organizations such as the United Nations.[7] Jones Sr. captured this state of mind in a satirical version of the Lord's Prayer he recited on July 4, 1968, that Paisley reprinted in his newspaper: "Forgive us our weakness in excusing weakness / Our treason in tolerating traitors / Our cowardice in cowering before 'world opinion.'"[8]

Paisley shared with Jones, McIntire, and other American ministers a desire to preserve the Protestant faith, defined in fundamentalist terms as belief in the literal truth of the Bible and in the imminent second coming of Jesus. Paisley and his American allies formed part of an international movement against the ecumenical World Council of Churches (WCC). They hated the WCC because it preached the social gospel, which led it to support social reforms such as civil rights and decolonization. While theology was central to the views of Paisley, Jones, and other militant fundamentalists, they shared their critique of the WCC's liberal internationalism with the broader transatlantic right. Their concerns were never simply theological, as indicated by the fact that Paisley, a Presbyterian, formed a key link with Jones, a Baptist.

Paisley's case highlights the importance of religion to the history of transatlantic white nationalism. Ever since the rise of European imperialism, those seeking to justify white rule worldwide have appealed to Christianity. It was the central marker of "civilization" that Europeans claimed they brought to the rest of the world. American and British imperialists specifically argued for the value of Protestantism as proving the cultural superiority of Anglo-Saxons not only to non-Christians but to Catholic imperial powers. To be sure, Christian justifications for Anglo-Saxon rule declined during the twentieth century with decolonization and secularization. And yet they still resonated on the right. Paisley and his American allies associated Protestantism with Anglo-Saxons, and specifically those of Scottish heritage. As Paisley proudly told his audience at Bob Jones, Ulster was "England's first colony" and the Scottish settlers of the sixteenth century were the "people [who] brought to Ulster the grand message of evangelical Protestantism and of liberty." Jones, in turn, declared himself proud to be of "Scotch-Irish stock," descended from those who had first colonized Northern Ireland before settling the American frontier. His university was founded in backwoods Greeneville, settled by many Ulster Scots. For Paisley and Jones, fundamentalist Protestantism embodied civilization and justified settler colonialism and settlers' descendants' retention of control where they lived. Ethnonationalism flowed naturally from their belief that Protestant nations needed to remain in godly hands.[9]

* * *

Ian Paisley dominated the Northern Irish political landscape from the 1960s to the 2000s. He was born in the town of Armagh in 1926, the son of James Kyle Paisley, a fundamentalist Presbyterian minister. Fourteen years earlier, the elder Paisley had joined the Ulster Volunteer Force, a mass army of Protestant Unionists determined to resist the imposition of Home Rule in Ireland, which would have given regional authority to the island's Catholic elite in Dublin. In 1916, Irish nationalists revolted, demanding and ultimately winning independence. But Ulster Protestants successfully resisted absorption into the new Irish Free State. Instead, six Ulster counties formed the new jurisdiction of Northern Ireland, which remained part of the United Kingdom but with its own regional parliament, Stormont, in Belfast. By design, Protestant Unionists controlled Northern Irish politics and institutions. But the region had a significant Catholic minority, roughly one-third of the population, and Irish nationalists north and south rejected the legitimacy of the island's partition.

Like his father, Ian Paisley was called to the ministry at a young age. His theological views were fundamentalist, stressing the literal truth of the Bible and the Calvinist doctrines of predestination and the inherent depravity of man. In 1951, he helped found a new denomination. Free Presbyterians broke from the Presbyterian Church of Ireland because of its growing ecumenicism. Free Presbyterians were militant separatists who refused fellowship with apostates and openly denounced them, making them controversial even among other fundamentalists. By 1966, the Free Presbyterians had grown from their original four congregations to twelve and Paisley was preaching to hundreds every Sunday in Belfast.[10]

Paisley's theology was inherently political. Though he claimed to attack only the Catholic Church and not individual Catholics, his anti-Catholicism was virulent. For example, in 1958 he denounced members of the British Royal Family as "committing spiritual fornication and adultery with the Antichrist" simply for meeting the pope. Such rhetoric undoubtedly reinforced anti-Catholic prejudice and reassured Protestants that they could not allow themselves to be ruled by Catholics. Paisley's anti-ecumenicism also pitted him against the region's more theologically liberal Protestant elite.

However, Paisley did not become a major political figure until the mid-1960s when he led militant Unionists against efforts to compromise with the region's Catholic minority, who suffered from employment and housing discrimination and from gerrymandering that artificially reduced their political representation. Paisley emerged as the leading Unionist opponent of the reformist prime minister of Northern Ireland, Terence O'Neill, who was elected in 1963 and pursued a modernizing policy that required accommodating the Catholic minority.[11]

Ironically, given Paisley's attacks on the social disorder created by the civil rights movement, he adopted a style of politics marked by confrontational demonstration. In 1966, he was jailed for leading an unauthorized march in Belfast against the General Assembly of the Presbyterian Church that deliberately provoked riots by processing through Catholic neighborhoods. He also entered electoral politics, winning election in 1970 to both the Northern Irish and U.K. parliaments. In 1971, he formed the Democratic Unionist Party (DUP) to oppose the Ulster Unionist Party, the traditional voice of Unionism. Paisley was also closely connected to Unionist paramilitary organizations that formed in the late 1960s, though he carefully maintained ignorance of any specific plans for violence. As an agitator and politician, Paisley won a far greater following than he had as leader of the Free Presbyterians, which remained a relatively small denomination. Paisley's ethnic populism appealed well beyond his theological brethren, though having a Calvinist minister as a leader held powerful symbolic value even for secular Unionists.[12]

Paisley's prominence coincided with the growth of the movement for Catholic civil rights in Northern Ireland that coalesced in the formation of the Northern Ireland Civil Rights Association (NICRA) in 1967, a coalition of middle-class Catholic activists and young New Leftists such as Bernadette Devlin. Though it included Republicans who sought the reunification of Ireland, the civil rights movement focused on achieving full equality within the United Kingdom. Like the American civil rights movement that inspired it, NICRA employed non-violent demonstrations to apply pressure on Stormont and Westminster. Challenged by Paisleyites on the right and NICRA on the left, the Unionist government in Northern Ireland found implementing reforms difficult and maintaining order impossible. There followed a decades-long low-grade civil war euphemistically known as the "Troubles," involving sectarian violence, the revival of physical force Republicanism in the form of the Provisional IRA, state repression, and the growth of Unionist paramilitaries. In 1972, Westminster suspended the Northern Irish Parliament and imposed direct rule.[13]

Historians have typically seen Paisley as historically significant only for his role in the politics of Northern Ireland and have thereby missed the part he played in the broader transatlantic right. Because of its many peculiarities, the history of Northern Ireland has been unusually prone to a methodological nationalism that downplays or ignores transnational connections. In addition, many have stressed the sectarian nature of political conflict in Northern Ireland to the exclusion of its ideological components. But Paisley was clearly a man of the international right and acknowledged himself as such. As he quipped to his audience at Bob Jones in 1969, "A person who is outspoken is labelled 'An extremist!' In our country they call you a right-winger. I am glad that I am on the right side."[14]

As historian Richard Jordan demonstrates, Paisley developed ties with leading right-wing American fundamentalists well before his rise to political prominence. These connections drew on a long history of exchanges between evangelicals in the U.S. and Ulster. In 1951, Paisley met Carl McIntire, who became a model and mentor to him. The bombastic and indefatigable Presbyterian preacher crusaded against ecumenicism as head of the American Council of Christian Churches (ACCC). To oppose the newly formed WCC, in 1948 the New Jersey minister founded the International Council of Christian Churches (ICCC), with which Paisley's Free Presbyterian Church later affiliated. McIntire bragged of 150,000 subscribers to his *Christian Beacon* newspaper, 1.2 million members in the ACCC, and 55 million members in the ICCC. Though the membership tallies were grossly exaggerated, these figures do reflect the numbers of people reached through ACCC and ICCC publications.[15]

McIntire formed a crucial historical link between the "old Protestant right" of the pre-World War II years represented by figures such as the Nazi-sympathizing minister Gerald L. K. Smith, and the "Christian right" that coalesced at the end of the 1970s behind televangelists and culture wars crusaders Jerry Falwell and Pat Robertson.[16] As historians have demonstrated, it is simply untrue that Protestant fundamentalists in the U.S. abstained from politics until the rise of the Christian right in the 1970s.

In fact, this myth has served the interests of the Christian right by erasing the unsavory politics of their predecessors, including their racism, anti-Catholicism, and anti-Semitism.

Paisley shared with McIntire and others in the ICCC a belief in the literal truth of the Bible, in the imminent second coming of Jesus, and in salvation through grace alone. But they also agreed on a policy of separatism that not only prevented them from associating with those preaching false doctrine but *required* them to actively condemn apostasy. For example, they denounced the prominent evangelical Billy Graham for his opposition to predestination and his willingness to share fellowship with apostates. The WCC's social gospel rankled with militant fundamentalists theologically and politically. Not only did it suggest that one could obtain salvation through good works, it also supported a liberal internationalism that favored decolonization and a world expansion of individual rights.

Through McIntire, Paisley came to know other leading American militant fundamentalists. In 1962, he met Bob Jones, Jr., at an ICCC meeting in Amsterdam at which they protested the WCC's decision to send observers to the Second Vatican Conference. Though the Joneses had a sometimes frosty relationship with McIntire, they collaborated on shared projects. Through the ICCC network, Paisley also met Billy James Hargis, the Oklahoma preacher and media personality whose right-wing radio and television shows were syndicated on hundreds of stations.

Paisley's connections with leading American figures helped bolster his stature in Northern Ireland. His international prominence in fundamentalist circles grew after his 1966 imprisonment for unlawful assembly bestowed on him a long-sought martyrdom. He had in fact sought imprisonment twice before, but in each case donors had paid the fines necessary to release him. McIntire visited Paisley in prison and Bob Jones, Jr., greeted him directly after his prison release to confer his honorary doctorate in divinity. Jones had already sponsored a speaking tour for Paisley in 1964, but now organized a second, more high-profile North American tour in 1967. Paisley returned for a third tour in 1968. During a five-week period that year, he visited twenty-three churches in nineteen states all over the U.S., though mostly in the Sunbelt region where conservative politics was strongest. In San Diego, he spoke at the church of Tim LaHaye, the John Birch Society member who later became famous for co-authoring the best-selling *Left Behind* novels about the end times that depicted the head of the United Nations as the literal Antichrist.[17]

For Paisley and his American allies, the defense of fundamentalist Protestantism as the one true religion had a strong racial character as they associated such religion with the traditional culture of people of Anglo-Saxon descent. In Northern Ireland, England's first settler colony, religion functioned similarly to race in other contexts. Protestantism was associated with the descendants of colonial settlers of the seventeenth century, who retained political and economic power, and Catholicism was associated with descendants of native inhabitants. Paisley spoke of the need for another Oliver Cromwell in Northern Ireland, harkening back to the English Protestant leader who had spearheaded the seventeenth-century settlement of Ulster and prosecuted a bloody campaign of ethnic cleansing against Ireland's Catholic population.[18] Paisleyites often depicted Irish Catholics as a different, inferior race. In the wake of civil unrest in Derry in the spring of 1969, the *Protestant Telegraph* described Northern Irish Catholics as "feral" and "savage ruffians" and joked that comparing them to blacks was an "insult to Negroes." The writer reported the observations of a military friend who observed

the Satanic scenes of rebel rage in Londonderry, and informed me that they eclipsed in ferocity and murderous intent, all that he had experienced among the allegedly uncivilized Arabs! Any reference to White Negroes applied to … [those] who attacked the police is a gross insult to all the coloured peoples of the world.[19]

Paisley's racialized thinking led him to detail *Ulster's Debt to America*, a book he wrote in 1976 on the bicentennial of the American Declaration of Independence. He stressed the contributions of Ulster Scots to the U.S. as against those of Irish-American Catholics. Throughout, he treated Ulster Scots as a distinct "race" with, if not biological differences, at least deeply held cultural characteristics including Calvinism, a love of liberty, and a willingness to defend their values through violence. The book's epigraph from Lord Rosebery, a leading turn-of-the-twentieth-century British imperialist politician and opponent of Irish Home Rule, praised "the branch of our [Scottish] race which has been grafted on to the Ulster stem" as "the toughest, the most dominant, the most irresist-ible race that exists in the universe at this moment." Relying on earlier histories such as Theodore Roosevelt's *The Winning of the West*, Paisley praised the Scotch-Irish for defeating "the awful barbarity of Indian warfare."[20] Bob Jones, Jr., wrote the introduction to Paisley's book. "For too long," he claimed, "the fabric of American history which is interwo-ven with that of Ireland has been coloured Green when ... the colour of America's Independence should be Orange even as much as Red, White and Blue."[21]

As Jones's argument that true American virtues derived from Ulster Protestants and *not* Irish-American Catholic immigrants shows, in the U.S. Protestantism was also conflated with race. In the nineteenth century, anti-Catholicism in the U.S. had thrived in opposition to emigration from Ireland. The 1924 Immigration Restriction Act, designed largely to restrict immigration from Catholic and Jewish southern and eastern Europe, was only repealed in 1965. The Ku Klux Klan of the 1920s was nearly as anti-Catholic and anti-Semitic as it was anti-black. During the 1920s, Bob Jones, Sr., was an active nativist who denounced "degener-ate, unassimilated foreigners."[22] Anti-Catholicism remained a common feature of the Protestant right into the 1960s and 1970s even as it shed its explicit anti-Semitism. Only later did many on the Protestant right drop their anti-Catholicism to make alliances with conservative Catholics on social issues such as abortion. Thus, even in the second half of the twen-tieth century, there were clear remnants of an American Anglo-Saxonism that drew sharp racial distinctions among those of European descent.

The Protestant right congealed around more than anti-Catholicism, though. The militant fundamentalists with whom Paisley allied were major leaders of the broader far right in the U.S. in which white national-ist views predominated. McIntire's popular and widely aired radio show broadcast on the same channels that featured Dan Smoot, who dominated the right-wing airwaves in the period between Father Coughlin and Rush Limbaugh. McIntire's virulent anti-communism led him to ally with Joseph McCarthy (despite McCarthy's Catholicism), the John Birch Society, the Young Americans for Freedom, and George Wallace. The Joneses, like McIntire, had deep and extensive ties to white supremacists. Two years before Bob Jones University conferred its honorary doctorate on Paisley, it had awarded one to Wallace, the former segregationist governor of Alabama who coalesced right-wing forces in his bids for the U.S. presidency. Through his connections with militant fundamentalists in the U.S., Paisley also formed relationships with secular right-wingers such as segregationist politicians Strom Thurmond and Lester Maddox and the right-wing anti-communist John Stormer. Opposition to the African American civil rights movement was a central feature of the politics of militant fundamentalists and was one cause, along with anti-communism, that linked them to broader right-wing politics.

* * *

The racist views of Paisley's American allies were consistently reproduced in his newspaper, the *Protestant Telegraph*, with readers left to draw parallels between the civil rights movements in the U.S. and Northern Ireland. The bi-weekly paper started publication in 1966 so that Paisley could spread his political views beyond his religious following. In the days before the internet, reprinting articles from abroad exposed an organization's rank-and-file to international perspectives. The newspaper reveals the views of its editor, Paisley, of his disciples who ran its daily operations, and of the broader movement who read it.

Ulster Unionist leaders typically sought to refute any parallels between the civil rights struggles of African Americans and Northern Irish Catholics. The Protestant Orange Order, insisted Brian Faulkner, Northern Irish prime minister from 1971 to 1972, was nothing like the Ku Klux Klan.[23] Paisley, on the other hand, allied himself to American white supremacists and consistently accepted civil rights parallels. The *Protestant Telegraph* was "proud" to be the first British newspaper to reprint a speech by Lester Maddox, the segregationist governor of Georgia who had made his name by assaulting African American theology students who sought to desegregate his fried chicken restaurant. In the speech, Maddox blamed the recent uprisings in American cities on those "who said that sit-ins, force-ins, and demonstrations on private property are no more radical than the secret ballot and advised the bums, criminals, and Communists to rouse the masses."[24] Northern Irish readers might well have concluded that the civil rights movement in their own country, which adopted similar tactics of non-violent resistance, was a radical conspiracy that intended to wreak violent disorder.

Bob Jones, Jr., wrote a regular column for the *Telegraph*, "A Look at the Book," that focused on biblical interpretation and often commented on political events. For example, he wrote in 1969,

> Most of the leaders in the widespread civil agitation—the so-called civil rights struggle—are not good men. They are evil men and their appeal is to the lowest instinct in human nature. They stir up strife and seek to destroy the country by holding out a promise of undeserved and unearned benefits.[25]

In another column, Jones claimed that rioting in American cities resulted not from poverty and injustice but from the inherent depravity of man abetted by "the forces of evil and ungodliness."[26]

The spread of urban uprisings and the emergence of the militant Black Power movement in the latter half of the 1960s helped American segregationists portray demands for racial equality as necessarily leading to violence. Yet the *Protestant Telegraph* also ran attacks on Martin Luther King, Jr., following his assassination in April, 1968. It published a caustic obituary of King by Bob Spencer, a Baptist minister from Huntsville, Alabama, whose church Paisley had visited that March when Paisley was made a "Freeman" of the city by Huntsville's mayor.[27] Spencer claimed that King was no true "Christian" because he preached the social gospel and alleged that King "loaded the gun of his own destruction by making himself the symbol of resistance to law and order." Paisley's newspaper also reprinted a speech made by the segregationist senator Robert Byrd that similarly blamed King for inciting violence. The message for readers was obvious: the growing movement for civil rights for Catholics in Northern Ireland, even when it practiced non-violence, was a sinister and ungodly force that severely threatened the social order.

Paisley's American allies were similarly invested in opposing the civil rights movement in Ulster. In 1969, McIntire's ACCC passed a resolution condemning the Northern Irish Civil Rights Association. Both Jones and McIntire appeared at secular protests in Northern Ireland in the late 1960s. McIntire saw the "same forces" at work against him in the U.S. as were working to "destroy Ulster," namely "liberals and radicals" who were "enemies of Christianity." In particular, McIntire compared Paisley's movement with his own struggle against the 1969 New Jersey state legislature's review of his university's (Shelton College) accreditation, a cause in which McIntire had enlisted followers of George Wallace and members of the white supremacist National States Rights Party.[28]

In 1969, Paisley's second imprisonment for leading an unauthorized demonstration incensed the right-wing California minister Rev. Ronald Cooke, who had been born in Northern Ireland but made his career in the U.S. In *Word of Truth*, an evangelical periodical he edited out of Pasadena, Cooke attacked conservative American Catholics who supported the civil rights movement in Northern Ireland. Cooke denounced as hypocritical a stance that "condemns Negroes and others for bombing and looting and burning in the U.S.A., but apparently has no condemnation for the rioting and burning and bombing in Northern Ireland." For Cooke, the issue was "Protestantism or Popery." Despite his apparent lack of literary skill, Cooke was inspired to write a poem that lionized Paisley as the "Prisoner of Crumlin" and demonized "modernistic spaniels [who] yap / About civil-rights / And all that claptrap / And hypocritical nonsense."[29]

In defending Paisley, his American allies saw themselves as supporting British nationalism and, through this, defending a longer transatlantic history of Anglo-Saxonism. Protesting a 1966 *Life* magazine portrait of Paisley, Jones insisted, "Northern and Protestant Ireland is loyal to the Queen ... Paisley is a Christian patriot persecuted by a traitorous Prime Minister [the Labour PM Harold Wilson] who collaborates with his country's enemies."[30] Meeting Paisley at Philadelphia airport for the start of his anti-Devlin speaking tour in 1969, McIntire organized a group of nearly 100 people to greet him and wave Union Jack flags, the quintessential symbol of both Ulster and British nationalism.[31]

Jones, Jr., praised Paisley as resisting "the ecclesiastical and political inroads which Roman Catholicism has been making in historically Protestant, royalist Northern Ireland."[32] Similarly, in McIntire's view, fundamentalist Protestantism was the "faith that made Britain great and free."[33] McIntire organized a letter-writing campaign for Paisley during his 1969 imprisonment. McIntire urged his radio listeners to write to the queen and to copy letters to President Nixon and to his show so that they could be read on the air. The fact that McIntire asked listeners to write to the queen, and not the prime minister, indicates the character of his Anglophilia. Like ethnic populists in the U.K. including Paisley, McIntire urged loyalty to the British nation but not the "traitorous" British government, and expressed nostalgia for an imagined past period of British national glory.

The way in which the cause of Ulster Unionism linked the broader transatlantic far right is illustrated by the story of David McCalden. Born in Belfast, McCalden attended university in London before emigrating to Los Angeles in 1978. There he established the Ulster-American Heritage Foundation, which sought to refute the claims of Irish Republican supporters and to argue that Ulster's Protestants were a distinct ethnic and cultural group entitled to rule their own nation. However, McCalden was later discredited when it emerged that he had been a member of the neo-Nazi National Front in Britain, had helped found the British National Party there, and remained a prominent Holocaust denier.[34]

* * *

Right-wing Protestants in the U.S. and Northern Ireland perceived their nations as sites of a broader international struggle taking place anywhere the rule of Anglo-Saxon Protestants was threatened. It was therefore hardly surprising that Paisley and his American allies were also deeply concerned with defending white rule in southern Africa. In 1965, Rhodesia unilaterally declared independence from the United Kingdom in order to preserve white rule. The United Nations declared Rhodesia an "illegal racist minority regime" and recommended its members apply sanctions, which both the U.S. and U.K. did.

Right-wingers in the U.S. and U.K. rallied around Rhodesia and South Africa. Paisley circulated defenses of white rule in Africa penned by his American allies. Jones told readers of the *Protestant Telegraph* that one sign of the sickness emanating from the social gospel was "the treatment which the United Nations is giving to South Africa and Rhodesia."[35] In 1968, the *Telegraph* reprinted an article by Hargis who recounted his trip to South Africa and Rhodesia and denounced international sanctions against the latter. In Hargis's view, "Before Prime Minister Smith and the white Rhodesian government came along, the Africans were savages. These white leaders have civilized them ... They have brought Christ to these people."[36] In order to bolster the new state, Hargis established the All-Africa Christian Crusade in the Rhodesian capital of Salisbury. Even though followers of militant fundamentalism were scarce in Rhodesia, the nation's leaders welcomed Hargis because of their desperate need for foreign allies.[37]

The *Protestant Telegraph* declared that it "stood solidly behind the State of Rhodesia" though "not because of its allegedly racialist policies."[38] To defend Rhodesia while denying its white supremacist character was clearly absurd. But a later *Protestant Telegraph* article addressed the issue of white rule more forthrightly, asking "Is it all right for black to rule black—but wrong for white to rule black?"[39] Rhodesia's example was especially pertinent in the case of Northern Ireland, because Rhodesia's leaders had claimed to be breaking with the government of the United Kingdom in order to preserve an older and purer ideal of British nationalism. UDI served as a model for Paisley and his supporters, whose loyalty to the British nation required active resistance to the British government. Paisleyites became particularly suspicious of British government betrayal after it imposed direct rule on Northern Ireland in 1972. Looking at what had happened in Rhodesia, as well as Kenya and Cyprus, one *Telegraph* writer concluded, "Britain has made friends of her enemies and enemies of her friends."[40]

The World Council of Churches condemned both Rhodesia and its larger neighbor, South Africa, which operated a system of racial apartheid. Paisley and his supporters were particularly outraged by the WCC's "Programme on Racism," which it adopted in 1968 and which entailed an active effort to dismantle white supremacist regimes in southern Africa. The WCC provided grants to national liberation movements, including those that used violent methods of resistance such as FRELIMO in Mozambique, SWAPO in Namibia, and the ANC in South Africa. These grants were particularly controversial for Northern Irish Protestants who feared that the WCC might one day feel justified in offering funds to the IRA.[41]

Paisleyites' deepest fears of conspiracy were stoked by this perceived alliance of Catholic-friendly ecumenicists, liberal internationalists, and radicalized blacks. A 1975 cartoon in the *Protestant Telegraph* showed the pope carrying a bag of money marked "WCC" to Africans in the jungle. Betraying a blatant racism rarely articulated in the newspaper's text, the cartoon depicted African guerrillas as actual gorillas with big lips and protruding jawlines.[42] Paisleyites saw themselves as under siege from the same "ecumenical-Romanist terrorists" operating in southern Africa. "What has been witnessed in South Africa," one writer alleged, "we too are seeing in Ulster … for the black terrorists we have the Provo IRA; and the WCC is the same all over."[43] One of Paisley's closest associates, Noel Doherty, emigrated to southern Africa in 1969. Doherty had printed the *Protestant Telegraph* until he was arrested in 1967 for providing explosives to a Loyalist paramilitary group. After his release from prison two years later, Doherty moved to South Africa where he established a printing business, reportedly first stopping in Rhodesia to fight "terrorists."[44]

Paisley's followers hoped white South Africans would similarly identify with their cause. One of Paisley's followers sought to inform a South African audience about the situation in Northern Ireland. He wrote an article for *The Covenant Message*, published in South Africa by the British-Israel-World Foundation, which promoted the belief that the peoples of northern Europe, especially Britain, were descended from the ten lost tribes of Israel. Popularized in the nineteenth century, British Israelism retained adherents in Britain and its former colonies, including the U.S. and South Africa. In twentieth-century iterations such as the Christian Identity movement, it offered a religious justification for racism by holding that English-speaking whites were God's chosen people.[45] In his article, Smyth sought to convince others in the lost tribes to see Northern Ireland as a pivotal site of struggle. He claimed, "The Lord has reserved unto Himself the axis on which the destiny of Anglo-Saxon-Celtic people of the Isles will turn. That axis is Ulster."[46] Given that the dominant force in white South African politics was Afrikaner nationalism, it is noteworthy that Smyth sought connections to South Africans with British ancestors, suggesting that Paisleyites were invested in a specific vision of English-speaking Anglo-Saxonism as much as the defense of European culture or Protestantism writ large.

* * *

Paisley's critique of civil rights and liberal internationalism also linked him to broader right-wing British nationalism, of which Ulster unionism had traditionally been a crucial component. Enoch Powell, for example, attacked the civil rights movements in both the U.S. and Ulster and saw them as linked. He did so in a populist register that depicted political leaders betraying the interests of whites. In his widely publicized "Enemy Within" speech of 1970 Powell described an international struggle against "the operation of the enemy on several different fronts." As with his earlier "Rivers of Blood" speech, Powell dwelled on the effects of non-white Commonwealth migration on the British national character. However, he also saw the U.S. and Northern Ireland as two key fronts in resisting the enemy, whom he defined as the liberal media and clergy, student protestors, union militants, and a complacent if not complicit political establishment. In both cases, he dismissed what he called the "'civil rights' nonsense." In the U.S., he claimed, "We have seen one city after another … engulfed in fire and fighting, as the material provided by the influx of Negroes in to the Northern states was flung into the furnaces of anarchy." Similarly, "In Ulster we are told that the deliberate destruction by fire and riot of areas of ordinary property is due to the dissatisfaction over allocation of council houses and opportunities for employment. It is nonsense—manifest, arrant nonsense."[47]

Powell actually ended his career as an Ulster Unionist MP. In 1974, he left the Conservative Party over its stance in favor of joining the European Economic Community (EEC) and stopped representing his Birmingham constituency in Parliament. Paisley and two other Unionists visited Powell to convince him to stand for election in South Down, a constituency south of Belfast.[48] Paisley collaborated with Powell in opposing British entry into the EEC, the forerunner of today's European Union. Paisley particularly objected to forming closer ties with Catholic nations in Europe, but he also shared Powell's concerns about surrendering British sovereignty, accepting a secondary role for British world power, and losing ties to the former settler colonies in the Commonwealth such as Australia, Canada, and New Zealand.[49] The *Protestant Telegraph* feared that joining the EEC would undermine Britain's "unique role in the world" that it owed to its "establishment of Christianity and its culture." "Evil powers," the writer feared, "are seeking to render impotent the British race."[50]

Though Commonwealth migration was not a major issue in economically depressed Northern Ireland, Paisleyites sympathized with the concerns Powell articulated in his infamous "Rivers of Blood" speech. For example, like Powell, the *Protestant Telegraph* opposed accepting South Asian migrants from Uganda despite the fact that most were British citizens and all were persecuted by Idi Amin's government:

Is Britain capable of accepting these alien cultures? The challenge with Popery is great enough, but what will the challenge with Hinduism and Buddhism be like? Is the British nation equipped to withstand this further invasion by an Un-Christian and Anti-Christian religion? *God save Britain from the attacks of the enemy.*

The writer referred to the previous "problem" experienced by cities such as Powell's Birmingham when "coloured West Indians darkened Britain's shores."[51] Paisleyites added to anti-migrant sentiment an opposition to mass emigration from the Republic of Ireland to Britain that "allow[ed] the rebel 'Irish' to invade England, to sop up jobs and cast their votes without restriction."[52]

Paisleyites felt aggrieved that the British government welcomed Commonwealth migrants while ignoring the interests of loyal subjects such as themselves. One 1973 *Protestant Telegraph* cartoon commented on British government opposition to the full integration of Northern Ireland, a policy advocated by Powell (and Paisley at the time) that would have seen Northern Ireland lose its devolved status but gain increased representation at Westminster and the assurance of remaining a full and permanent part of the United Kingdom. The cartoon contrasts British government opposition to integrating Northern Ireland to its welcoming of migrants to Britain: 2,000,000 Asians, 500,000 West Indians, and 2,000,000 "S. Irish Aliens." Panels depict Prime Minister Edward Heath with an exaggeratedly long nose welcoming a man from each group rendered in racial caricature: a dark-skinned, portly Asian in a turban; an even darker-skinned, white-lipped West Indian; and a disheveled Irishman with a shamrock tattoo. The final panel depicts the traitorous prime minister declaring, "Integrating British citizens from Ulster? My dear fellow, the whole idea is out of the question."[53]

Paisley's movement shared with the transatlantic right of the era not simply a commitment to a set of shared causes, but an emotional sense that those who held traditional virtues were losing ground to an international conspiracy of hidden enemies. "The war is ... everywhere," declared one *Protestant Telegraph* article,

> in Latin America, Africa, and in the United Nations, where it urges "urgent and decisive" action against South Africa ... We see it at work in every liberal philosophy ... in the [anti-Vietnam War] Moratorium demonstration and the [left-wing Ulster civil rights] People's Democracy movement; *in the training of young Roman Catholic men in Ulster in Black Panther urban guerrilla tactics.*[54]

This conspiratorial perspective only enhanced Paisleyites' sense of Ulster's world-historical significance.

Satan was the ultimate conspirator, whose involvement was never doubted by Paisley and his theological brethren. Hence, the *Protestant Telegraph* warned of "Satan's cunning plot to drag us into the 'Babylonish' Common Market."[55] Satan's presumed manipulation of world events could easily link all disturbing developments. Paisleyites typically perceived the Catholic Church as the main conspiratorial force, implausibly seeing it as responsible for the radical upsurge in France in May 1968 (along with communists). "They are Everywhere," declared one article. "Ulster, Vietnam, Watergate, South Africa, Biafra, and Israel—What's the connection? The interference of the agents of the Vatican." To be sure, hardly all members of the transatlantic right, let alone all of Paisley's political followers, thought a literal Armageddon was in the offing. But conspiratorial concepts resonated throughout the more secular transatlantic right as in Enoch Powell's vision of a common "enemy" at work on several international fronts. This is one major reason why Protestant fundamentalists played such a key role in the transatlantic right.

After resisting every effort at compromise to bring peace to Northern Ireland, including the Good Friday Agreement of 1998, Ian Paisley reversed course in 2007, agreeing to serve as first minister of Northern Ireland in a power-sharing arrangement with Sinn Féin, the political wing of the IRA. After he left the Northern Ireland Parliament in 2010, Paisley was awarded a peerage, allowing him an aristocratic title and a seat in the British House of Lords. After his death in 2014, the image of Paisley as a peacemaker had largely replaced the earlier one of him as a rabble-rouser.

It is therefore tempting to see his place as part of the transatlantic right as only belonging to the past. However, the party Paisley founded, the DUP, the largest political party in Northern Ireland, played a key role in the success of the Brexit referendum, which was a project of the contemporary transatlantic right that expressed its characteristic hostility to supranational organizations and concern with protecting the homeland from immigrants who threatened Britain's racial character. The DUP's support for Brexit is especially remarkable given that, by raising again the possibility of Irish reunification, it threatened its most central political interest.

One of the DUP's leading Brexiteers is Ian Paisley, Jr., who assumed his father's seat in the British House of Commons in 2010. Paisley, Jr., invited controversy in 2018 when he retweeted an Islamophobic tweet by the British far right celebrity Katie Hopkins: "March 2018. London has a higher murder rate than New York ... And Ramadan's not yet begun."[56] Paisley, Jr., welcomed the election of Donald Trump and has publicly invited him to visit Northern Ireland. He bragged that Trump admired his father and dubbed him a "political legend."[57]

There is thus continuity as well as change in the transatlantic right and the role of Protestant fundamentalists in Northern Ireland within it. The issues are no longer the same as they were in Paisley's heyday. Explicit anti-Catholicism has faded and it is no longer possible to defend white rule in southern Africa. Most U.S. fundamentalists followed Pat Robertson's lead in renouncing the defense of scriptural segregation, recognizing that overt racism was harming their political position at home as well as evangelical efforts abroad. But ethnonationalism remains a potent force among the ideological descendants of Paisley and his allies, reflected in its hostility to racially undesirable immigrants, Islamophobia, and opposition to liberal internationalist organizations.

The fact that Paisley's main concern was defending one group of whites against another should not lead us to conclude that he had nothing to do with white nationalism. Rather, it should convince us that white nationalism was always part of a wider complex of ideas offered by the transatlantic right, including ethnic populism, post-colonialism, and resistance to liberal internationalism. Of course, these are precisely the ideas that helped enable the connected triumphs of Brexit and Trump.

Notes

1 Ian Paisley, *Northern Ireland: What is the Real Situation?* (Greenville, SC: Bob Jones University Press, 1970), 18, 15.

2 Mark Taylor Dalhouse, *An Island in a Lake of Fire: Bob Jones University, Fundamentalism, and the Separatist Movement* (Athens, GA: University of Georgia Press, 1996), 156–8. Jones's quote is from p. 155. The university admitted black students in 1975, but continued to battle the Internal Revenue Service in court because the university banned interracial dating, a policy it kept in place until 2000 in the wake of public controversy over presidential candidate George W. Bush's decision to speak at the university.

3 Simon Prince, "'Do What the Afro-Americans Are Doing': Black Power and the Start of the Northern Ireland Troubles," *Journal of Contemporary History* 50 (2015): 516–35; Brian Dooley, *Black and Green: The Fight for Civil Rights in Northern Ireland and Black America* (London: Pluto Press, 1998).

4 Tara Keenan-Thompson, *Irish Women and Street Politics* (Dublin: Irish Academic Press), 159–61.

5 Paisley, *Northern Ireland*, 11.

6 John M. Lee, "Cardinal's Views Scored in Ulster," *New York Times*, August 25, 1969, 14.

7 On ethnic populism, see Bill Schwarz, *The White Man's World* (Oxford: Oxford University Press, 2011).

8 "Invocation by Dr. Bob Jones at a Dinner Honouring General Walker held in Boston *Fifth Annual New England Rally for God, Family and Country*, July 4," *Protestant Telegraph*, October 6–7, 1968.

9 Paisley, *Northern Ireland*, 7; Bob Jones, "Foreword," in Ian R. K. Paisley, *America's Debt to Ulster* (Belfast: Martyrs Memorial Press, 1976), n.p.

10 Steve Bruce, *Paisley: Religion and Politics in Northern Ireland* (Oxford: Oxford University Press, 1994), 89.

11 Marc Mulholland, *Northern Ireland at the Crossroads: Ulster Unionism in the O'Neill Years, 1960–69* (Basingstoke: Palgrave, 2000).

12 Richard L. Jordan, *The Second Coming of Ian Paisley: Militant Fundamentalism and Ulster Politics* (Syracuse, NY: Syracuse University Press, 2013); Ed Moloney, *Paisley: From Demagogue to Democrat?* (Dublin: Poolbeg Press, 2008); Bruce, *Paisley*.

13 Simon Prince, *Northern Ireland's '68: Civil Rights, Global Revolt, and the Origins of the Troubles* (Dublin: Irish Academic Press, 2007); Niall Ó Dochartaigh, *From Civil Rights to Armalites: Derry and the Birth of the Irish Troubles* (Cork: Cork University Press, 1997); Bob Purdie, *Politics in the Streets: The Origins of the Civil Rights Movement in Northern Ireland* (Belfast: Blackstaff Press, 1990).

14 Paisley, *Northern Ireland*, 7.

15 Jordan, *The Second Coming of Ian Paisley*; Richard Lawrence Jordan, *Paisleyism and Civil Rights: An Ambassador Unchained* (Newcastle: Cambridge Scholars Press,

2018); Markku Ruotsila, "Carl McIntire and the Fundamentalist Origins of the Christian Right," *Church History* 81 (2012): 381.

16 Ruotsila, "Carl McIntire"; Markku Ruotsila, *Fighting Fundamentalist: Carl McIntire and the Politicization of American Fundamentalism* (New York: Oxford University Press, 2016).

17 *Protestant Telegraph*, March 2, 1968, 2.

18 Micheál Ó Siochrú, *God's Executioner: Oliver Cromwell and the Conquest of Ireland* (London: Faber and Faber, 2008).

19 "Here and There With Mountain Rover," *Protestant Telegraph*, May 17, 1969.

20 Ian R. K. Paisley, *America's Debt to Ulster* (Belfast: Martyrs Memorial Press, 1976), 28.

21 Ibid., n.p.

22 As quoted in Dalhouse, *Island in a Lake of Fire*, 28.

23 Brian Faulkner, *Memoirs of a Statesman* (London: Weidenfeld and Nicolson, 1978), 16.

24 "Governor Maddox of Georgia, U.S.A. Speaks His Mind," *Protestant Telegraph*, September 30, 1967, 6–7, 10–11.

25 Bob Jones, Jr., "A Look at the Book," *Protestant Telegraph*, May 31, 1969, 5.

26 Bob Jones, Jr., "A Look at the Book," *Protestant Telegraph*, November 16, 1968, 8.

27 "Dr. Paisley Made Freeman of Huntsville, U.S.A.," *Protestant Telegraph*, April 13, 1968, 3.

28 "Last Appeal For Students," *Christian Beacon*, September 4, 1969, 1.

29 "An American Editor Lashes Out," *Protestant Telegraph*, June 14, 1969, 6–7 (reprinted from May, 1969 edition of *Word of Truth*).

30 "Bob Jones Defends Ian Paisley in the U.S.A.," *Protestant Telegraph*, September 10, 1966, 4.

31 "Hymn-Singers, McIntire Welcome Paisley to Philadelphia," *Philadelphia Bulletin*, September 7, 1969 (reprinted in *Christian Beacon*, September 11, 1969, 3).

32 Bob Jones, Jr., "Ian Paisley," *Bob Jones Alumni Newsletter*, 1967, 40.

33 "Protest Telegrams from Dr. Carl McIntire, President, International Council of Churches," *Protestant Telegraph*, March 21, 1970, 3.

34 Andrew J. Wilson, "Ulster Unionists in America, 1972–1985," *New Hibernia Review* 11 (2007): 69–71.

35 Bob Jones, Jr., "A Look at the Book," *Protestant Telegraph*, August 24, 1968, 9.

36 "South Africa and Rhodesia: Report of a Fact-Finding Tour by Dr. Billy James Hargis, Christian Crusade, U.S.A.," *Protestant Telegraph*, April 13, 1968, 8.

37 Richard Jordan, "A Militant Crusade in Africa: The Great Commission and Segregation," *Church History* 83 (2014): 978–85.

38 "Rome and Rhodesia," *Protestant Telegraph*, June 4, 1969, 2.

39 "Vote Gimmick in Rhodesia," *Protestant Telegraph*, January 22, 1972, 9.

40 "They've Done it Before," *Protestant Telegraph*, December 8, 1973, 3.

41 Norman Taggart, "The World Council of Churches' Programme to Combat Racism and Irish Methodist Mission," *Wesley and Methodist Studies* 4 (2012): 91–112.

42 Cartoon illustrating "Churches and Terrorism," *Protestant Telegraph*, July 1975 ("Twelfth Issue"), 8.

43 "Same All Over," *Protestant Telegraph*, May 24, 1975, 4.

44 Moloney, *Paisley*, 134; Peter Taylor, *Loyalists* (London: Bloomsbury, 1998), 30. Even if reports that Doherty had fought in Rhodesia were untrue, the fact that this made for a plausible rumor in Belfast remains significant.

45 Michael Barkun, *Religion and the Racist Right: Origins of the Christian Identity Movement* (Chapel Hill, NC: University of North Carolina Press, 1997).

46 Clifford Smyth, "The United Kingdom in Crisis," *Protestant Telegraph*, December 20, 1969, 7 (reprinted from *Covenant Message*).

47 Enoch Powell, "The Enemy Within," speech, June 13, 1970, www.enochpowell.info/Resources/May-June%201970.pdf (accessed August 10, 2017). See also Camilla Schofield, *Enoch Powell and the Making of Postcolonial Britain* (Cambridge: Cambridge University Press, 2013).

48 Robert Shepherd, *Enoch Powell* (London: Hutchinson, 1996), 453. Paisley and Powell clashed later in the 1970s, as Paisley saw Powell as too English and insufficiently committed to Ulster nationalism.

49 See, for example, "No! to EEC," *Protestant Telegraph*, February 2, 1975, 2.

50 "The Common Market?," *Protestant Telegraph*, June 12, 1971, 6.

51 "By the Way …," *Protestant Telegraph*, February 17, 1968, 2.

52 "In Brief …," *Protestant Telegraph*, October 7–20, 1973, 2.

53 Cartoon, *Protestant Telegraph*, October 27–November 7, 1973, 1.

54 Michael Clark, "The War is Not Just in Vietnam," *Protestant Telegraph*, March 19, 1970, 6.

55 *Protestant Telegraph*, June 12, 1971.

56 "Ian Paisley Sorry for Tweeting Ramadan Remark by Katie Hopkins," *Irish Times*, April 3, 2018, www.irishtimes.com/news/politics/ian-paisley-sorry-for-retweeting-ramadan-remark-by-katie-hopkins-1.3449119 (accessed August 11, 2018).

57 "Ian Paisley Welcomes Election of 'Down to Earth' Trump," *Irish Times*, November 12, 2016, www.irishtimes.com/news/world/uk/ian-paisley-welcomes-election-of-down-to-earth-trump-1.2864680 (accessed April 15, 2020).

Nostalgia for white rule

6

"One last retreat": racial nostalgia and population panic in Smith's Rhodesia and Powell's Britain[1]

Josiah Brownell

RHODESIA HAS ALWAYS floated somewhere in between the realms of reality and fantasy. This ethereal quality can be attributed in part to the self-mythologizing stories white settlers told themselves about their own rebellion; partly to the overdrawn tales these settlers told people in the West about life in Rhodesia; and partly to the parables some people in the West told themselves, and continue to tell themselves, about a utopian Rhodesia that never existed. Rhodesia was the object and subject of other fantasies as well. Incongruously, despite its self-assured public face, Rhodesia was a white settler colony that always had very few white settlers actually living in it. This was a very real problem for the territory that went beyond mere imperial classification and colonial administration, but instead concerned its fundamental nature. This perceived racial imbalance between white settlers and indigenous Africans became an existential problem for the regime after its illegal break with Britain in 1965, and efforts to remedy this population imbalance were a top priority as it attempted to strike out on its own. When the rebellion collapsed in 1980, Rhodesia was finally able to shed its imperfect worldly body and fully enter the spirit world of myths and memories where it continues to play a powerful emotive role for Western white supremacists. This chapter explores the stories the settler regime told prospective white immigrants overseas about life in Rhodesia, the stories it told prospective white emigrants from Rhodesia about the lands to which they were considering returning, the stories the regime used to define and defend its white immigration policy at home, and the stories some in the West told, and still tell, about Rhodesia as a Great Lost Cause. It will demonstrate how these different stories told about Rhodesia, by people inside and outside of the territory, as they were told then and as told now, all orbit around the same transatlantic racial population panic that began to form in the late 1960s.

The British colony of Rhodesia had governed its internal affairs since the 1920s, and at one stage came very close to achieving full Dominion status. Yet even though it was nearly independent, it was never fully so. From 1953 to 1963, Rhodesia had been one of the three component territories of the Central African Federation, alongside Northern Rhodesia (Zambia) and Nyasaland (Malawi). When the British dissolved the Federation at the end of 1963, Zambia and Malawi were granted full independence under African majority rule, but Rhodesia continued on in its ambiguous quasi-independent status. This legal limbo between dependency and full independence was a source of frustration and anxiety for many white settlers who were unsure of their constitutional future, a situation seen by many to be more perilous when viewed against the backdrop of their fragile white demographic base.[2] In response to these fears, on November 11, 1965, Rhodesian Prime Minister Ian Smith unilaterally declared Rhodesia's independence from Britain (UDI), beginning a rebellion that would last fifteen years.[3] After the settler regime's illegal break with Britain, Rhodesia functioned as though it was an independent state, yet Britain and the international community denied its existence and held to the fiction that the British Crown maintained sovereign control over the territory.

Ian Smith made it clear that he had not seen much in modern Britain to take pride in since the end of World War II. Smith and the Rhodesian Front predicated their right to independence in part upon their wartime sacrifices; that by fighting and dying in the war in support of their mother country, white settlers had earned their independence in a way that other non-white members of the Commonwealth supposedly had not.[4]

Furthermore, Rhodesians argued that unlike most of the rest of the former empire, they still felt a bond with Britain through their shared history.[5] This accorded with Enoch Powell's argument that the great majority of people from the New Commonwealth were hostile toward Britain, and that these ungrateful countries in the Commonwealth continued to "twist the lion's tail with impunity" internationally, while their emigrants were overrunning Britain itself, and according to Powell, the former imperial metropole was participating in its own humiliation.[6] After World War II, Smith saw this kind of "appeasement and surrender" all around him, and as he famously said in his speech announcing UDI in 1965: "To us has been given the privilege of being the first Western nation in the last two decades to have the determination and fortitude to say 'So Far and No Further.'"[7]

With the rest of the world seemingly moving in one direction on racial matters, toward greater civic and political inclusion of non-whites in the West and toward colonial self-determination in the former European empires, southern African politics were moving in the exact opposite direction. Whites in southern Africa were busy consolidating their power and implementing policies explicitly intended to exclude non-white African political and civic participation at the very same time as non-white immigrants from the Global South were flowing into the West. Southern Africa's enemies therefore lined up nicely alongside the enemies of Western conservatives—the Soviet Bloc, the United Nations, African nationalists, international civil rights leaders, and Western liberals—creating a natural affinity based upon race, social conservatism, and anti-communism. It was those sections of the British population who were most appalled by non-white immigration to Britain and the attendant changes that came with it who found the idea of Rhodesia holding the racial line to be most appealing.[8]

It is a peculiar aspect of Rhodesian history that it could never be properly synchronized with the West, which added to its sense of unreality.[9] For Western conservatives, particularly white supremacists, the rebellion began as a historical anachronism, a vision of the past that evoked a form of racial nostalgia. In the white supremacist imaginary, with UDI Rhodesia was seen to have essentially paused time to avoid Powell's warning of the parade of racial horrors that was poised to destroy a multicultural Britain. Once the guerrilla war fought between the regime and African liberation armies began in earnest in 1972, whites in Rhodesia were imagined by these same Western conservatives to be martyrs.[10] When the regime collapsed in 1980 and became the new state of Zimbabwe, Rhodesia instantly became a Great Lost Cause, and it skipped forward from being of the past to being portrayed by some whites in the West as a vision of a dystopian future.

Among the states of southern Africa, it was always Rhodesia much more than South Africa (and the Portuguese colonies) that captured right-wing imaginations in the West at the time and since. Rhodesia took pains to present itself overseas as having a milder racial character than apartheid South Africa, suggesting that it was continuing with a sort of old-style paternalistic racism that was more easily defended in the West.[11] White Rhodesians prided themselves on being pragmatic about race, driven not by any overarching ideology but by commonsense notions derived from experience.[12] Allison Shutt's book, *Manners Make a Nation*, illustrates how central the idea of the supposedly friendly, courteous, and pragmatic treatment of Africans in the territory was to white Rhodesians' self-image.[13] This in part explains the regime's official rhetoric emphasizing how their society valued merit over race, and evolutionary societal progress over what the regime argued was the chaotic revolutionary upheavals north of the Zambezi. As English speakers recognizably akin to other outposts of the Anglo-world, Rhodesia was also more culturally translatable to British, American and Australian audiences than the Afrikaner-dominated, inward-looking South African Republic. Almost becoming a metonym for his regime and the rebellion, Ian Smith, the laconic World War II veteran-turned-farmer-turned-politician, was also immensely popular among conservatives in the English-speaking world. Another part of Rhodesia's appeal to Western conservatives, both during the rebellion and after it collapsed, was that the Smith regime was seen as a young, plucky underdog—a small, unrecognized settler regime born into a hostile continent, and rejected by the international community and Western leaders.[14] As a result, Rhodesia's rebellion has always cast a much larger shadow than its small size or short duration would seem to warrant.

It was audiences of potential white migrants inside and outside of the territory, both those thinking of coming to Rhodesia or those leaving it, to whom the regime tried to make the case that it alone was preserving white supremacy even while there was "appeasement and surrender" all around. As detailed below, Rhodesia's immigration promotion efforts tapped into the idea that the old Britain was gone forever, but their pitch told prospective immigrants that the traditions and lifestyles they remembered did still exist—but only in southern Africa. Among other things, this meant rhetorically placing their settler society back in time as a last bastion of white supremacy, as the "one last retreat."[15]

* * *

During the fifteen-year UDI rebellion, white Rhodesian discourses on the fear of being "swamped" by non-whites because of soaring birth rates were strikingly similar to some discourses then occurring in Britain, where there was a growing backlash against the influx of non-white immigrants.[16] Wendy Webster has identified how the British media presented images of white settler homes under siege in colonial wars and of white homes under siege by non-white immigrants in Britain as being parallel to one another, with both white communities "shown as beleaguered and vulnerable."[17] These images reflected a new and wider transatlantic right-wing fear that non-white populations were overrunning white populations, not just in their former colonial outposts but at home as well, the latter being what Webster refers to as "the reversal of the colonial encounter."[18] Against this backcloth, Bill Schwarz correctly points out that in Britain the UDI crisis and the backlash against non-white immigration "became superimposed."[19]

Rhodesia's and Britain's shared racial population anxieties fit within widespread popular fears in the West starting in the late 1960s regarding population growth rates in the Global South and rates of non-white migratory flows into the West. One major factor in the timing of these public fears inside and outside of Rhodesia was the 1968 publication of the bestselling book *The Population Bomb* by an American, Paul Ehrlich, which popularized the notion that the earth was headed toward a neo-Malthusian resource crisis.[20] In this mode of thinking, higher birth rates and lower death rates simply meant there were not enough resources to go around.[21] Importantly, Ehrlich's book came out in the same year as Enoch Powell delivered his famous "Rivers of Blood" speech that predicted a violent dystopian future in Britain if non-white Commonwealth immigration were allowed to continue.

While Ehrlich's fears concerned absolute global numbers, and Powell's concerned the spatial distribution of these numbers, they could be coherently knitted together in the politics of racial migration. It is useful here to quote directly from Powell's "River of Blood" speech, which relays an anecdote about white fears of the non-white migratory influx:

A week or two ago I fell into conversation with a constituent, a middle-aged, quite ordinary working man employed in one of our nationalised industries. After a sentence or two about the weather, he suddenly said: "If I had the money to go, I wouldn't stay in this country." I made some deprecatory reply to the effect that even this government wouldn't last forever; but he took no notice, and continued: "I have three children, all of them been through grammar school and two of them married now, with family. I shan't be satisfied till I have seen them all settled overseas." In this country in 15 or 20 years' time the black man will have the whip hand over the white man.[22]

In 1970, former Commonwealth Relations Secretary Duncan Sandys expanded upon this population panic idea in Britain by identifying the connection between non-white inflows and white outflows to and from the United Kingdom. He said in a statement that it was "sheer lunacy" to encourage Britons to emigrate abroad while the British government was simultaneously allowing 40,000 Asians and blacks into the country, adding: "When your bath is overflowing you don't rush to get a mop. You first turn off the tap."[23]

White Rhodesians were obsessed with white migration flows and non-white birth rates.[24] Whites never accounted for more than 5 percent of the total Rhodesian population and being outnumbered by an enormous ratio was a source of deep anxiety within the settler community.[25] It was of existential importance to the regime to maintain a constant flow of whites into Rhodesia and to stem the flow of whites out of Rhodesia. Rising white numbers created confidence in the political future of the regime, helping convince more whites to stay in the country, while dropping white numbers spooked the white community and led to greater emigration. In Rhodesia it was often repeated that white migration numbers served as a "barometer" for the political fortune of the settler regime.[26] For them, a corollary to the idea of a Global South population growing out of control inside and outside of its borders was the notion of the relative scarcity of white migrants in the global migration market, making them a precious global resource that must be poached from abroad and hoarded at home. So, when the Rhodesians saw this overflow of white migrants from Britain, they rushed to grab their mop.

The Rhodesian regime constantly worried not only about its ability to mop up the new emigrants spilling out of Britain and elsewhere, but also its ability to hold onto the whites it already had. As one editorial in the *Rhodesia Herald* commented, and to put further strain on the migrants-as-liquid analogy, Rhodesia had a "hole in the bucket."[27] Even so, it was almost an article of faith in Rhodesia that emigrating residents leaving the territory would realize the grass was not greener abroad and soon return. However, the regime did not passively leave this to fate. The Rhodesian media and the Smith regime constantly produced and reproduced Powellite stories of how modern Britain was a racial and social dystopia.[28]

In 1978, two well-known Rhodesian political cartoonists, Louis Bolze and Rose Martin, produced a collection of political cartoons titled *The Whenwes of Rhodesia*. This book focused on the humorous aspects of the white Rhodesian diaspora, in particular how they did not fit in overseas, and most interestingly, how they did not really want to.[29] Their collection relied upon common stereotypes and clichés about the culture shocks experienced by Rhodesians abroad that would have been instantly recognizable to their white Rhodesian readers. While the book gently poked fun at the emigrants themselves—portraying them as beer-bellied, thin-legged, khaki-short-wearing bumpkins—most of the cartoons homed in on what they saw as the cultural degeneration and social decay of the West. One cartoon, for instance, depicted a doctor from Rhodesia who had moved to Britain looking out at his new office's waiting room, which was packed tightly with black and brown patients suffering from all sorts of ailments. The doctor snarls to his nurse: "And to think that I never once went out to Harari [the African township outside of Salisbury] in my twenty years in Salisbury."[30] Another cartoon showed a white Rhodesian family standing on a London street corner, suitcases in hand, looking with disapproval at the mass of black and brown pedestrians on the sidewalk, with the mother commenting: "When we were in Salisbury at least one saw a white face occasionally."[31] Together these illustrations offer a darkly humorous look at what its creators imagined it was like for Rhodesians to experience first-hand Enoch Powell's frightening vision of modern Britain.

Popular depictions of contemporary Western culture in Rhodesia in other media also highlighted what they saw as the flouting of traditional values and the transgression of racial and sexual boundaries. In Bill Schwarz's words, like other white settlers, Rhodesians "believ[ed] themselves to be the true custodians of the deep core of British values."[32] Part of this enervating tendency Rhodesians identified in the West was an alleged passive surrender of Western culture to the "invasion" of ex-colonials who were moving to their former imperial capitals in large numbers. One article in the *Herald* from 1979 quoted a returning emigrant from Britain as saying, "It's not funny when you're paying £15 a week for a poky little room to be told by the Pakistani landlord that he's going to ration your bathwater." On the basis of this and several other personal stories, this same article pointed to a possibly optimistic trend that many former Rhodesian residents were returning, "preferring to brave the uncertainties of a country at war than accept the way of life overseas."[33] Better Smith's Rhodesia at war than Powell's postwar Britain.

Some Rhodesians suspected that the Rhodesian media pushed this narrative too hard. One letter writer to the *Rhodesia Herald* pointed out:

> Are we not heartily sick of the well-worn technique employed by RTBC/RTV of emphasizing ad nauseam the troubles and difficulties of the rest of the world, so that by contrast Rhodesia emerges as a paragon of virtue and rectitude? … If Britons are degenerate and bankrupt, if Americans are longing for release from their colour problems and the terrible dilemma of Vietnam, if Frenchmen really feel crushed between de Gaulle and Communism, what fantastic opportunities for immigration present themselves to Rhodesia … Why isn't there a flood? Are these discontented, thwarted millions really just too indolent to stretch out and pick the golden fruit that beckons them? … Is it just possible that there are imperfections here?[34]

Outsiders noticed this defensive, even insecure, pride as well. An article in the British magazine *Punch* highlighted the Rhodesian sport of bashing the West. Among other critiques of Rhodesian society, Alan Coren's article remarked that "derision of England and things English is perhaps Rhodesia's only creative activity."[35] He relayed a story of a Rhodesian traveler returning to Salisbury airport from abroad, announcing that: "all Europe was bloody awful. Both immigration officer and traveler roared with laughter."[36] The overriding theme of these Rhodesian discourses about the West was clear: stay put, the Britain you remember is gone forever.

Rhodesia's migration policies were not formed in isolation. Regime officials were very aware of the global and regional migration markets in which they were operating.[37] In the competitive global migration market, Rhodesia had several disadvantages compared to the other major destinations, such as Australia, New Zealand, South Africa, Canada, and the United States (all of which were, like Rhodesia, former British settler colonies). New immigrants from Britain had to circumvent British domestic laws and international sanctions designed to thwart emigration to Rhodesia, take on the social stigma associated with moving to the controversial rebel regime, and be willing to gamble on an uncertain political and economic future.[38] It was much easier, for example, for Britons to move to Australia, a settler society that was itself still guided by an overtly racist immigration policy until 1973. But regime officials also understood that their primary selling point was one that was unique to southern Africa: they could offer a return to the imperial way of life. Unlike the other former white dominions, Rhodesia held out the possibility of a certain type of time travel, of going back to "Britain *as it was*."[39] This ideological and temporal escape from the modern West quite obviously was not predicated upon the rebel regime being devoid of non-whites, but instead the idea that in Rhodesia whites still held the "whip hand."

The dramatic changes in racial politics that took place after World War II, in the rise of anti-colonial nationalism globally but also in the expansion of civil rights within Britain, created the temptation for both proponents and opponents of these changes to translate them through temporal analogies. For example, in a 1971 speech, Enoch Powell explicitly cast Birmingham, England, as becoming in twenty or thirty years as racially torn as Detroit, Michigan, were non-white immigration to continue.[40] For Powellites, Britain's racial past was more appealing than its present or certainly its probable future. To this audience, it was precisely because Rhodesia's preservation of white privilege seemed to place it in an earlier time that it was so appealing. So, being slightly out of time was embraced by Rhodesia as part of the regime's immigration promotion strategy.

These were the waters where Rhodesia fished for white migrants, and this was how it baited the hook. For example, an advertisement in the right-of-center British magazine *The Spectator* posted by the Rhodesian Department of Immigration Promotion in 1973 described Rhodesia as though it was an imperial idyll out of time. It read:

Rhodesia. It isn't easy to find that haven to escape to any more. Most of the world's idyllic retreats are getting a little tarnished—and prices aren't what they were once, to say nothing of taxes. But there is one last retreat where Britain's way of life is still treasured and life has a special tempo of its own. Where endless sunny days and peaceful ways let one forget the problems of life elsewhere. Rhodesia. A land of leisurely pursuits and sophisticated facilities; of outstanding service and good neighbourliness; where money still goes a lot further and taxes are low. There are spacious homes, domestic help, modern health amenities, fast communications and uncrowded cities. The arts are catered for and sport is second to none, no matter what you fancy. Rhodesia is dedicated to preserving a way of life we all cherish. We would like you to be a part of it.[41]

An advertisement that ran in the *Daily Mirror* in 1967 read:

Rhodesia invites you ... to pull up your roots and move to a country where life is still a challenge. Where hard work and initiative still bring their just rewards. Where opportunities for advancement and capital investment are virtually limitless ... to live in a modern, sophisticated society where people still smile. Enjoying the benefits of a superb climate, low taxation and good salaries, a fine standard of living, educational, health and sporting facilities ... to make a new life in a country with a great future.[42]

The British government and the United Nations were very aware of the importance of white migration to Rhodesia's political survival and attempted to shut down these advertisements.[43] One that ran in Britain on June 19, 1968, days after new laws were passed in Britain clamping down on immigration promotion, directly responded to Prime Minister Harold Wilson's push to shut off emigration to Rhodesia. It was titled: "Shh! ... ask you-know-who about Rhodesia." The advertisement continued:

Bet he couldn't tell you. But we can. Sure we have problems. Who hasn't? Ask him. You would be knocked flat at the progress and stability of a peaceful country, and wonder why he made all the fuss. You would find many old friends from John-o-Groats to Land's End heads down, tails up plugging away in every profession. Pay us a visit. Come as a tourist.

It added that Rhodesians are a '"hats off to the past, coats off to the future' kind of people."[44] Rhodesia's appeal to potential white immigrants was to a certain past, or more accurately to a future where they could remain in an imagined past forever.

* * *

This was, in part at least, a bluff. Despite the regime's confident rhetoric, racial power relationships in Rhodesia were not at all static. Beneath the veneer of pool parties and a leisurely sporting culture lurked widespread racial population fears among white Rhodesian society. During its fifteen years of pseudo-independence, Rhodesia constantly endeavored to increase or at very least hold steady its white population, all the while trying in vain to stem the tide of black population growth. The language of racial "swamping" was ubiquitous in the articulation of these white fears of African population growth. In the Rhodesian context, high African birth rates were often characterized as being akin to rising swamp waters threatening to submerge all in their path. To address this supposed inundation, the Rhodesian regime implemented a mass white immigration policy that was paired with the aggressive promotion of family planning in African communities, which together formed the twin pillars of its demographic war of numbers.

In a Rhodesian parliamentary debate on immigration policy in January 1969, the Rhodesian minister of immigration, P. K. Van der Byl, outlined the settler state's critical need for more skilled immigrants as well as those with capital and professional qualifications. He explained that white immigrants were the ones who brought with them the necessary knowhow, experience, and money the Rhodesian economy needed to continue to grow, and most crucially it was whites alone who had the ability to create jobs for the rapidly increasing African population. During the course of the debate, an Opposition African MP asked Van der Byl if in light of the serious shortage of skills and capital he described, the government ever considered opening up immigration to skilled and moneyed Africans from outside of Rhodesia to fill these critical openings and provide the same tonic to the economy. Van der Byl responded by saying that bringing in African immigrants to Rhodesia would be "a case of bringing coals to Newcastle."[45]

Van der Byl's flippant and offensive double entendre only made sense if all Africans, skilled or unskilled, rich or poor, professionals or without any education at all, were considered to be undifferentiated pieces of coal in a place that already had plenty of coal. According to his logic, it was solely Africans' skin color that made them redundant in Rhodesia, and so it did not matter if any one African was skilled and moneyed or any one white was unskilled and penniless. Collectively, whites, by virtue of being white, had immense political value to the regime; and Africans, by virtue of being African, had a negative political value for the regime.

More than a year before UDI, the Smith government secretly began to define the criteria for the granting of permanent residence visas to new immigrants: the first criterion for new immigrants was always that they must be white.[46] But in its immigration policy, as in other areas, the Rhodesian state publicly attempted to launder racial categories through economic categories. Its supposed emphasis on merit rather than race simply meant that racial divisions were made to overlap perfectly with economic skills.[47] This thin window dressing was enough to preserve the distinction, held precious by most white Rhodesians, that their regime was not as radically racist as was the South African state under apartheid.[48] Because of its precarious position as an illegal state, Rhodesia was also more sensitive to world opinion than South Africa, and in issuing official statements regime officials were careful never to appear to be too far outside the discursive norms of the West. This meant that, for instance, the *Rhodesia Herald* could disingenuously claim: "It is fundamental to the established Rhodesian way of life that merit should be the only criterion for any individual's advancement."[49]

The regime's two major population initiatives in some ways ran counter to one another.[50] Its policy of promoting family planning relied upon a degree of trust and cooperation from the African population, and blatantly racist attempts to bolster the white population through immigration jeopardized the parallel policy of slowing African growth rates. Despite the government's efforts to de-link family planning from mass white immigration, African MPs regularly attacked the government for spending money on new white immigrants when Africans were repeatedly being told to limit their numbers. As one Rhodesian Front minister tried to explain to an Opposition MP, "Unfortunately this is a potential source of misunderstandings between the races, because the Africans may well feel that these [two policies of white immigration and black family planning] taken together, represent a determined drive to reduce the large difference in numbers between them and Europeans."[51] The persistence of this "misunderstanding" constantly annoyed regime officials. In an effort to clear up what he referred to as "confusion" over the two policies, Jack Howman, the minister of immigration, said in 1968: "Immigration was necessary to bring in people with the skills and knowledge the country required. Family planning was necessary if the needs of the people of the country were to be met and a reasonable standard of living assured to them."[52] In the same debate, the minister of health responded to accusations that the two policies were being pursued in tandem to achieve racial ends less patiently, calling it "a wild, irresponsible charge which I have had to deal with year after year."[53]

P. K. Van der Byl was minister of immigration from 1968 to 1974, which were the peak years of post-UDI immigration.[54] As an Afrikaner, Van der Byl's appointment in and of itself had political ramifications because it represented a shift away from the British bias that defined earlier immigration policy in Rhodesia. While he was a strong advocate for, and indeed a symbol of, a new polyethnic vision of white Rhodesia, Van der Byl was a racial hardliner of the first order. As it was, the shift from an exclusively British identity to the coalescence of a polyethnic white racial identity in Rhodesia after UDI necessitated some delineation of its borderline with non-white racial classifications. Yet this endeavor was not as straightforward as it is often assumed, since racial categories were never physiologically certain, and distinctions along this borderline were decided in an ad hoc and arbitrary fashion. In addition, official classifications of who was white and who was not differed according to whether or not the designated individuals or groups were prospective immigrants or were already residing in the territory.

In the context of the population war of numbers, there were very strong incentives for the regime to increase white numbers within Rhodesia even if this meant secretly defining and redefining who was considered white.[55] For instance, Turks, Arabs, and Persians all often passed for whites in Rhodesia.[56] Likely some members of the Colored community also could pass as white at certain times and in certain situations. In a fascinating discussion in 1973, Prime Minister Ian Smith's cabinet weighed the benefits of a new policy of the "progression on merit of persons other than Europeans to the European community," with a particular focus on the Colored community. As a result of the discussion, the cabinet decided to allow certain members of the Colored community to assimilate to the white section of society. While these individual crossings of the racial line differed in some respects from top-down recategorizations of various groups, they both illustrate the instability and ambiguity of these seemingly rigid categories.

The regime's reasoning regarding racial boundaries can be illustrated in the case of the Swartz family, who had left South Africa because they violated that country's anti-miscegenation law. In this 1969 case, a family consisting of a half-Asian spouse and a white spouse and their Rhodesian-born baby was unilaterally denied permanent residency by Van der Byl. His rationale was that Rhodesia's policy of banning mixed families "should be applied without exception. Once a single exception was allowed the pressure would build for more and more concessions." He also worried that "Rhodesia must not be allowed to become a refuge for persons from South Africa who were prepared to break the law of their own land."[57] In criticizing Van der Byl's denial of the family's visas, the rest of the cabinet decided that he read the Swartzes' case incorrectly, concluding: "The basic division in Rhodesia was between black and white and it was essential that the white population should be increased in every way pos-sible way. There was something to be said, therefore, for not discouraging entry of people who would adhere to the European group."[58] While they conceded that "There was no advantage to the country or to the European group in the admission of pure Asiatics," they opined that "with persons of mixed blood the position could be very different ... [For example, the Swartzes'] baby is now Rhodesian by birth and 75% European." Though they decided that this particular decision could not be undone, the cabinet agreed that in future people similarly situated as the Swartzes should be granted residency permits because "people in [their] position would move into the European class and be an asset to the country." To the rest of the cabinet, the Swartzes were close enough to being white to be of value.

The borders of the white group were more amorphous than even the cabinet's crude percentiles, and had more to do with perceived merit than skin color. In 1970, Ian Smith asked the cabinet whether, in light of the "high standards" of both Japanese and Chinese people, government policy should henceforth treat those whole groups already in Rhodesia as a part of the white community.[59] In weighing the arguments behind this reclassification, the cabinet noted that Japan was an industrialized country and that Rhodesia might in the future rely upon trade with the East. After some discussion, the cabinet concluded that "Chinese and Japanese residents should be classed as Europeans."[60] With the collapse of Portuguese Africa in the mid-1970s, a new influx of immigrants began to show up in Rhodesia seeking residence permits. After some debate, it was decided that white Portuguese immigrants were to be allowed in, as would Chinese doctors, but Indo-Portuguese from Goa and Colored Portuguese would be rejected.[61] Reclassifying certain selected Asian groups as sud-denly being European was a policy unique in the Anglo world, though it resembled in some respects the evolution of American views regarding the whiteness of Jewish and Irish Americans.[62]

While some non-white groups already in Rhodesia had the possibil-ity of assimilating to the white community as a matter of policy, *new* Asian or Colored immigrants were still denied permanent residence status as a matter of course. This was because the regime had no interest in recreating what it saw as the degradation of British society by allowing in more non-whites. One Rhodesian Front backbencher laid down his Powellite interpretation of Britain's immigration policy next to what he saw as Rhodesia's:

> England is exporting its brains and taking in its place unskilled labour and people who do not fit into the country, so that today race riots are becoming a common feature of news items which occur in English newspapers. We are doing something quite different. We are bringing people into this country who help the economy, who help all the inhabitants of the country, who provide labour for all the inhabitants of the country, further labour, both black and white.[63]

Van der Byl certainly agreed. He forthrightly stated in 1971 that "Asiatics, Coloureds and Indians are not admitted as immigrants to this country."[64] Similarly, even after the government settled on a policy of allowing certain existing members of the Colored community into white society, there was no change in immigration policy regarding foreign Coloreds.[65] In 1969, Van der Byl actually boasted to the Rhodesian Front Annual Congress that he received "ceaseless requests" from industry leaders to allow skilled Coloreds to enter Rhodesia from South Africa to fill economic needs and that he rejected all their requests.[66] In one specific incident, he was able to block the residence permit of a Colored medical worker hired to fill an open medical position at the Ministry of Health, even though no other qualified candidate existed.[67] He also successfully pushed for the blocking of a possible influx of Indians into Rhodesia from Zambia.[68] Indeed, in 1969, despite the fact that imported capital was a major justification for white immigration and the need for foreign exchange was a pressing concern, Van der Byl declared that the idea of bringing in rich Indians to Rhodesia was "ridiculous."[69]

Against this patently racist backdrop, the various ministers in charge of immigration nonetheless took great pains to try to convince African MPs that their all-white immigration policy was not racist but was necessary for the economy. In public discourses, immigration proponents used the pseudo-economic argument that every white immigrant brought with him or her African jobs. Their evidence derived from countrywide ratios of white employers and black employees, something which obviously reflected the state-instituted racist economic structure of Rhodesia. From these ratios, they then made the fallacious leap that all whites, even newly arrived immigrants, magically created a certain number of black jobs. In this way the preexistence of economic discrimination was used to justify further discrimination in the realm of immigration policy.[70] It was only in this context that a Rhodesian Front MP could make the absurd statement: "Immigration is vital to this country. It is vital that we close the population gap between the African on one side and the European on the other. I am not being racial in this. I am dealing with it from the point of view of the development of the country."[71]

At the peaks of the Rhodesian economic pyramid there were gaps that remained open, but reserved for white immigrants, in spite of the fact that more and more Africans were obtaining the qualifications and skills necessary to fill these positions. As a result, African school-leavers with advanced degrees filled the unemployment queues in the cities, vying for the limited opportunities available to them, while at the same time the regime was actively soliciting new white immigrants. The existence of these skilled Africans was a visible repudiation of the purported rationale of the state's racial population policies. Since they were closed off from higher-skilled jobs, this population was forced either to move from Rhodesia to where their skills would be put to use or remain underemployed or unemployed in Rhodesia.[72] Particularly galling to government ministers were the calls by African MPs to attract skilled black immigrants from outside Rhodesia to fill gaps in the economy. This line of argument cut to the heart of the government's racially motivated immigration policy by further divorcing skills from race. It was in this context that Van der Byl uttered his sardonic coals-to-Newcastle line.[73]

Rhodesian Front supporters were exasperated that urban Africans, many of whom were skilled, would not take up rural work and in effect re-enter the conceptual box that was created for them. One letter writer to the *Herald* wrote: "[Africans] prefer to be parasites" in the towns rather than work on farms.[74] Another letter to the editor claimed that education was "a curse to the African," as it raised expectations unduly and made the educated not want to "toil and sweat."[75] For this reason the Rhodesian regime crossed out urban African unemployment as being artificial. In 1969, the minister of internal affairs, Lance Smith, even called the claim of African unemployment "a damned lie."[76] In Rhodesia it would have been unthinkable, of course, to suggest that unemployed urban whites, even those with no skills at all, take jobs on white farms. Taking this line of thinking to its logical conclusion, one letter writer gave this advice: "To resentful young African school-leavers I would say '… go North, young man …' And to the Rhodesian Government, I would put this suggestion. Would it not be a good idea to offer assisted passages (to Britain for instance) for a million or so Standard 6 African academics?"[77]

Another satirical letter to the *Herald* a week before UDI reveals some of these same population anxieties and their relationship to Rhodesia's international status. Suggesting a solution to the constitutional impasse, the letter writer called for Britain to send Rhodesia two million whites and in exchange Rhodesia would send Britain two million blacks. By increasing white numbers and decreasing black numbers, this plan would secure settler rule forever, and furthermore, "[Britain's] great love for the black Rhodesian makes the position very easy [for them to accept]."[78] Camilla Schofield shows us that this same language of calling non-whites "parasites" on the British welfare state, scammers, and "bad citizens," can be found throughout the letters of support received by Powell following his "Rivers of Blood" speech, with white Britons portrayed as the only ones dutifully paying into the system.[79]

In the logic of the numbers war, white skin obviously mattered more than actual skills. The 1969 Rhodesian Front Annual Congress unanimously passed resolutions for less selective white immigration and more job categories to be reserved only for whites. In a speech to the Congress, Van der Byl called for a policy that would be "as unselective as possible [for whites]," denying residence only to "rogues, scalawags, and criminals."[80] As heard in the regime's defenses of its immigration policies, whites were needed in Rhodesia because they possessed an indefinable quality that had something to do with initiative and industriousness, and little to do with actual economic or academic qualifications. These qualities could not simply be learned through any formalized schooling, and no certificate could confer these attributes.[81] This was, of course, a necessary fallback position once the objective measures of merit began to be met by more Africans and other non-whites. In an interview in 1969, Van der Byl even questioned the very meaning of merit. He argued:

> Naturally one believes in merit but firstly one has to find a way of assessing merit ... When it comes to meritocracy, in that it is aimed at African-European relationships, one must be ever wary of confusing book learning with education and education with civilization, because they are not the same. I believe meritocracy must contain as a major ingredient, civilization.[82]

Race was therefore not only a proxy for merit but was ipso facto proof of merit or lack thereof.

A telling analogy between these two racial migration flows was offered in a *Rhodesia Herald* editorial from January 1969. The editorial drew a parallel between non-white immigration into Britain and white immigration into Rhodesia, comparing Britain's economic need for, and popular resistance to, importing non-white labor with Rhodesia's alleged need for, and African resistance to, an all-white immigration policy.[83]

> Up to a point of protest, the situation in Rhodesia is parallel with Britain's. Rhodesia too depends on the work and skills of immigrant races, who come here for the same general reasons that it has in Britain. White immigration is necessary for the good of Rhodesia's indigenous population far more so than is Coloured for Britain's. But if it is not to arouse antagonism on the British model it should increase individual opportunities for our indigenous population to share in the general advancement created by its lifting of Rhodesia out of the Stone Age in three generations.[84]

176

In conclusion, the editorial expressed the relatively liberal view in Rhodesia that "To encourage white people to come to basically black Rhodesia and take jobs which indigenous Rhodesians are eager to do and can be trained to do is the height of social folly." While expressing some sympathy with African frustrations over black unemployment running alongside white immigration, this editorial illustrates a massive racist blind spot common to most white Rhodesian discourses on immigration, taking for granted the underlying assumption that race equated perfectly with skills. Importantly, this column did not explore how these two migrations were related on a causal level, namely how a racial population panic prompted by a non-white influx into Britain fed into Rhodesia's desperate campaign to attract white Britons, and how this exchange was laundered through the language of economics and development.

* * *

Whom did the Rhodesian regime attract with its racially nostalgic immigration appeals? The regime certainly understood the relationship between prospective immigrants' political dispositions and the potential for migration, knew its target audiences, and, as shown above, pitched its appeals in such a way as to draw them to Rhodesia. And new immigrants who came to Rhodesia after UDI tended to reflect more right-wing political and ideological dispositions. Rhodesian author, and former Salisbury mayor, Frank Clements noted that after UDI there was a general population transfer of so-called liberals out of the country and more conservative or "apolitical" types coming in.[85] Because Rhodesia's white population was so small and was always so fluid and transient, the opportunity for national reinvention was greater there than perhaps any other place on earth at the time, and so any study of the evolution of white Rhodesian politics over this time period needs to consider if these were the same people whose views had changed, or if they were in fact different people.[86]

It is obviously impossible to fully reconstruct immigrant motivations for moving to Rhodesia, but there is anecdotal evidence that both political push factors and economic pull factors played a major role in driving white migration to Rhodesia during the rebellion. But how different were these two factors? In its immigration appeals quoted above, Rhodesia presented itself to the outside world as a place "where hard work and initiative still bring their just rewards," in contrast to socialist Britain which was seen to dull initiative and coddle the lazy. But in the context of Rhodesia this was of course racially coded, since the Rhodesian economy artificially propped up white labor and closed off African competition so that only white hard work brought just rewards. In this way, the economic and the political motivations for moving to Rhodesia are difficult to untangle. It could be argued that Frank Clements' use of the term "apolitical" to describe those whites who came to Rhodesia for economic reasons, purportedly not caring about the settler state's racial politics, was a touch misleading, since they were in fact expressing a certain political disposition, namely that they were willing to move to an illegal regime that was ostracized by the world because of its racial character to take full advantage of its racist economic structure. One British immigrant who made the move from Lancashire to Rhodesia in 1968 and was profiled in the *Herald* illustrates this entanglement. He said modern Britain was awful, "socialism gone mad," and that his decision to leave was in part prompted by the increasing "flood" of non-white immigrants to Britain.[87] Another immigrant from Britain who arrived in 1968 was open about his reasons for emigrating to Rhodesia. As the *Herald* reported: "The two main reasons for his coming to Rhodesia, he said, were a general dissatisfaction with Britain, where there had been a detrimental leveling of standards, and his wife's glowing reports of Rhodesia."[88]

* * *

From 1972 to 1980 the Rhodesian regime fought and eventually lost a bloody guerrilla war against African liberation armies. With its defeat Rhodesia's magical hold on the imaginations of Western conservatives did not dissipate, but instead grew stronger. The brutal reign of Robert Mugabe that followed white rule played into this narrative, and to many conservatives in the U.S. and Britain this served to retrospectively justify white settler rule. With the Fast Track Land Reform beginning in 2000, the Mugabe regime began seizing white-owned farms. The plight of these evicted white farmers in Zimbabwe garnered a great deal of attention, especially in certain conservative circles, and stories of these white farmers under siege are very similar in theme and message to the anecdote Powell quoted in his "Rivers of Blood" speech about the besieged elderly Wulfrunian woman. For the white supremacist fringe, these farm seizures were read as a racial warning. For example, one American white supremacist website, Occidental Dissent, features a now viral photo of a white Zimbabwean woman holding onto her two young children as a crowd of menacing Africans gather outside the front gate of her farm. It is captioned: "Remember Rhodesia? Switch the main players, especially aggressors, around, and you have the likely scenario of a future America where Whites, especially Southerners, are the demonized minority."[89]

But romanticizing the Rhodesian rebellion is not simply the work of the white supremacist fringe. Revisionist myths about Rhodesia have long been maintained and energized by the very active presence of white Rhodesians in the diaspora. When Mugabe was finally pushed out of office in November 2017, this sparked a renewed interest in his legacy and the legacy of the regime that came before him. To mark Mugabe's fall, which came nearly forty years after Rhodesia's collapse, the *National Review*, a magazine which when it was under the direction of William F. Buckley, Jr., and William A. Rusher was perhaps Rhodesia's biggest booster in the United States, published a long, gauzy, and uncritical retrospective of the Rhodesian rebellion.[90] Clearly the ghosts of the rebellion linger, especially in cyberspace.[91]

* * *

Widespread Western fears of population growth in the Global South in the 1960s, the real and perceived effects of non-white immigration to Britain, and the numbers of whites leaving Britain for Rhodesia were

179

interrelated phenomena. Rhodesia's immigration appeals targeted people in the West who, like Powell's anonymous constituents, were the most disturbed by the demographic changes occurring at home, those to whom the idea of having a Pakistani-born landlord was an inversion of the proper order of the world. Among many of those experiencing this racial population panic, Rhodesia seemed to be an anachronistic bastion of old-style white supremacy, even though whites formed a very small numerical minority. As this chapter has argued, the absurdity of Britons leaving for Africa to avoid Powell's warning of "the black man [having] the whip hand over the white man" should be viewed as part of the larger reaction to global demographic changes, the end of empire, and the rise in political rights claims of minority groups in the West. In the end, these British migrants to Rhodesia misinterpreted Powell's omen, as it was not the Thames but the Zambezi that would be foaming with blood by the end of the 1970s.

Notes

1 British National Archives at Kew, FCO 36/1716, advertisement, *Spectator*, dated December 22, 1973.

2 For more on the bizarre legal status of Rhodesia during the rebellion, see J. Brownell, "'A Sordid Tussle on the Strand': Rhodesia House During the UDI Rebellion (1965–1980)," *The Journal of Imperial and Commonwealth History* 38.3 (2010): 805–24.

3 For an excellent overview of the role of race in the complicated constitutional politics of Rhodesia, see L. White, *Unpopular Sovereignty: Rhodesian Independence and African Decolonization* (Chicago: University of Chicago Press, 2015).

4 Camilla Schofield writes of how important popular memories of World War II were for Enoch Powell's vision of who did and did not belong in the English nation, and more concretely who deserved the fruits of the postwar welfare state as payback for their wartime sacrifices (whites), and who did not deserve them (New Commonwealth immigrants), a notion that conveniently ignored the sacrifices of non-white soldiers. Camilla Schofield, *Enoch Powell and the Making of Postcolonial Britain* (Cambridge: Cambridge University Press, 2013), 22. For the significance of the timing of Rhodesia's UDI on Remembrance Day, November 11, see J. Brownell, "'The Magical Hour of Midnight': The Annual Commemorations of

Rhodesia's and Transkei's Independence Day," in Toyin Falola and Kenneth Kalu (eds.), *Exploitation and Misrule in Colonial and Postcolonial Africa* (Basingstoke: Palgrave Macmillan, 2018), 243–76.

5 Smith tried hard to associate Rhodesia with "the best of Churchill's Britain." W. Webster, *Englishness and Empire, 1939–1965* (Oxford: Oxford University Press, 2005), 206. For how this Rhodesia/Churchill connection was emphasized visually, see J. Brownell, "The Visual Rhetoric of Settler Stamps: Rhodesia's Rebellion and the Projection of Sovereignty (1965–80)," in Yu-Ting Huang and Rebecca Weaver-Hightower (eds.), *Archiving Settler Colonialism: Culture, Space and Race* (New York: Routledge, 2018).

6 Powell quoted in Schofield, *Enoch Powell*, 197.

7 Ian Smith's UDI announcement speech, November 11, 1965.

8 Rhodesians noted that austerity measures in Britain in 1968 resulted in an increase in emigration, but Rhodesia found it difficult to fully take advantage of this trend. See J. Brownell, *The Collapse of Rhodesia: Population Demographics and the Politics of Race* (London: I.B. Tauris, 2011), ch. 5, "Rhodesia's Immigration Policy: 'To Save Civilisation in this Country.'" See also "Emigration Queues in London," *Rhodesia Herald*, November 27, 1968. The *Rhodesia Herald* noted that British emigration dropped with the rise to the premiership of Tory Edward Heath. "Fewer Leaving UK Under Tory Rule," *Rhodesia Herald*, October 20, 1970.

9 For a study of Rhodesia's asynchronicity with the West, see J. Brownell, "Out of Time: Global Settlerism, Nostalgia, and the Selling of the Rhodesian Rebellion Overseas," *The Journal of Southern African Studies* 43.4 (2017): 805–24.

10 It should be noted that while nearly all white supremacists were also anti-communist, by no means were all anti-communists white supremacists. A great deal of sympathy for the plight of Rhodesia came from anti-communists who were not white supremacists. For the centrality of anti-communism to the Rhodesian Front's ideology, see D. Lowry, "The Impact of Anti-Communism on White Rhodesian Political Culture, c. 1920s-1980," in S. Onslow (ed.), *Cold War in Southern Africa: White Power, Black Liberation* (London: Routledge, 2009), 84–109.

11 Rhodesia's paternalistic racism found many Western defenders, perhaps most notably in William F. Buckley's *National Review*. South Africa also served as a useful right flank in other contexts. Wendy Webster points out that in the aftermath of the Notting Hill and Nottingham white riots of 1958, the British media touted Britain's relatively tolerant attitude regarding race as compared with the American South and South Africa. Webster, *Englishness and Empire*, 173, 179.

12 P. Godwin and I. Hancock, *Rhodesians Never Die: The Impact of War and Political Change on White Rhodesia, 1970–1980* (Oxford: Oxford University Press, 1993).

13 A. K. Shutt, *Manners Make a Nation: Racial Etiquette in Southern Rhodesia, 1910–1963* (Rochester, NY: University of Rochester Press, 2015).

14 For example, a flyer from the US-based, far right Friends of Rhodesian Independence claimed: "[T]he truth is that the Rhodesian experience exactly parallels our own history: pioneer settlers carving a civilized Nation out of hostile wilderness, then being abused and betrayed by their mother country, and asking only of the outside world that it not pass judgment before getting all the facts." Columbia University, Group Research Inc. Archives, Box 146, Folder FRI, Friends of Rhodesian Independence flyer, "We Hold These Truths to be Self-Evident … But …" (undated).

15 For Rhodesia's temporalizing discourses, see Brownell, *Out of Time*; Bill Schwarz, *The White Man's World* (Oxford: Oxford University Press, 2011).

16 Daniel McNeil reveals how the Rhodesian information services communicated to members of the right-wing British Monday Club that there was a natural alliance between those who opposed non-white immigration to Britain and support for Rhodesia. D. McNeil, "'The rivers of Zimbabwe will run red with blood': Enoch Powell and the Post-Imperial Nostalgia of the Monday Club," *Journal of Southern African Studies* 37.4 (2011): 731–45.

17 Webster, *Englishness and Empire*, 152.

18 Webster, *Englishness and Empire*, 149. Webster is paraphrasing a quote she attributes later to Louise Bennett, 159.

19 Schwarz, *White Man's World*, 396.

20 P. Ehrlich, *The Population Bomb* (New York: Ballantine Books, 1968). For an overview of these neo-Malthusian fears in Rhodesia specifically, see Brownell, *The Collapse of Rhodesia*, ch. 3.

21 The British imperial state had long been interested in controlling the demographic contours of its colonial populations. For a longer historical look at the relationship between population science and colonial policy, see Karl Ittman, *A Problem of Great Importance: Population, Race, and Power in the British Empire, 1918–1973* (Berkeley, CA: University of California Press, 2013).

22 Full text in "Enoch Powell's 'Rivers of Blood' Speech," *The Telegraph*, November 6, 2007.

23 "Encouragement of Migration from UK called "Sheer Lunacy,'" *Rhodesia Herald*, March 23, 1970.

24 For a broader study of Rhodesia's demographic war of numbers, see Brownell, *The Collapse of Rhodesia*.

25 J. Brownell, "The Hole in Rhodesia's Bucket," *Journal of Southern African Studies* 34.3 (2008): 591–610 (603).

26 See, for example, "Biggest Gain of Immigrants for Ten Years," *Rhodesia Herald*, December 20, 1968.

27 Editorial, "There's a Hole in the Bucket," *Rhodesia Herald*, June 13, 1970.

28 Rhodesians were constantly looking back over their shoulders. As Luise White correctly points out: "When white people, whatever their politics, immigrated to independent Rhodesia, their recollections followed a particular pattern: 'I came from a bad place, now I am in a good place.'" L. White, "The Utopia of Working Phones: Rhodesian Independence and the Place of Race in Decolonization," in M. D. Gordin, H. Tilley, and G. Prakash (eds.), *Utopia/Dystopia: Conditions of Historical Possibility* (Princeton, NJ: Princeton University Press, 2010), 106.

29 L. Bolze and R. Martin, *The Whenwes of Rhodesia* (Bulawayo: Books of Rhodesia Publishing Co., 1978).

30 Bolze and Martin, *Whenwes*, 83.

31 Bolze and Martin, *Whenwes*, 23.

32 Schwarz, *White Man's World*, 398.

33 "Gapping it in Reverse: Emigrants Finds Grass no Greener," *Rhodesia Herald*, October 18, 1979.

34 Letter to the editor from H. L. Tuckey, "If All Is Well in Rhodesia Why Do Immigrants from Troubled Europe Hesitate?," *Rhodesia Herald*, July 22, 1968.

35 Quoted in "Hard Words on Rhodesia," *Rhodesia Herald*, November 18, 1970.

36 Ibid.

37 See Brownell, *The Collapse of Rhodesia*, ch. 5.

38 Ibid.

39 Schwarz, *White Man's World*, 406 (emphasis in the original).

40 Powell quoted in Schofield, *Enoch Powell*, p. 214.

41 British National Archives at Kew, FCO 36/1716, *Spectator*, December 22, 1973.

42 LAB 8/3195, *Daily Mirror*, December 1967.

43 Brownell, "The Hole in Rhodesia's Bucket."

44 "Scores Respond to Rhodesia Advert in British Paper," *Rhodesia Herald*, June 19, 1968.

45 Parliamentary Debates, Committee of Supply Vote, January 17, 1969.

46 Ian D. Smith papers, Rhodes University, Grahamstown, South Africa, Box 017, Cabinet minutes, July 8, 1964.

47 In another example, in 1963 the Rhodesian cabinet decided to de-racialize the pay scales for their police forces. In so doing, they decided to "remove racial discrimination but to introduce a substitute barrier, such as an economic one ... Therefore, the proposed rates of pay would be based on income rather than colour." Smith papers, Box 015, Cabinet minutes, June 18, 1963.

48 The 1961 and 1965 constitutions were both based on non-racial franchise qualifications, but with economic barriers built-in to achieve the same effect. The 1969 republican constitution abandoned this for a purely racial franchise.

49 Editorial, "Acceptable to All," *Rhodesia Herald*, April 26, 1966.

50 On the complexities and contradictions inherent in the Rhodesia regime's African family planning policies, see A. Kaler, *Running After Pills: Politics, Gender and Contraception in Colonial Zimbabwe* (Portsmouth, NC: Heinemann, 2003).

51 "Budget Debate Showed Up Unemployment Danger: Problem Likely to Grow," *Rhodesia Herald*, July 29, 1968.

52 "In Parliament Today: Immigration and Family Planning 'Confused,'" *Rhodesia Herald*, July 31, 1968.

53 Ibid.

54 He was to take over the post again in the much leaner years from 1977 until the end of the regime in 1979.

55 For a fascinating study of what whiteness meant in Rhodesia, including its relationship to the idea of the maintenance of standards and efficiency, in particular working telephones, see White, "The Utopia of Working Phones."

56 See F. Clements, *Rhodesia: A Study of the Deterioration of a White Society* (New York: Praeger, 1969).

57 Smith papers, Box 23, Cabinet minutes, "Mr. and Mrs. Swartz," January 13, 1970.

58 Smith papers, Box 22, Cabinet minutes, November 13, 1969.

59 Smith papers, Box 23, Cabinet minutes, "Chinese and Japanese Residents," September 8, 1970.

60 Smith papers, Box 23, Cabinet minutes, "Chinese and Japanese Residents," September 8, 1970.

61 Smith papers, Box 26, "Immigration Policy: Permanent Residence: Non-Europeans," September 11, 1973.

62 See, for example, K. Brodkin, *How Jews Became White Folks and What That Says About Race in America* (New Brunswick, NJ: Rutgers University Press, 1998); N. Ignatiev, *How the Irish Became White* (London: Routledge, 2008).

63 MP Ellison, Parliamentary Debates, Committee of Supply Vote, August 1, 1969.

64 "Racial Bar is Rigid," *Rhodesia Herald*, September 6, 1971.

65 Smith papers, Box 26, Cabinet minutes, "Immigration Policy: Permanent Residence: Non-Europeans," September 11, 1973.

66 "More Jobs for Whites and Wider Immigration are Called for," *Rhodesia Herald*, October 25, 1969.

67 "Racial Bar is Rigid," *Rhodesia Herald*, September 6, 1971.

68 Smith papers, Box 22, Cabinet minutes, January 14, 1969.

69 Parliamentary Debates, Committee of Supply Vote, January 17, 1969.

70 See Brownell, *The Collapse of Rhodesia*, ch. 5. See also "Budget Debate Showed Up Unemployment Danger: Problem Likely to Grow," *Rhodesia Herald*, July 29, 1968; "Immigration 'Of Benefit' to Africans—van der Byl," *Rhodesia Herald*, August 9, 1969; Parliamentary Debates, Vol. 72, "Sadie Report," August 13, 1968.

71 Parliamentary Debates, Committee of Supply Vote, August 1, 1969. For more on Rhodesians' construction of race as a stand-in for the notion of standards, see White, "The Utopia of Working Phones."

72 See, for example, Editorial, "Education, but Few with Jobs," *Rhodesia Herald*, October 12, 1966; "Skilled Africans Leaving Country," *Rhodesia Herald*, March 2, 1971.

73 His obfuscation used humor, while others dealt with these questions more harshly. See "Brains in Question," *Rhodesia Herald*, August 13, 1970.

74 "Stop Influx of Africans," *Rhodesia Herald*, letter by M. Moore, June 5, 1969.

75 "Education a Curse to the African," *Rhodesia Herald*, December 23, 1969.

76 "Minister Denies Serious African Unemployment," *Rhodesia Herald*, June 12, 1969.

77 Standard 6 was the final year of primary school. Letter to the editor, "Why Should Africans Not Emigrate in Search of Jobs?," *Rhodesia Herald*, January 5, 1970.

78 Letter to the editor by D. H. Watson, "Exchange 2 Million of Populations," *Rhodesia Herald*, November 1, 1965.

79 Schofield, *Enoch Powell*, 230.

80 "More Jobs for Whites and Wider Immigration are Called for," *Rhodesia Herald*, October 25, 1969.

81 Parliamentary Debates, "Sadie Report," August 13, 1968.

82 *Evening Post*, February 16, 1962. Quoted in H. Wessels, *PK Van Der Byl: African Statesman* (Johannesburg: 30 Degrees South Publishers, 2010), 95.

83 Editorial, "Immigration Warning from Britain," *Rhodesia Herald*, January 29, 1969.

84 Ibid.

85 Clements, *Deterioration*, 243.

86 An average of 4.1 percent of Rhodesia's total white population left the country each year over the twenty-four years from 1955 to 1979, and an average of 4.6 percent entered the country every year. Brownell, *The Collapse of Rhodesia*, 73.

87 "Family Leaves Britain for Children's Sake," *Rhodesia Herald*, October 24, 1968.

88 "New Rhodesians—VI," *Rhodesia Herald*, October 14, 1968.

89 Occidental Dissent, occidentaldissent.com (accessed October 16, 2017).

90 Helen Andrews, "Where Zimbabwe Went Wrong," *National Review*, December 18, 2017.

91 John Ismay recently examined the resurgent popularity of Rhodesia and Rhodesiana among American white nationalists in a long article in *The New York Times Magazine*. See "Rhodesia's Dead—But White Supremacists Have Given It New Life Online," April 10, 2018, www.nytimes.com/2018/04/10/magazine/rhodesia-zimbabwe-white-supremacists.html (accessed April 15, 2020).

7

Transatlantic white supremacy: American segregationists and international racism after civil rights

Zoe Hyman

I N JUNE 2015, Dylann Roof murdered nine African American parishioners at the Emanuel African Methodist Episcopal church in Charleston, South Carolina. Interest in this 21-year-old quickly grew as the media exposed him as a white supremacist who hoped the massacre would start a "race war".[1] The police soon discovered Roof's journal and website – lastrhodesian. com – which outlined his racist ideology and featured photographs of Roof posing with the Confederate flag and wearing clothes embellished with the outdated flags of apartheid South Africa and the illegal state of Rhodesia.[2] Roof was born in 1994 – the year majority rule finally came to South Africa and fourteen years after minority white rule ended in Rhodesia. That a 21-year-old with no personal memory of, or connection to, the era of apartheid would adorn his clothes with flags of these white supremacist states tells us much about the racial right's long-standing identification with, and nostalgia for, apartheid-era southern Africa. Furthermore, it illustrates the importance of understanding historical and contemporary white supremacy as a transnational phenomenon that, in part, draws its strength from the adoption of an international, rather than a regionally or nationally defined, concept of white nationalism.

American racists have long fixated on apartheid southern Africa. From the mid-twentieth century, when legal and practical segregation came under threat in the United States, segregationists looked to South Africa, and then Rhodesia, as bastions of white supremacy that they wished to emulate and support. These states, and their commitment to continued white rule, offered an ideological route out of desegregation and legally mandated racial equality at home and offered segregationist organizations alternative visions for the future. During the civil rights era, the Citizens' Council led the opposition to racial reform in the American South. Its publications regularly promoted white rule in Africa and published inflammatory stories about the perceived dangers of black majority rule on the continent. In 1960, a Citizens' Council newspaper reported that "Black Supremacy" in the Congo was celebrated by "natives [...] going on a spree of unbridled savagery" resulting in whites being "raped, murdered, assaulted and made to suffer unspeakable personal indignities".[3] Nearly half a century later, the Council of Conservative Citizens (CofCC) – the successor organization of the civil rights era Citizens' Council since the 1980s – reported that since the African National Congress won power in South Africa "crime and violence had run rampant" and "[c]annibalism is on the rise". A warning that "IT CAN HAPPEN HERE!" and "Someday, American Whites will be a minority" accompanied horrific images purporting to be murdered white South Africans.[4] Such fearmongering had historically been used to encourage white supremacy during slavery, secession, Reconstruction, and the civil rights movement; it was now being used once again in response to post-civil rights and post-colonial black political and economic power.

Dylann Roof was influenced by this fearmongering. "I was not raised in a racist home or environment", Roof wrote in the opening line of his online "manifesto".[5] But an FBI investigation revealed that six weeks before the shooting, Roof accessed an online CofCC article about "black-on-white" crime in Charleston and "successfully managing the coming race war".[6] He was radicalized by white supremacy online:

> The first website I came to was the Council of Conservative Citizens. There were pages upon pages of these brutal black on White murders. I was in disbelief [...] From this point I researched deeper and found out what was happening in Europe. I saw that the

same things were happening in England and France, and in all the other Western European countries.[7]

Roof also looked further afield. Like the CofCC, and the Citizens' Council before it, Roof did not regard contemporary South Africa (or the US and Europe) as a lost cause for white supremacy and saw apartheid South Africa as a model worth emulating:

> Look at South Africa, and how such a small minority held the black in apartheid for years and years [...] if anyone thinks that think [*sic*] will eventually just change for the better, consider how in South Africa they have affirmative action for the black population that makes up 80 percent of the population. It is far from being too late for America and Europe.[8]

In the minds of American racists, then, South Africa (and Rhodesia) were both models to aspire to and cautionary tales. Central tropes of racist rhetoric – that the end of white rule resulted in economic, political, and social collapse, interracial sex, endangerment of white women, and white "genocide" – alongside fidelity to white rule in Africa were honed by the Citizens' Council in the 1950s and 1960s, continued by the CofCC in the last third of the twentieth century, and adopted by Roof in the twenty-first century. Consequently, Roof is intimately connected to the history and evolution of the Council's brand of transatlantic white supremacism. Despite his chosen domain name, he is far from "the last Rhodesian"; the mythologizing of white supremacist governments in southern Africa continues unabated among the extreme and more mainstream right.[9] Rather, Roof's ideology, inspiration, and actions reaffirm the need to view the evolution of white supremacy in transnational terms.

* * *

To illustrate this evolution, this chapter focuses on the various incarnations of the Citizens' Council movement and pays special attention to its transatlantic alliances with South Africa, Rhodesia, and Britain after 1965. It also uncovers individuals and organizations that entered the Council's orbit, from pro-apartheid newspaper editors in mid-century South Africa, to fascists in 1990s' Britain, and so-called "alt-right" activists in the twenty-first century. It reveals that the Council's network was wide-reaching and diverse, and that a new brand of white supremacism was engaging.

When segregation faced defeat in the US, American racists looked to South Africa and Rhodesia for affirmation of their ideological commitment to white supremacy. When apartheid looked precarious in the 1980s, they found like-minded counterparts in Britain. After 1965, then, a triangulated relationship of white supremacy unfolded across the Atlantic between the US, southern Africa, and Britain. It was premised on the notion that white ethnonationalism was borderless and that white supremacy anywhere was best supported by promoting white supremacy everywhere. As overt racism became increasingly untenable after the civil rights era, this new outlook served to unify disparate and marginal groups into something that had at least the appearance of a more sizeable and coherent global white nationalist movement. This purposeful repackaging of white supremacy into "white nationalism" and increasing attempts to avoid explicitly racist language and enter intellectual spaces as so-called "alt-right" political actors enabled racists to normalize the ideology of white supremacy. In doing so, they claimed middle-class respectability and political legitimacy. Indeed, white nationalists in the US viewed international alliances as emblems of the legitimacy and respectability of their own local movements.

In exploring the process of alliance-building this chapter reveals three key things. First, American racists have long understood their struggle in international terms and have played a significant role in creating a global white supremacy (or "white nationalism" as image-conscious adherents often call it) that combines race with nationality by promoting shared racialized versions of their nationalities. Secondly, it recognizes that the domestic and international agenda of the racist right often dovetailed with that of the US government, which prioritized anti-communist alliances over human rights, racial equality, and democratic processes during the Cold War and thereafter. Thirdly, it underscores that white supremacists cannot be dismissed as subjects unworthy of serious consideration. Rather, white nationalism – increasingly presented as legitimate identity politics – has woven in and out of the mainstream over the years, and devotees are using the current political climate to stage a more forceful comeback. Indeed, white supremacists are best understood as long-term regional, national, and international actors, not a people tied to the rise and fall of segregation as a practice and segregationism as an ideology.

This chapter also contributes to the reconceptualization of segregation and massive resistance historiography. Scholarship on African American civil rights now stretches the chronological and geographical boundaries of the movement beyond the "Montgomery to Memphis" timeframe and the confines of the American South.[10] This has de-centred Martin Luther King, Jr, and the infamous showdowns of the Deep South, and revealed grassroots activism, women's activism, the economic and labour dimensions of civil rights, black power, and protest in the rest of the United States.[11] This idea of a "long" civil rights movement stimulated comparable ideas of a "wide" civil rights movement as scholars connected domestic activism to geopolitical struggles for Cold War supremacy and the internationalization of black protest.[12] However, scholarship has only just begun to consider how opponents of racial equality attempted to emulate black internationalism and connect their struggle to white supremacy overseas.[13] Building on scholarship that has uncovered a long and wide civil rights struggle, this chapter illuminates an equally long and wide segregationist movement. It was flexible and adapted to a post-civil rights United States that had mandated legal equality but was unclear about how that equality would manifest in everyday life. It was globally minded during the civil rights era, and evolved by strategically adopting an internationalized white supremacist agenda thereafter. These two frameworks, which have reconsidered the chronology and geography of the African American freedom struggle, can usefully be mapped on to the enduring struggle of white supremacists to better historicize evolving aspects of post-war racism and contextualize the global white nationalism that is currently ascendant.

* * *

Roof's interest in South Africa and Rhodesia alerted the general population in the US and beyond to a largely unknown strand of modern racism – the fascination with and nostalgia for apartheid – which is often presented as a new trend in white supremacist imagery.[14] However, there is nothing new about identification with apartheid-era southern Africa, with the Citizens' Council promoting the affiliation from its inception. The Citizens' Council was the leading segregationist organization in the American South during the civil rights movement. Formed in Sunflower County, Mississippi, in July 1954, it was an immediate response to the Supreme Court's decision in *Brown* v. *Board of Education* that segregated schooling was unconstitutional. Implicit in this decision was that if segregation in schools was wrong, segregation anywhere was wrong. Though *Brown*'s impact on school desegregation is contested, its symbolic importance is widely accepted.[15] *Brown* catalysed massive resistance among white southerners, and the Citizens' Councils played a central role.[16] Chapters spread rapidly across the South to become a real threat to black freedom and equality. Neil McMillen concluded that Council membership never exceeded 250,000;[17] but far from being a fringe organization, the group counted "governors, congressmen, judges, physicians, lawyers, industrialists, and bankers, as well as an assortment of lesser men [and women] who crowded membership rosters and packed municipal auditoriums to dedicate themselves to the preservation of 'states' rights and racial integrity'".[18]

The Council projected an image of middle-class respectability focused on constitutional rights and "separate but equal" segregation. Council leader Tom Brady believed that "unless we keep our ranks free from the demagogue, the renegade, the lawless and the violent" it would be dismissed as a criminal and fearful organization, akin to the Klan.[19] This ethos gave the Citizens' Council remarkable clout during the 1950s and 1960s. Although the concern over respectability would slowly wane, it enabled the group to endure after legal segregation ended and overt racism became unsustainable. Indeed, Stephanie Rolph's recent definitive history of the Council demonstrates the organization's ability to find new relevance in a post-civil rights America, showing that a commitment to white supremacy was strengthened, not weakened, by the civil rights movement.[20] One way that the Council sought legitimacy was by adopting a foreign policy agenda that masked support for international white supremacy with Cold War anti-communism. This effectively brought the Council in line with the US government, which prioritized its Cold War alliances. Influential policymakers in the US government saw in South Africa and Rhodesia allies whose strategic position and natural resources were crucial to anti-communist influence in Africa and armaments manufacturing at home. The US did impose sanctions on Rhodesia, and eventually on South Africa too, but there was never unanimity on these issues and this provided space for right-wing organizations such as the Council to claim alignment with official US policy.[21]

The inaugural four-page newspaper published by the Citizens' Council in October 1955 included two substantial pieces about South Africa courtesy of Sydney E. D. Brown, editor of the pro-apartheid *South African Observer*, printed in Cape Town. Brown depicted whites in South Africa and the US South as people facing the same challenges, arguing that "those who own and control the press throughout the world are able to guide and misguide at will".[22] The cry of "fake news", then, is not new. Brown listed their shared enemies:

United Nations, Unesco, the empires of Wall Street and Moscow and their dupes, viz. internationalists, liberals, liberal democrats and leftists generally, have marked out South Africa as an enemy because it is a bastion of white conservatism; because it believes in national sovereignty and western Christian civilization; and because it will not accept the Fabian, Socialist and Communist doctrine of Equality.[23]

In a separate letter, Brown encouraged segregationist southerners, praised them for organizing, and suggested a more sinister, vigilante approach of "exposing the names and identities of the individuals and groups whose master plan it is to destroy the European race".[24] Southern segregationists certainly pursued Brown's suggestion of exposing race traitors, and white activists in the civil rights movement faced ostracism and sometimes violence.[25]

Brown's *South African Observer* was not a mainstream newspaper and these early transnational links reveal a noteworthy relationship between the American and South African right wings. Indeed, this first publication was the start of regular reference to, and support of, white minority rule in Africa. Letters from South African correspondents followed and lent an air of professional journalism to the Council newspaper.[26] Segregationists, like many other Americans, were interested in foreign affairs and articulated their concerns. By featuring stories about white rule and racial problems elsewhere, the Citizens' Council showed that the South was not an anomaly. Additionally, increasingly entrenched white supremacy in South Africa demonstrated the possibility of an alternative future, validated hopes that segregation could be preserved, and legitimated the continuity of the Council throughout the 1960s.

Buoying the Council's agenda further was a US government that prioritized Cold War alliances and an American public that was comparatively ill-informed about southern Africa. As late as 1979, the Carnegie Endowment for International Peace think tank reported that "Africa ranks very low in terms of public interest, and the image of a backward primitive continent is still widely held".[27] US foreign policy towards South Africa was at least partly responsible for this. In May 1948, the National Party won power in South Africa and began implementing the apartheid policies that would dominate the country for nearly half a century. Six months later, Harry Truman won the US election and his foreign policymakers established relations with the new apartheid state. The Department of State established three fundamental objectives: to maintain and develop the "friendly relations" which existed between the two countries; to encourage "South African bonds of sympathy" with other Western powers and its continued participation in the United Nations; and to promote South Africa's economic development alongside the growth of its foreign trade.[28] This became a blueprint for US foreign policy towards South Africa over the subsequent decades. Lip service was paid to the immorality of apartheid but condemnation was consistently blunted by the perceived importance of South Africa as a Cold War ally.[29] Segregationist rhetoric was also in step with conservative publications such as *National Review*, segregationist politicians such as George Wallace and James O. Eastland, and Republican power brokers such as Jack Abramoff and Grover Norquist who opposed sanctions against Rhodesia in the 1960s and South Africa in the 1980s.[30] In sum, white supremacist support for South Africa appeared mainstream rather than marginal.

After taking office in January 1969, Richard Nixon continued his predecessors' failure to support majority rule and promoted "cooperation instead of confrontation" with the white governments of southern Africa.[31] A growing feeling that the liberalism of the civil rights era had failed was bolstered by Nixon's law-and-order rhetoric and assertion of "colour-blindness" and an increasing rejection among African Americans of civil rights-era protest in favour of Black Power and black liberation politics. In her study of African Americans in the era of decolonization, Brenda Gayle Plummer revealed that while "racial liberals sought black inclusion", a new generation of blacks with "militant transnational racial politics" emerged.[32] Widespread ignorance over Black Power meant that it was (often incorrectly) seen as a philosophy of black separation, and this further encouraged those who had long argued that blacks, like whites, preferred segregation.[33] Black rejection of integrationist efforts appeared to vindicate segregationist claims that roughly two decades of civil rights activity had worsened race relations and satisfied nobody.

With overwhelming evidence that neither the US government nor southern politicians were committed to widespread racial reform at home or abroad, African American observers were rightly cautious about the gains of the civil rights era. After decades of struggle, in little more than a year the key legislative goals of the civil rights movement had been achieved with the Civil Rights Act in 1964 and the Voting Rights Act in 1965. Discrimination and disenfranchisement were outlawed and African Americans, women, and ethnic and religious minorities now had legally mandated social, labour, and political equality. Yet not all observers were optimistic about the future. In November 1965 the African American *Chicago Defender* speculated that the whole world was simply following the "U.S. Dixie Script":

> Today the South is being cursed with the rise of certain organiza-
> tions that not only threaten the peace and purpose of the Negroes of
> the South but of the nation and the world. Race prejudice Southern
> style is becoming the pattern of race prejudice for the world. The
> "Apartheid" that is afflicting South Africa is largely fashioned after
> the "Aparthied" [*sic*] of the Southern United States.[34]

Gordon Hancock's editorial warned black Americans and other minorities to be vigilant and reminded readers of the enduring power of white
supremacy: "When the Confederate armies were [defeated] the South's
fight was transferred to the newly emancipated Negro slaves. This war
in the form of cruel propaganda has been waged bitterly ever since."
Hancock cautioned that there were

> four active organizations of the South all with one common
> purpose—to undo what was done at the end of the War of
> Rebellion. Although these nefarious organizations cannot turn
> back the hands of time, they can make great trouble and tribula-
> tion for the struggling Negro [...] The White Citizens' Council,
> The John Birch Society, the Ku Klux Klan and Nazism. All of
> these are being built around one common purpose—and that is to
> hold the Negro back and shackle him in his race toward the goal
> of full citizenship.[35]

Hancock's warning was prophetic. These organizations could not undo
the progress of the civil rights revolution, but neither did they fade
away. US white supremacy was never a fixed ideology, but a flexible
system of racial control that has been modified over time. Just as the end
of slavery repackaged white supremacy as Jim Crow segregation, the

defeat of Jim Crow saw white supremacy refashioned once again by New Right conservatism, the carceral state, and institutionalized racism.[36] Correspondingly, white supremacists at the grassroots have adapted and evolved in order to maintain relevance in mainstream politics and society in the post-civil rights era.

* * *

By the mid-1970s, the Citizens' Council was still operating, though certainly with depleted ranks and less influence. In June 1976, the new editor of its publication, *The Citizen*, asked "Will [the] U.S. Sacrifice Her Friends for 'Détente'?" George W. Shannon wrote, "When historians of the future ponder the decline and fall of the great nations of the Twentieth Century they may wonder what madness so possessed the people of the United States that, in 1976, they should have joined forces with their enemies and turned on their friends."[37] In this context, friends were South Africa and Rhodesia – bastions of white supremacy and anti-communism on the African continent – and enemies were those who supported "one man, one vote" there. South Africa and Rhodesia were not only "friends" because they maintained the white supremacist society that the Citizens' Council mourned. Shannon astutely tied this part of the Atlantic world together, noting that all three countries were "founded by white European immigrants" and that South Africa and Rhodesia had followed America's example in declaring independence from Britain. Why, Shannon asked, did the US now condemn them for following its lead? "Perplexing as these questions may be to future generations", Shannon continued, "they are of more vital concern to Americans living today who conceivably may still have time to reverse the course on which we have embarked." The future Shannon feared was one "torn by racial strife and violence as a result of having yielded to black *minority* pressures within its own borders".[38] A question more perplexing than Shannon's could be why the Citizens' Council was still printing glossy, colour publications in 1976, long after one might reasonably have expected the organization to have withered away.

Segregationism as an ideology has deep historical roots. Rolph has demonstrated that the tendency to map the civil right years (c. 1954–65) on to the Citizens' Council has produced a distorted view that fundamentally misunderstands the organization's aims and reach.[39] Nearly a century ago, Ulrich B. Phillips concluded that the "central theme of Southern history" was white supremacy: that the South "shall be and remain a white man's country".[40] Given the integral role of racial oppression in US history, the relatively recent abolition of slavery, the very recent removal of legalized segregation, and the persistence of de facto segregation, it would be remarkable if segregationists had withered away. Simultaneously, the existence of the organization ensured the continued promotion of the ideology. It should not, then, be a surprise that the Council movement was still alive (if not enormously vibrant) in 1976 and that Shannon believed (as Roof did four decades later) that they might still "reverse the course" of integration at home and majority rule in southern Africa.

The idea that integration and equality were not inevitable is vitally important in white supremacist discourse. So idealized were South Africa and Rhodesia that *The Citizen* celebrated prime ministers John Vorster and Ian Smith with large portrait images on the front cover of its June 1976 issue. The publication hailed them as the "Free World's Guardians of Southern Africa".[41]

Although it was unusual to dedicate almost all of the 32-page publication to foreign issues, it represented the Council's enduring commitment to white supremacy abroad. As the 1970s ended, founding member of the Jackson Citizens' Council, William J. Simmons, was interviewed for a Mississippi oral history programme. Simmons, having worked full time for the Council since 1955 and previously served as editor and publisher of *The Citizen*, was now the organization's administrator and wouldn't retire until 1990.[42] His interview revealed the centrality of southern Africa to US white supremacists. Simmons recalled participating in a United Nations Association session in Canada and quipped that the French and English in Montreal "can't integrate with each other, and yet they think it's kind of strange that white–black in the South don't integrate". Simmons said:

[T]here was a South African named De Villier, and he and I were jointly attacked. We were accused of being like South Africa and this terrible thing called apartheid [...] Well this happened more than once and it aroused my curiosity. And I thought, "Well, if this is the collar we're going to wear, I want to see what sort of collar it is."

Simmons and his wife, Bobbe, embarked on a three-and-a-half-month tour of South Africa and Rhodesia in 1966, conducting interviews with citizens, the press, and even politicians including Ian Smith in Salisbury.[43] Simmons thought apartheid "worked very well" because so many different tribes "will not integrate with each other". The choice of words – *will* not – emphasized the choice on the part of blacks as well as whites to segregate. He commented on the lasting friendships he made, his great fondness for the region, and wistfully noted, "South Africa reminds me of this country as it was probably fifty years ago. Their styles – even their lampshades – look like early 1920s."[44]

Simmons was not only longing for 1920s-era décor. His nostalgia for a bygone era of racial hierarchy offered a favourable contrast to the negative changes that he perceived in the twenty-five years since *Brown*. He highlighted "the complete deterioration of public schools [...] massive white flight [...] The bussing of children [...] reverse discrimination" and bemoaned the gerrymandering of school districts and voting districts "to enhance black political power".[45] Nevertheless, the social system Simmons wanted to resuscitate was barely dead and certainly not yet buried; the American political system had failed to challenge systemic racism. The Council had a five-point programme in 1979, which was not particularly far fetched: oppose race mixing, avoid violence, maintain and restore legal segregation, defend states' rights, and correct the court and Congress. Only restoring legal segregation was unachievable, but de facto segregation remained a reality. Simmons thought that the target of more conservative justices on the Supreme Court was "pie in the sky" and that defending states' rights was "very difficult".[46] However, a mere eighteen months later, Ronald Reagan's election initiated a conservative revolution that has not yet ended. When asked if the Council's enduring existence had contributed to the relatively low levels of integration and race mixing, Simmons replied that he thought it had, "Probably by maintaining a public position and keeping alive the knowledge in people's minds that there is an open stand being taken."[47] Indeed, the Council ensured that a defence of segregation based on middle-class ideas of family values, law and order, individual rights, states' rights, and anti-communism remained on the agenda. Long after the Councils became less visible, they were still having an impact on the ground.

* * *

Throughout the 1970s, local Citizens' Council chapters increasingly connected their own experiences to those of whites overseas. In 1974 the Texas chapter's *Councilor* reported that England and Australia suffered the same "universal" problems with school integration as America. In Australia, Aboriginal primary school children were described as "slow-learning" and accused of "form[ing] gangs to beat up white children". In South London, West Indian students were accused of lacking a work ethic, being violent and anti-social towards white students, and disrupting the education of their peers.[48] This article was reprinted from *Britain First*, the National Front (NF) newspaper. The NF formed in 1967 after several smaller extreme right groups, including the Racial Preservation Society and some branches of the Anglo-Rhodesian Society, merged. The group enjoyed its heyday during the 1970s, gaining a few council seats but never achieving representation in Parliament. By 1974, the NF *was* the extreme right in England.[49] *Britain First*'s editor was Richard Lawson, who has remained prominent in the British fascist movement, and the *Councilor* included Lawson's address in Croydon in an effort to encourage correspondence.[50]

The Citizens' Council was undoubtedly attracted by the NF's anti-black and anti-immigration literature as well as its attempts to make inroads into British politics. While South Africa was a model to emulate, Britain served as a cautionary tale and barometer for the US. In a 1971 editorial about

Britain's future under Conservative Prime Minister Edward Heath, John J. Synon (a regular *Citizen* contributor) warned that the UK, in decline for more than twenty years and "gutted" by labour unions, faced economic collapse. "Can [Heath] pull the wheezing John Bull onto his feet?" Synon asked. He was not convinced Heath could.[51] "The answer is Enoch Powell, the hard-nosed segregationist", readers were told. Indeed, it was Powell who could create "a New-Model England". Why should readers in the US care about UK politics? Because "England's fate is precursor of things to come in this country", Synon told them. "Our ailments and England's ailments are on a parallel course."[52]

The "New-Model England" would not be created by Powell. By 1978, change was afoot and the front cover of the *Citizen* was dedicated to a portrait of Margaret Thatcher.[53] Asking "Can Margaret Thatcher Liberate Great Britain?", Shannon's editorial now used Britain as a potential role model rather than a cautionary tale. He explained that "White British resistance to a mounting flood of black and brown immigrants may become the force that will give England its first woman Prime Minister." He commented on the widespread "white resentment" over immigration, the "recurring racial violence which has rocked Britain", and the rise of the National Front, which Shannon described as an "extremist pro-white political party". But he took heart from these developments: "American politicians who think forced racial integration is a dead issue might take a cue from developments in England."[54] In 1978, South African apartheid was fairly robust, but US segregation was long (legally) dead and white minority rule in Rhodesia was all but over (the rebellion ended in 1979). Britain, meanwhile, offered a new possibility for white domination – one that was attractive because it came not from the starting point of defending an *existing* white supremacist hierarchy, but from the actions of *new* politicians such as Thatcher and new grassroots forces such as the National Front. American racists saw in Britain, as in southern Africa, the roots of their shared "Anglo-Saxon" heritage, and a sense that the fortunes of whites in the US, southern Africa, and Britain were intertwined fostered the growth of global white nationalism in which Anglo-Saxonism featured heavily.

In addition to the Citizens' Council, other groups with mainstream political aims began to publicize Anglo-Saxon nationalism as an international movement, thereby putting the segregationist South in line with global trends rather than at odds with modernity. In 1979, the Southern National Party (SNP), a group founded in Mississippi and headquartered in Memphis, Tennessee, dedicated more than half of its newsletter to nationalist aims around the world:

> The idea of Southern Nationalism is [...] part of a world-wide moral force of immense force and potency. It is by no means an isolated idea, or an eccentric notion born of nostalgia for the old Confederate South; Southern Nationalism is part and parcel of a vast international trend based on the desire to preserve its separate entity.[55]

The SNP's cheaply printed newsletter collated reprints from other publications dating from June 1973 to January 1979, but the group had some notable impact. It was established in November 1969 as a third political party in Mississippi in opposition to court-ordered school desegregation that was to take place by 1 February 1970, interracial marriage, and other challenges to the racial status quo. Its stated aim was to lure conservative southern voters from the Democratic and Republican Parties and the group brought short-lived injunctions against interracial marriage.[56] The SNP, like the Citizens' Council, demonstrates that segregationists still occupied space in mainstream society and politics by continuing to oppose the *Brown* decision and equality legislation of the mid-1960s, framing its argument in anti-communist terms, and promoting the idea of innate white superiority. In January 1970, the SNP organized a 1,500-strong rally in Jackson, Mississippi, to oppose school integration. Its literature complained that "The Federal Government is acting towards the South in a fashion similar to that of Russia toward its victims" and reminded readers that "[t]he Southern Anglo-Saxon race produced the brains and the ethical standards that run America". The SNP was aligned with Mississippi's governor, John Bell Williams, who said in a state-wide televised address that he would aid the state legislature in setting up private schools because "Most of us resent this denial of our rights."[57]

The SNP's anti-totalitarianism and promotion of Anglo-Saxon supremacy reveal key hallmarks of right-wing organizing in the post-civil rights era. Appealing to individual and states' rights, and national security concerns, presented the group as patriotic to those who preferred to avoid overtly racist language. Meanwhile, the explicit calls for white supremacy appealed to those less concerned with respectability. SNP's newsletter on nationalism was adorned with emblems of countries in Europe, North America, and Africa. The first editorial on European nationalism reported on the Bureau of Unrepresented European Nations, a group established in Brussels to lobby for regionalists in areas including Alsace-Lorraine, the Basque country, Brittany, Wales, and Cornwall.[58] "The unrepresented nations of Europe and the South have much in common", readers were told, and a call to action was issued: "The time is now for an organization that speaks for working class, populist causes."[59] The newsletter also reprinted the front page of an August 1978 issue of *Bulldog*, the newspaper of the Young National Front, which reported that "hundreds" of youths and, in particular, large numbers of young women were joining the NF.[60] While *Bulldog* was hardly a mainstream publication, the SNP also reprinted articles from mainstream press outlets including the *Christian Science Monitor*, *Washington Post*, *National Review*, and the *New York Times* about Welsh nationalism, separatism in continental Europe, the goals of the Scottish National Party, secession in Australia, Sami autonomy in Lapland, nationalist protests in Quebec, and white homelands in South Africa. At the beginning of the 1970s, the South African Bureau for Racial Affairs (SABRA), a think tank formed by "total apartheid" proponents at Stellenbosch University in 1948, was turning the apartheid policy of black homelands on its head and considering the future prospect of white Afrikaner homelands, or what outgoing chairman and university professor G. Viljoen called "operation Israel".[61] By 1980, SABRA was pressing ahead with plans for a "racially pure" white homeland in the middle of South Africa to be called Orania. While most Afrikaners dismissed the plan as unrealistic, Orania was created in 1991 and, after spending twenty years as a sleepy backwater, the population doubled in the 2010s with 10 per cent growth annually.[62] Though still a small settlement, Orania demonstrated that pockets of white supremacy could be built and maintained even when state-sanctioned racism ended. Articles that highlighted white supremacist movements in Britain or South Africa told readers that white nationalism was flourishing in the western world and attracting a new generation; accordingly, the work of American white supremacists appeared relevant and capable of creating change.

* * *

The endurance of the Citizens' Council, the emergence of groups such as the Southern National Party, and the fact that right-wing politicians still supported the aims of their white supremacist constituents meant that the groundwork existed for the emergence of the reinvigorated Council of Conservative Citizens in 1985. The 1980s witnessed a shift in racist organizing as groups went underground, reformulated, and re-emerged as much more overt and populist white supremacist organizations. The CofCC relaunched using the mailing list of its predecessor, the Citizens' Council, at a time when the defeat of apartheid and its supporters in the US was becoming apparent. Meanwhile, the perceived negative impact of globalization, and the abandonment of détente that accompanied renewed Cold War tensions in the early 1980s, presented far right groups with another opportunity to engage with foreign policy and further internationalize their agenda.[63] The CofCC evolved into an overtly white supremacist group, but was initially adept at disguising its extremism. Founder Gordon Lee Baum, a personal injury lawyer from St Louis, Missouri, who had been Midwest field organizer for the original Citizens' Council, explained that the CofCC was "a responsible and effective voice and active advocate for the no longer silent conservative majority".[64] It was still conjuring Nixon in 2012, writing that "The Council of Conservative Citizens, the no longer silent majority, is a genuinely active national organization—effectively organizing and winning!"[65]

Despite the new name, many of the same characters and themes appeared. The South Louisiana chapter used its January 1985 *Citizens Report* to educate readers on the "truth" of South Africa: it had no native population as it was empty before the Dutch arrived, and the majority of blacks, like whites, supported apartheid and celebrated progress under it. An article by Robert B. Patterson – a founder of the original Council – warned that "The cry of 'civil rights and human rights' has destroyed stable authoritarian governments all over the world in recent years. They are replaced by Marxist 'Peoples' Republics'."[66] Virulent anti-communism, which always formed a significant part of the segregationist movement, enabled white supremacists to continue to connect support for apartheid governments with official US foreign policy. The *Citizens Report* regularly warned that the ANC and its allies such as Archbishop Desmond Tutu were "controlled by the Soviet Union" and that communists hoped to "stir up a racial war" in South Africa.[67]

The CofCC's efforts to endear South Africa to the American public dovetailed with a sophisticated and costly campaign by South Africa's Department of Information to "sell" South Africa to Americans.[68] The South African government employed the US public relations firm Sydney S. Baron & Company in March 1976 to improve its image and appeal in the US by acting as a public representative of the apartheid state. It encouraged American business engagement with South Africa and favourable US media coverage of the country. It also promoted visits by prominent Americans and reported on US attitudes towards South Africa. The New York firm was paid $365,000 for one year's service.[69] The wider information scandal, which saw the South African government attempting to buy politicians and news outlets around the world between 1973 and 1978, eventually led to the resignations of the minister for information, Connie Mulder, the secretary for information, Eschel Rhoodie, and the prime minister, B. J. Vorster.[70] The *Citizen* celebrated Mulder on its September 1978 cover and reprinted a lengthy article in which he said that the "Communist World" sought "the suppression of this white South African nation as a distinct entity in its own right; or to put it more bluntly, genocide".[71] Muldergate didn't deter South Africa:

throughout the 1980s and into the 1990s the National Party employed public relations and legal firms – mostly in Washington DC – to lobby against sanctions.[72] However, 1986 was a critical year for US–South Africa relations. The US Congress – overriding Reagan's veto – enacted the Comprehensive Anti-Apartheid Act in October. After decades of relatively mild condemnation of apartheid, the US government would now disassociate from South Africa politically, economically, and militarily as well as morally.[73]

Despite expensive efforts to bolster South Africa's image in the US, negotiations were already underway to end apartheid with free elections (although this would not happen until 1994) and by the mid-1980s, the CofCC saw its long-term model of white supremacy failing. The *Citizens Report* warned that losing South Africa's minerals would "ground the Air Force, close hospitals and restaurants [and] directly affect the employment of 3.2 million Americans in industries that use these materials". At best, sanctions would lead the US down a "road to destruction" and at worst would present a situation whereby a "Black Communist majority in the U.N." would force the US to "give five or ten states to the Blacks in our country to create a black nation inside the U.S.". Failure to do so would mean sanctions being imposed on the US that would cut off all oil and strategic materials for industry.[74] These conspiratorial warnings emphasized the idea that whites in the US could suffer the same imagined fate as whites in South Africa.

Having suffered the domestic demise of white supremacy, American white supremacists became increasingly concerned with shoring up white South Africans. Exemplifying an attempt to combat the large anti-apartheid movement that had existed in the United States since the 1960s, populist activist Robert J. Hoy founded the American-Afrikaner Union (AAU) in Alexandria, Virginia, in 1986. The AAU supported Afrikaner nationalists' plans for white homelands in the Transvaal and Orange Free State, sought to combat negative views of apartheid in the US, and pursued tangible links between white nationalists in the US and South Africa.[75] Hoy wrote to *Focus on South Africa*, a propaganda publication churned out by the South African Department of Foreign Affairs:

There is much goodwill here for SA's people and a real desire to see a solution to your problems [...] Your problems are remarkably like our own and I would welcome correspondence from South Africans and Americans who would like to learn more about the American-Afrikaner Union. In these difficult times, understanding is important in order to open communication between our two peoples.[76]

Hoy was a photo-journalist from Vienna, Virginia. He was particularly known for his involvement with the 1974 Kanawha County school textbook controversy, when parents in Charleston, West Virginia, opposed, boycotted, and partially reversed a decision to diversify student reading in elementary schools with multiracial and multi-ethnic texts. The protest that began in April 1974 turned violent by October. Shootings, arson, bombings, and vandalism featuring Klan and Nazi symbols closed some schools and, in December, the Klan publicly supported the protesters.[77]

Hoy was not personally invested in the books; he was invested in the protesters. Hoy co-founded the Populist Forum on 1 January 1974 to "provide writing and press relations services to populist movements". The organization's first activities included Boston's anti-bussing movement and the textbook protests, and it sought to "bring social and economic conservatives together" and make single-issue focus groups "aware of each other's existence and the possibilities and strengths arising from cooperation".[78] This networking would make Hoy a useful part of the New Right and, later, the extreme right. The old right, Hoy concluded in 1982, was "doomed". He promoted a new kind of movement and outlined his populist and conservative ideology in a chapter for *The New Right Papers*, a book edited by his Populist Forum co-founder, Robert W. Whitaker, and printed by the leading mainstream publishing house St Martin's Press:

Populism is not an historical aberration or a form of political extremism. It is a traditional and genuinely American political phenomenon. An American who ignores it is not a conservative,

but an elitist of the right [...] Neither liberals nor old-line conservatives are in a position to successfully articulate or manifest the
frustrations of Middle America. The New Right is. It can tap into
a tremendous reservoir of frustration, which can mean political
power.[79]

Whitaker served in the Reagan administration as special assistant in the
Office of Personnel Management and he was not alone as a New Right pro-
ponent in the federal government. A *New York Times* article from October
1983 concluded that Reagan's "most enduring impact" would not be "his
budget cuts or vigilance against the Russians" but rather "a network of
young conservatives that is only now emerging in Washington". Morton
Blackwell, Reagan's special assistant and liaison to conservative groups,
agreed that Reagan's legacy would be that he "'credentialed' a whole generation of conservatives [...] and they're going to have a lasting impact".[80]

Hoy was a cultural conservative, a descriptor adopted by New Right
strategists to distinguish their conservatism from the old right. Mason
explains that "Key to cultural conservatism is promoting values through
policy that defines particular ideas about family, sexuality, gender, reproduction, and work as essential to American life and national survival."
Unlike the old right's "doomsday defeatism", cultural conservatives
were "proactive rather than reactive".[81] Part of this proactivity was mainstream appeal and political engagement, and it represented a shift from
civil rights-era segregationist organizing. Former segregationists sought
legitimacy by joining this new force and being absorbed into a Republican
Party that attracted southern whites in increasing numbers after 1965 with
a "southern strategy" that appealed to unreconstructed racists, evangelicals, those concerned with changing gender relations, and middle-class
suburbanites who favoured a "colour-blind" approach to maintaining
inequality.[82] This was a broad church, and Hoy was part of this new
force – the New Right. Hoy and Whitaker certainly had a lasting impact,
but on modern white supremacy rather than in mainstream politics. This
demonstrates the travel between the mainstream and the margins that
sustained white supremacy in the twentieth and twenty-first centuries.

Hoy's journey from the mainstream to the margins is not well understood, but reveals that, like many on the far right, he was a "serial joiner". Hoy joined a number of far right US groups, worked with National Front fascists in Britain, and supported ex-Klansman David Duke's presidential bid in 1992.[83] In addition to the aforementioned Populist Forum and AAU, Hoy worked for the Liberty Lobby, an organization that published racist, anti-Semitic, and Holocaust denial literature and contributed articles and photographic essays to its *Spotlight* magazine praising neo-Nazism in the US and the National Front in Britain.[84] By 1992, he was chairman of Republican Action for the '90s, a Washington-based group once chaired by Newt Gingrich, which endorsed Duke's campaign.[85] Weaving in and out of the conservative mainstream, his chapter in *The New Right Papers* positioned him alongside New Right leaders including William A. Rusher (publisher of *National Review*), Paul Weyrich (co-founder of the Moral Majority), and Samuel T. Francis (a journalist-turned-white supremacist who went on to lead the CofCC).[86]

Through the AAU, Hoy hoped to educate Americans about Afrikaner history, just as the Citizens' Council and CofCC did. In a photo essay, he compared Afrikaners fighting for freedom in the Anglo-Boer or South African War (1899–1902) to southerners fighting for "independence" during the Civil War (1861–65), telling readers that "no two people on earth have more in common than white Americans and South African Boers" and, critically, "Boers and white Americans share a common racial background".[87] This was not a new alliance. Historians have shown that, during the South African War, while the white American public and Congress had favoured the "underdog Boers", US political leaders favoured a pro-British neutrality, and the "racial bond" of Anglo-Saxonism framed policymakers' discussion of the war.[88] And southerners saw themselves in Boers: "a white nation rooted in agriculture that was undergoing industrialization and urbanization" and a shared experience of living alongside blacks and relying on black labour.[89] Since Boers defined themselves against – and fought – the British, the Anglo-Saxonism and Afrikaner nationalism that Hoy endorsed were not obvious bedfellows. However, shifting political ideas about whiteness earlier in the twentieth century laid the groundwork for the more encompassing white nationalism that characterizes the racial right today. When the Union of South Africa formed in 1910, politicians faced the dilemma of how to reconcile two separate and competitive white communities – Afrikaners who opposed Anglo dominance and English-speaking South Africans who feared Afrikaner nationalism. "The answer lay not in assimilation", historian Hermann Giliomee wrote, "but in ethnically separate institutions in the white community that were committed to 'South Africa first'."[90] By the time apartheid was implemented in 1948, "South Africa first" meant white power. The Nationalist message was clear; whites "were to be one group with one territory" while blacks were to be split into myriad "homelands", which were presented as evidence of black South African self-rule.[91] So, when Hoy wrote that "white people cannot survive in South Africa or America unless we have our own homeland", he was drawing on a century of history and propaganda.[92]

Hoy's propagation of a white homeland partly stemmed from his anti-immigration stance and this undoubtedly aroused his interest in British race relations. His AAU literature encouraged association with English nationalism. "AMERICANS, HELP THE NATIONAL FRONT IN IT'S [sic] BATTLE FOR BRITAIN", Hoy told readers in a 1990 newsletter, adding an image of Uncle Sam with an "I want you for the National Front" tagline. Hoy travelled to England where he produced a photo essay on "The Battle for Britain" for the NF's magazine, *Vanguard*, to which he encouraged his American readers to subscribe in an effort to forge kinship across the Atlantic.[93] With a seemingly insatiable appetite for white supremacist organizing, and the failure of his AAU to save apartheid, Hoy was soon associating with the CofCC and moving back towards the mainstream.

The historical trail picks Hoy up again in December 1997 alongside CofCC board member, American Renaissance founder, and still-prominent white supremacist Jared Taylor. Hoy and Taylor attended a forum in Annandale, Virginia, on President Bill Clinton's Initiative on Race, which sought recommendations for "one America" in the twenty-first century.[94] The Q&A session enabled conservative voices to be heard. Hoy was agitated, complaining that whites were losing "our homeland".

The *Washington Post* quoted Hoy on its front page: "There's no one up there that's talking about the white people! We don't want to be a minority in our own country!" As police escorted him out, Hoy represented the siege mentality that white supremacists had adopted by the end of the century warning, "We're going to be a minority soon!"[95] Advisory Board member Susan Johnson Cook remarked that Hoy's "angry white voice [was] the kind of thing we are trying to stay away from". Hoy agreed that he was indeed angry because "no whites are coming in". For Hoy, the change wrought by immigration was a fundamental problem: "I think what we are talking about is the South Africanization of America. Whites are scared to death to speak about it."[96] Hoy's outburst came from multicultural Annandale where, collectively, people of colour did constitute a small majority of 56 per cent (24% Asian, 17% Latino, 15% black) while whites made up 44 per cent of the population.[97] This only enhanced Hoy's minority mentality, and represented an important shift in South Africa's position in the white supremacist imaginary: it now offered a vivid picture – along with Zimbabwe – of the perceived catastrophe of black political power.

* * *

For the first time in nearly half a century, South Africa no longer represented the hopes of white supremacists. Instead, efforts in Britain to mainstream white power offered a new strategy. The British National Party (BNP) had been formed by former NF leader John Tyndall in 1982. It was the most prominent extreme right group in Britain in the 1980s but failed to achieve electoral success. The French Front National demonstrated that the "construction of political legitimacy, brought about in part through a process of self-induced internal moderation" was a prerequisite for electoral gains, but Tyndall would not temper the BNP's image or ideology.[98] Nick Griffin ousted Tyndall in 1999, aiming to "modernise" and "normalise" the BNP "as a legitimate political party". He made clear, though, that such airbrushing would not alter the party's main objective of fascism.[99] One strategy was to create "satellite organisations" to support the BNP and extend its influence.[100] This call was heard by British neo-fascist Mark Cotterill, who would, in time, journey across the Atlantic and into the CofCC. Like Hoy, Cotterill was a white supremacist career-ist. He joined the NF as a 17-year-old in 1978 and remained a leading organizer until 1992; he founded and ran the right-wing Patriotic Forum from 1992 to 1995; he dabbled with mainstream politics by joining the Conservative Party in 1993; and he ran unsuccessfully as an Independent Conservative in Torbay in 1995 before his past led to his expulsion.[101] Cotterill "encouraged entryism of the Tory party by the far-right" and his time with the Tories schooled him in the "genteel arts of fundraising and traditional party politics, organising cheese and wine parties and tombo-las". After failing to win election in Torbay, he joined the BNP and moved to Washington DC in 1995.[102] Cotterill took his method of "entryism" to the US and, in January 1999, founded the American Friends of the British National Party (AFBNP).

In Cotterill's words, the AFBNP aimed to promote "our Western culture, heritage and civilization". The organization and its newsletter *Heritage and Destiny* had three aims: to serve as an intellectual and analyti-cal forum independent of established political parties; to "promote interest in the historical achievements and cultures of our nations and race, and thereby help to instill a proper understanding of and positive pride in our European ethnic identity"; and to support "candidates and parties that stand against the evil forces which are bent on destroying our Western Christian culture, our European heritage and our race".[103] However, the AFBNP's main goal was fundraising and it channelled money back to the BNP in the UK. This would ultimately be the organization's undoing. In August 2001 the Southern Poverty Law Center (SPLC) asked the US Justice Department to investigate whether the AFBNP was violating the Foreign Agents Registration Act, which requires those acting or lob-bying on behalf of foreign political groups to register their activities. The SPLC report accused the AFBNP of raising approximately $100,000 for the BNP. Mark Potok, who authored the report, said, "Hate knows no borders", adding, "We have never seen a fundraising scheme of this size operating in the open."[104] Cotterill resigned from the AFBNP in the wake of the SPLC's report and was given a ten-year exclusion order in September 2002. He left the US that November.[105]

Nevertheless, Cotterill made a considerable impact in a short time. The SPLC reported that he was doing what no leader on the American extreme right had managed since the Second World War: "unifying a significant number of American extremist factions". The AFBNP "provided a meeting ground for hate groups as disparate as the neo-Nazi National Alliance and the more mainstream, neo-Confederate League of the South". Cotterill wrote in his internet newsletter, "It is not an American fight or a British fight or a German fight. It is a white fight, and we have got to win it." He promoted "racial nationalism" (his preferred term) and insisted that people wear "deck shoes, chinos and a polo shirt" rather than combat, paramilitary, or Nazi-style gear that would enable the media to disparage them. Cotterill appealed to American racists attempting to maintain relevance and respectability in a new millennium.[106]

Exemplifying the fluid nature of modern membership in extremist groups, Cotterill became involved with the CofCC shortly after he arrived in the US. It was clear to CofCC leaders Gordon Baum and Robert Patterson that they needed new blood; the membership was overwhelmingly ageing southern men. Cotterill (using the false name Mark Cerr) set up a youth chapter in Washington, and brought approximately 100 young people into the organization. After the SPLC revealed Cotterill's true identity in December 1998 he resigned as a CofCC leader but remained a member. It is highly unlikely that his fascist links offended CofCC members, but the damage to the organization's image was unacceptable. Baum had worked hard to reinvigorate the CofCC as a legitimate political organization. At a November 1998 national board meeting in a Jackson, Mississippi, hotel he was unnerved when David Duke arrived. "Damn you, Dave", Baum said. "Don't say you're involved with us. The politicians won't show up. We use these politicians."[107] Negative press coverage, not Duke's neo-Nazism, was the problem.

The CofCC prized associations with politicians, but the relationship was irreversibly damaged when the press revealed that a number of US politicians had addressed, and been members of, the group. During the winter of 1998–99 newspapers revealed that Representative Bob Barr (R-GA), Senate Majority Leader Trent Lott (R-MS), and Mississippi Governor Kirk Fordice had all spoken at CofCC events.[108] Described as "generally off the national radar" before the revelations, Barr and Lott were forced to renounce the CofCC and South Carolina's Republican national committeeman, Buddy Witherspoon, resigned his membership after pressure from party leaders.[109] The outcome of this was twofold. First, substantial press coverage from local and national papers propelled the CofCC into a position of prominence such groups hadn't enjoyed since mid-century. Secondly, it effectively ended public relations with politicians, and thereby ended the Council's commitment to token moderation. As such, Cotterill was welcomed back.

On 4 December 1999, the AFBNP attended the CofCC's semi-annual conference in Huntsville, Alabama, where, according to Cotterill, the AFBNP "sold a large number of BNP publications" and met "our enthusiastic Southern members with whom we had previously only corresponded or spoken to on the phone".[110] In the same month, Cotterill (using his alias Cerr) was again chairperson of the Washington CofCC and presided over a meeting in Arlington. He provided attendees with a brief history of the organization before opening the floor to speakers who overwhelmingly focused on anti-Semitic issues.[111] As the veneer of respectability disappeared, Cotterill continued to use the AFBNP to support the CofCC. He publicized CofCC meeting dates and its website on his own website, which serves as a reminder that the extreme right was now operating in the internet era. It profoundly transformed the nature of extremist politics and political culture.[112] People such as Cotterill bridged the gap between real-world hate and online hate.

While never a large group (most AFBNP meetings reported between sixty and eighty attendees), it attracted big names and gathered funds (Cotterill usually reported collections of $500–$1,000 per meeting).[113] The first meeting of the new millennium, on 29 January 2000, took place in Arlington. Speakers included Stephen King of the London BNP complaining that "Third World immigration" would mean white Britons would be outnumbered by mid-century, and Sam van Rensburg (a former officer in apartheid South Africa's Special Forces and leader of the neo-Nazi National Alliance) who "spoke about the rapid decline of [...] South Africa since black supremacists took it over".[114] BNP Chairman Nick Griffin addressed the AFBNP on 22 April 2000, "calling on all American nationalists of British decent [sic] to rally round the American Friends of the BNP and give whatever support they can". Cotterill reported that Griffin met American racists such as "White Civil Rights leader" David Duke.[115] The terminology was deliberate here, and Cotterill's newsletters reveal the intentional linguistic shifts that re-characterized white supremacists as mainstream actors. "Black supremacists" were extremists while the "white civil rights" characters who gathered at AFBNP meetings were moderates. And adopting the terminology of African American civil rights and utilizing the strategy of identity politics alongside other (minority and/or oppressed) groups continues to be used to legitimize racist activity.

Over the course of about five years, Cotterill's impact was extensive. As a Brit in America, he promoted "racial nationalism" and his recruitment efforts for the CofCC, fundraising efforts for the BNP, and ability to weave between innumerable organizations in the US and connect them across the Atlantic helped solidify a lasting transatlantic alliance of white supremacists. Like many others, Cotterill was aided by the rise of the internet. When the press exposed southern politicians' links to the CofCC at the end of 1998, Cotterill told the *Washington Post* that before the story broke, the website for his Washington DC chapter had received 4,000 hits over the previous four months, but had now received 10,000 hits in the preceding week alone.[116] Certainly, the internet grew the white supremacist network, but it also documented it and preserved evidence of a tangled web of people, publications, and organizations. Indeed, when the SPLC's Mark Potok reflected on the AFBNP's controversial fundraising, which had been boastfully documented on its website, he concluded, "they operated very stupidly".[117]

* * *

It would be satisfying to be able to conclude that white supremacists are stupid and will orchestrate their own downfall. Unfortunately, it isn't so. But scholarship that renders more visible white nationalism – particularly the links between its historical and contemporary manifestations – can help rectify common misconceptions that racists look like racists and are easily identifiable by their dressing like outdated relics of the Ku Klux Klan; that they sound like racists by using overtly racist, or obviously coded, language; and that racists are unintelligent and believe in white supremacy because they are uneducated. White nationalism in the era of Brexit and Trump is multi-dimensional. Organizations such as the Citizens' Council/Council of Conservative Citizens and supporters such as Hoy and Cotterill reveal that the racist right has been highly adaptive, thoughtfully reactive, and capable of maintaining relevance long after the death of Jim Crow and the end of apartheid.

As the twenty-first century began, there barely remained even a veneer of mainstream respectability and American racists moved deeper online and further to the fringes. An amateur-looking CofCC website reported in 2010 that in South Africa, black-owned farms had failed, whites were being executed, and black groups were calling for the mass murder of whites.[118] Stories about a "race war", white "genocide", anti-white results of "extreme affirmative action", and the kidnap and killing of white teenage girls all recall some of the key extremist talking points on the racist right: miscegenation, race extinction, and so-called reverse discrimination.[119] The internet provides space where comments are unfiltered and racist rhetoric can reach many more people, as evidenced by Dylann Roof's statement that the CofCC website introduced him to "pages upon pages of these brutal black on White murders".[120] Reports in the media that linked Roof to the CofCC gave the organization a much-needed publicity boost, just as revelations of political affiliation did in 1998 and 1999. A new, polished website has appeared that belies the inflammatory stories it features and represents a renewed effort at respectability and professionalism. The *Citizens' Informer* publication reveals that Donald Trump's campaign revitalized the CofCC further:

Right now, the White race is facing an extinction event in their homelands [...] Here in the USA, we're basically doing nothing to prevent our own genocide. At least, at the moment, we think we have Donald Trump to do battle for us. He's awakened long suppressed residual instincts in us.[121]

White supremacists and anti-Semites must have been further encouraged when Trump appeared to vindicate them after the August 2017 "Unite the Right" rally in Charlottesville, Virginia, which featured white nationalists, Klan members, and neo-Nazis. Trump infamously told the press that there were "some very fine people on both sides".[122]

Extremists in the US were not hiding in the anonymity of the internet but moving back to the physical, rather than digital, domain. There were swastikas and Confederate flags at the rally, and some wore paramilitary garb. But many more adopted Cotterill's preferred uniform of chinos, polo shirts and clean-cropped haircuts. Criminologist George Michael noted that being presentable and articulating their arguments as reasonable was very important in order to encourage new adherents of white supremacy.[123] This echoes Tom Brady's argument in the 1950s that the Citizens' Council must avoid being associated with the lawless Klan; Simmons's argument in the 1970s that the Council was maintaining a law-abiding "public position"; the Council of Conservative Citizens' attempt in the 1990s to keep its neo-Nazi acquaintances hidden from public view; and Cotterill's instruction at the turn of the century that supporters swap the swastikas for representations of middle-class respectability.

Just as AFBNP gatherings provided a meeting ground for various right-wing organizations and individuals, Trump campaign rallies enabled like-minded people to meet face-to-face in a mainstream political context.[124] The "residual instincts" that Trump catalysed were kept alive by white supremacists who were bolstered, not broken, by the defeat of Jim Crow in 1965. Some organizations were short-lived and achieved little more than symbolic transnationalism (the American Afrikaner Union), while others managed to have a significant impact at particular moments in time (AFBNP). Organizations such as the Citizens' Council/Council of Conservative Citizens have endured in part by never completely abandoning the possibility of mainstream political "entryism". Interest in the CofCC after the Roof massacre revealed that CofCC president Earl Holt III had donated $65,000 to Republican contenders including Ted Cruz, Rick Santorum, and Rand Paul.[125]

The CofCC still wants real political influence and frames its objectives in mainstream ways. Its statement of principles, formalized in 2005, is clearly right wing but lacks overtly extremist language. It promotes Christianity, states' rights, free trade, small government, a hawkish foreign policy, and opposes homosexuality, interracial relationships, and non-Western immigration. The second point of its fourteen-point declaration states: "We believe that the United States is a European Country and that Americans are part of the European people."[126] This promotion of white supremacist unity across borders is the culmination of post-1965 racist organizing. Presently, white supremacy, xenophobia, and anti-Semitism are re-entering the mainstream with renewed vigour and legitimacy, repackaged as non-threatening "identitarian" or "alt-right" politics. As this examination of American racists' long-term engagement with white supremacist regimes, organizations, and individuals in southern Africa and Britain shows, it is important to revisit the roots and transnational reach of white supremacist organizations and individuals in order to better illuminate the evolution, and present state, of transatlantic white supremacy.

Notes

1 FBI interview with Dylann Roof, www.postandcourier.com/church_shooting/dylann-roof-says-he-chose-charleston-emanuel-ame-for-massacre/article_6fab5 32c-be05-11e6-ab05-575a173993ee.html (accessed 10 October 2018).

2 Dylann Roof, "Journal", www.postandcourier.com/dylann-roof-s-journal/pdf_c5f655oc-be72-11e6-b869-7bdf860326f5.html (accessed 26 July 2019) and "Manifesto", www.nytimes.com/interactive/2016/12/13/universal/document-Dylann-Roof-manifesto.html (accessed 28 November 2018).

3 "Lessons from the Congo", *Citizens' Council* 5.10 (July 1960): 1.

4 "The White Slaughter", 4 June 2004, archived from the original, http://web.archive.org/web/20040606234944/http://cofcc.org:80/shelby.htm (accessed 7 December 2018).

5 Roof, "Manifesto", 1.

6 Mark Potok, "Carnage in Charleston", www.splcenter.org/fighting-hate/intelligence-report/2015/carnage-charleston (accessed 5 November 2018).

7 Roof, "Manifesto", 1.

8 Ibid., 3.

9 For commentary on Rhodesia-themed memorabilia, see John Ismay, "Rhodesia's Dead—But White Supremacists Have Given It New Life Online", 10 April 2018: www.nytimes.com/2018/04/10/magazine/rhodesia-zimbabwe-white-supremacists.html (accessed 5 November 2018), and Ethan Cox and Erin Seatter, "Rhodesia Nostalgia 'Screams Out Extreme Hatred', Say Zimbabweans", 8 November 2018, https://ricochet.media/en/2409/rhodesia-nostalgia-screams-out-extreme-hatred-say-zimbabweans (accessed 30 July 2019). White supremacist websites, such as *American Renaissance*, regularly promote apartheid nostalgia. See, for example, "Apartheid South Africa: Reality vs. Liberation Fantasy", 19 December 2013, www.amren.com/news/2013/12/apartheid-south-africa-reality-vs-libertarian-fantasy/ (accessed 30 July 2019). And spurred on by President Donald Trump's propagation of the white genocide myth in South Africa, the *Daily Stormer* celebrated the president's request that the State Department investigate seizure of land from, and mass killings of, white farmers: https://dailystormer.name/its-happening-trump-tweets-about-white-genocide-in-south-africa/ (accessed 30 July 2019).

10 Jacquelyn Dowd Hall, "The Long Civil Rights Movement and the Political Uses of the Past", *Journal of American History* 91.4 (2005): 1233–63.

11 See, for example, Tiyi M. Morris, *Womanpower Unlimited and the Black Freedom Struggle in Mississippi* (Athens, GA: University of Georgia Press, 2015); Thomas Sugrue, *Sweet Land of Liberty: The Forgotten Struggle for Civil Rights in the North* (New York: Random House, 2008); Gavin Wright, *Sharing the Prize: The Economics of the Civil Rights Revolution in the American South* (Cambridge, MA: Harvard University Press, 2013).

12 See, for example, Mary L. Dudziak, *Cold War Civil Rights: Race and the Image of American Democracy* (Princeton, NJ: Princeton University Press, 2000); Nicholas Grant, *Winning Our Freedoms Together: African Americans and Apartheid, 1945–1960* (Chapel Hill, NC: University of North Carolina Press, 2017); Clive Webb, "Britain, the American South, and the Wide Civil Rights Movement", in Cornelius A. van Minnen and Manfred Berg (eds), *The U.S. South and Europe:*

Transatlantic Relations in the Nineteenth and Twentieth Centuries (Lexington, KY: University Press of Kentucky, 2013), 243–64.

13 See, for example, Daniel Geary and Jennie Sutton, "Resisting the Wind of Change: The Citizens' Councils and European Decolonization", in van Minnen and Berg (eds), *The U.S. South and Europe*, 265–82; Stephanie R. Rolph, "The Citizens' Council and Africa: White Supremacy in Global Perspective", *Journal of Southern History* 82.3 (2016): 617–50; Clive Webb. "Jim Crow and Union Jack: Southern Segregationists and the British Far Right", in Paul Jackson and Anton Shekhovtsov (eds), *The Post-War Anglo-American Far Right: A Special Relationship of Hate* (Basingstoke: Palgrave Macmillan, 2014), 67–83.

14 Chris McGreal, "Charleston Shootings: The Apartheid Era Flags that Have Found New Life with America's Racists", *Guardian*, 19 June 2015, www.theguardian. com/world/2015/jun/19/charleston-shootings-the-apartheid-era-flags-that-have-found-new-life-with-americas-racists (accessed 5 November 2018); Ismay, "Rhodesia's Dead".

15 See *Journal of American History* 91.1 (2004) for a roundtable reassessment of *Brown* in its fiftieth anniversary year.

16 Michael J. Klarman, "How Brown Changed Race Relations: The Backlash Thesis", *Journal of American History* 81.1 (1994): 81–118.

17 Neil R. McMillen, *The Citizens' Council: Organized Resistance to the Second Reconstruction, 1954–64* (Urbana, IL: University of Illinois Press, 1971), 153.

18 Ibid., 11.

19 Ibid., 22.

20 Stephanie R. Rolph, *Resisting Equality: The Citizens' Council, 1954–1989* (Baton Rouge, LA: Louisiana State University Press, 2018).

21 Zoe Hyman, "American Segregationist Ideology and White Southern Africa, 1948–1975", PhD diss., University of Sussex, 2012, esp. 31–71.

22 "The Myth of 'World Opinion'", *Citizens' Council* 1.1 (October 1955), 2.

23 Ibid.

24 S. E. D. Brown, "From South Africa", *Citizens' Council* 1.1 (October 1955), 4.

25 State-funded organizations such as the Mississippi State Sovereignty Commission collected information on black and white civil rights activists in the state, and well-known white activists including James Reeb, Viola Liuzzo, Michael Schwerner, and Andrew Goodman were murdered by southern racists.

26 For example, John R. Parker from Transvaal became a regular contributor from August 1960. *The Citizen* 5.11 (August 1960).

27 James E. Baker, J. Daniel O'Flaherty, and John de St Jorre, "Public Opinion Poll on American Attitudes Toward South Africa" (Washington, DC: Carnegie

Endowment for International Peace, 22 May 1979), 1. Archive of the Anti-Apartheid Movement, 1956–98, Bodleian Library of Commonwealth and African Studies, Oxford University, MSS AAM 1359: USA: Correspondence and Papers, 1963–1995.

28   Policy Statement by the Department of State on the Union of South Africa, 1 November 1948, in *Foreign Relations of the United States (FRUS)*, 1948, Vol. V, Part 1 (Washington, DC: US Government Printing Office, 1948), 524, http://digital.library.wisc.edu/1711.dl/FRUS (accessed 15 April 2020).

29   See Alex Thomson, *U.S. Foreign Policy Towards Apartheid South Africa, 1948–1994: Conflict of Interests* (New York: Palgrave Macmillan, 2008), for a study of policymaking for each administration from Truman to Clinton.

30   For southern politicians' support for Rhodesia, see Hyman, "American Segregationist Ideology and White Southern Africa", 189–234. For pro-apartheid and anti-divestment campaigners, see Sam Kleiner, "Meet the Conservatives Who Campaigned for Apartheid South Africa", *The Nation*, 9 July 2013, www.thenation.com/article/meet-conservatives-who-campaigned-apartheid-south-africa/ (accessed 30 July 2019).

31   Donald R. Culverson, "The Politics of the Anti-Apartheid Movement in the United States, 1969–1986", *Political Science Quarterly* 111.1 (1996): 127–49 (127).

32   Brenda Gayle Plummer, *In Search of Power: African Americans in the Era of Decolonization, 1956–1974* (New York: Cambridge University Press, 2013), 344. See chapter 7 for radical black responses to the failures of civil rights protest and legislation, and chapter 8 for responses to, and engagement with, black liberation movements across Africa. See Keeanga-Yamahtta Taylor, *From #BlackLivesMatter to Black Liberation* (Chicago: Haymarket Books, 2016), ch. 2, for a discussion of the impact of Nixon and the rhetoric of "colour-blindness" on civil rights in the US.

33   See Jeffrey O. G. Ogbar, *Black Power: Radical Politics and African American Identity* (Baltimore, MD: Johns Hopkins University Press, 2005), 124, for public confusion between black determination, nationalism, and separation.

34   Gordon Hancock, "World Racism Following the U.S. Dixie Script?", *Chicago Defender*, 27 November 1965, 31.

35   Ibid.

36   See Michelle Alexander, *The New Jim Crow: Mass Incarceration in the Age of Colorblindness* (New York: The New Press, 2010).

37   George W. Shannon, "Will U.S. Sacrifice Her Friends for 'Detente?'", *The Citizen* 21.9 (June 1976), 4.

38 Ibid., 4, 6. Emphasis in original.

39 See Rolph, *Resisting Equality*, Introduction.

40 Ulrich B. Phillips, "The Central Theme of Southern History", *American Historical Review* 34.1 (1928): 30–43 (31).

41 *The Citizen* 21.9 (June 1976).

42 "Oral History with Mr William J. Simmons", 26 June 1979, 1. University of Southern Mississippi Center for Oral History and Cultural Heritage, https://digitalcollections.usm.edu/uncategorized/digitalFile_804061a4-ab3f-4e45-bc98-6d271c92fd8f/ (accessed 15 April 2020).

43 Ibid., 87.

44 Ibid., 88.

45 Ibid., 72.

46 Ibid., 76–7.

47 Ibid., 76.

48 "England Has Same Problems as U.S. in Efforts to 'Integrate' Schools" and "Aussie Schools Have Same Troubles as U.S. and England", *The Councilor*, 11.7–8 (May 1974), 326. Hall-Hoag Collection, MS.76.5: Anti Integrationist Organization (AIO) Box: 76.5–1X, Folder: HH 752: The Councilor.

49 Thomas Linehan, "Cultures of Space: Spatialising the National Front", in Nigel Copsey and John E. Richardson (eds), *Cultures of Post-War British Fascism* (New York: Routledge, 2015), 53–4; Nigel Fielding, *The National Front* (Abingdon: Routledge, 2016 [1981]), 19–20.

50 *The Councilor* 11.7–8 (May 1974), 326.

51 *The Citizen* 15.8 (May 1971), 19–20.

52 Ibid., 21.

53 *The Citizen* 23.8 (May 1978).

54 Ibid., 13–14.

55 Southern National Party newsletter, n.d., 1. University of Mississippi, Race Relations Collection, Box 5, Folder 1.

56 Billy G. James, "New Southern Party Calls for School Rally", *Atlanta Constitution*, 2 January 1970, 18A; "Governor of Mississippi Backs Private Schools", *New York Times*, 4 January 1970, 78; Leroy Morganti, "White, Negro Wed in Mississippi", *Atlanta Constitution*, 3 August 1970, 8A.

57 "Governor of Mississippi Backs Private Schools".

58 SNP newsletter, 2; David Hanley, *Beyond the Nation State: Parties in the Era of European Integration* (Basingstoke: Palgrave Macmillan, 2008), 158.

59 SNP newsletter, 2.

60 SNP newsletter, 11.

61 For the history of SABRA, see Hermann Giliomee, *The Afrikaners: Biography of a People* (London: Hurst, 2003), 483. For consideration of white homelands, see South African Institute of Race Relations, *A Survey of Race Relations in South Africa, 1972* (Johannesburg: South African Institute of Race Relations, January 1973), 56–7.

62 Humphrey Tyler, "Apartheid Switch: South African Call for 'Whites Only' Homeland", *Christian Science Monitor*, 14 July 1980, www.csmonitor. com/1980/0714/071443.html (accessed 10 January 2020); Dennis Webster, "'An indictment of South Africa': Whites-only Town Orania is Booming", *Guardian*, 24 October 2019, www.theguardian.com/cities/2019/oct/24/an-indictment-of-south-africa-whites-only-town-orania-is-booming (accessed 10 January 2020).

63 See Andrew L. Barlow, *Between Fear and Hope: Globalization and Race in the United States* (Lanham, MD: Rowman and Littlefield, 2003); Odd Arne Westad, *The Global Cold War: Third World Interventions and the Making of Our Times* (Cambridge: Cambridge University Press, 2007 [2005]), 331–63.

64 www.splcenter.org/fighting-hate/extremist-files/individual/gordon-baum (accessed 30 July 2019); Gordon Lee Baum to Robert Hatch, 4 September 1990, Hall-Hoag Collection, MS.76.43, Box 76.43–3, Folder: Council of Conservative Citizens.

65 "What is the Council of Conservative Citizens?", 24 February 2012, http:// conservative-headlines.com/2012/02/what-is-the-council-of-conservative- citizens/ (accessed 31 August 2017).

66 *Citizens Report* 29.1 (January 1985), Hall-Hoag Collection, MS.76.5:A10, Box 76.5–1, Folder: South Louisiana Citizens' Council, Inc. (76.5/27/2-SER).

67 *Citizens Report* 29.8 (August 1985), 1; 34.2 (February 1990), 2.

68 See Ron Nixon, *Selling Apartheid: South Africa's Global Propaganda War* (London: Pluto Press, 2016).

69 American Committee on Africa news release, 2 August 1976; contract, 17 March 1976; E. M. Rhoodie to Sydney S. Baron, 20 February 1976, in South African Apartheid Collection, Yale University, 1999-M-122, Box 10: Propaganda, Sydney S. Baron Co., Inc., folder 156.

70 The Internews International Bulletin 6:5 (March 1979), in South African Apartheid Collection, Yale University, 1999-M-122, Box 9: Propaganda, US, General folder 143.

71 Cornelius. P. Mulder, "South Africa Lights the Way to Pluralistic Society", *The Citizen* 23.12 (September 1978), 1, 10.

72 Pearson & Pipkin, Inc., to anonymous, August 1998, in South African Apartheid Collection, Yale University, Series 1: South African Government, 1961–1991,

Box 1: Embassy/Consulate 1987–1990; "S. Africa's Low-Profile Lobbyists", *Washington Post*, 15 July 1991.

73 Culverson, "The Politics of the Anti-Apartheid Movement in the United States", 146. The Comprehensive Anti-Apartheid Act prohibited new corporate investment in South Africa, American bank deposits from South African governmental agencies, the importation of South African products, including coal, steel, and uranium, and ended the landing rights of South African airlines in the US and of American airlines in South Africa. The Act and popular sentiment led to massive disinvestment in South Africa and American companies leaving.

74 *Citizens Report* 29.8 (August 1985); 34.2 (February 1990); 29.1 (January 1985); 29.7 (July 1985); 34.2 (February 1990).

75 Letter from Robert J. Hoy, *Focus on South Africa* (South Africa: Department of Foreign Affairs, 1989), n.p., https://books.google.co.uk/books?id=QFM qAQAAMAAJ&q=%22American+Afrikaner+Union%22&dq=%22American+ Afrikaner+Union%22&hl=en&sa=X&ved=oahUKEwjorLyHgdneAhVtMewK HSyCAWkQ6AEIODAD (accessed 15 April 2020); SCLC, *The Southern Christian Leadership Conference National Magazine* 19.1 (1990), 162, https://books.google. co.uk/books?id=oXwOAQAAMAAJ&q=%22American-%20Afrikaner+Union %22&dq=%22American-%20Afrikaner+Union%22&hl=en&sa=X&ved=oahU KEwielNjwptneAhXHKewKHQUuCG8Q6AEIMDAB (accessed 15 April 2020).

76 Letter from Hoy, *Focus on South Africa*.

77 Carol Mason, *Reading Appalachia from Left to Right: Conservatives and the 1974 Kanawha County Textbook Controversy* (Ithaca, NY: Cornell University Press, 2009), 3–7.

78 Robert J. Hoy, "Lid on a Boiling Pot", in Robert W. Whitaker (ed.), *The New Right Papers* (New York: St Martin's Press, 1982), 86–8.

79 Ibid., 102.

80 David Shribman, "… and Recruit for the Government", *New York Times*, 12 October 1983, B6.

81 Mason, *Reading Appalachia from Left to Right*, 190.

82 For assessments of the southern strategy, see Angie Maxwell and Todd Shields, *The Long Southern Strategy: How Chasing White Voters in the South Changed American Politics* (New York: Oxford University Press, 2019), and Matthew Lassiter, *The Silent Majority: Suburban Politics in the Sunbelt South* (Princeton, NJ: Princeton University Press, 2006).

83 Matthew Levie, "David Duke: Winning by Losing", *Chicago Tribune*, 21 January 1992, NW15.

84 Tyler Bridges, *The Rise of David Duke* (Jackson, MS: University Press of Mississippi, 1994), 133; Jeffrey Kaplan (ed.), *Encyclopedia of White Power: A Sourcebook on the Radical Racist Right* (Walnut Creek, CA: Altamira Press, 2000), 42; Russ Bellant, *The Coors Connection: How Coors Family Philanthropy Undermines Democratic Pluralism* (Cambridge, MA: South End Press, 1991 [1988]), 71.

85 Levie, "David Duke"; for reference to Gingrich, see Craig Shirley, *Citizen Newt: The Making of a Reagan Conservative* (Nashville, TN: Nelson Books, 2017), 261.

86 Elizabeth Bryant Morganstern, "Samuel T. Francis", in Kathleen R. Arnold (ed.), *Anti-Immigration in the United States: A Historical Encyclopedia* (Santa Barbara, CA: Greenwood, 2011), 508.

87 American-Afrikaner Union newsletter, issue 28, December 1990. Hall-Hoag Collection, MS.76.72.HGER, Box 76.72–1, Folder: American Afrikaner Movement.

88 William N. Tilchin, "The United States and the Boer War", in Keith M. Wilson (ed.), *The International Impact of the Boer War* (Abingdon: Routledge, 2014 [2001]), 108–9; Stuart Anderson, "Racial Anglo-Saxonism and the American Response to the Boer War", *Diplomatic History* 2.3 (1978), 222.

89 Jennifer Ann Sutton, "The Empire Question: How the South African War, 1899–1902, Shaped Americans' Reactions to U.S. Imperialism", PhD diss., Washington University in St Louis, 2012, 161–2, 164.

90 Giliomee, *The Afrikaners*, 400.

91 William Beinart, *South Africa in the Twentieth Century* (Oxford: Oxford University Press, 2001), 162–4.

92 American-Afrikaner Union newsletter, issue 28, December 1990. Hall-Hoag Collection, MS.76.72.HGER, Box 76.72–1, Folder: American Afrikaner Movement.

93 AAU pamphlet, 1990. Hall-Hoag Collection, MS.76.72.HGER, Box 76.72–1, Folder: American Afrikaner Movement.

94 https://clintonwhitehouse2.archives.gov/Initiatives/OneAmerica/PIR.pdf (accessed 15 April 2020).

95 Peter Baker, "With Outburst at Fairfax Forum, Race Initiative Finally Hits a Nerve", *Washington Post*, 18 December 1997, A1.

96 Terence Samuel, "Race Debate Heats up at Virginia Session", *St. Louis Post-Dispatch*, 19 December 1997, A15. https://search.proquest.com/docview/403750237/E00B0 6328DF24EB1PQ/1?accountid=14511 (accessed 7 July 2020); Steven A. Holmes, "Conservatives' Voices Enter Clinton's Dialogue on Race: Testy Debate Focuses on School Vouchers", *New York Times*, 18 December 1997.

97 Chris Matthews (Chicago Tribune Service), "If Race Dialogue Is to Work, Clinton Must Keep Talking", *Salt Lake Tribune*, 21 December 1997, A17.

98   Nigel Copsey, *Contemporary British Fascism: The British National Party and the Quest for Legitimacy* (Basingstoke: Palgrave Macmillan, 2008 [2004]), 44.

99   Ibid., 100, 102. Copsey discusses terminology ("fascism", "right-wing extremism", and "national-populism") in chapter 4, noting (76) that the legitimate-sounding "British nationalism" was the preferred term of those who wanted to avoid being called "fascist".

100 Ibid., 108–9.

101 Paul Waugh, "BNP's Strategy of Prejudice was Sinister but Simple", *Independent*, 1 September 2001, www.independent.co.uk/news/uk/politics/bnps-strategy-of-prejudice-was-sinister-but-simple-9209427.html (accessed 15 April 2020).

102 Ibid.; Michael Prescott, "Tories Welcome 'Racist' Man from the National Front", *The Times*, 15 August 1993, https://search.proquest.com/docview/317977963?accountid=14511 (accessed 7 July 2020).

103 *Heritage and Destiny* 1 (summer 1999), 1.

104 Kevin Johnson, "Va. Group Accused of Illegal Efforts for Racist U.K. Party", *USA Today*, 30 August 2001, A4; "US Fundraisers give BNP £70k", *Daily Record* (Glasgow), 31 August 2001, 33.

105 https://nationalvanguard.org/2016/06/will-the-real-thomas-mair-please-stand-up/ (accessed 15 April 2020).

106 "American White Supremacists Have History of International Conflict", 29 August 2001, www.splcenter.org/fighting-hate/intelligence-report/2001/american-white-supremacist-groups-have-history-international-conflict (accessed 15 April 2020).

107 www.splcenter.org/fighting-hate/intelligence-report/1999/racist-council-conservative-citizens-finds-home-mainstream-politics (accessed 15 April 2020).

108 "GOP Happy to Hold Hands with Racists", *Atlanta Journal Constitution*, 28 March 1999; ibid.

109 Thomas B. Edsall, "Conservative Group Accused of Ties to White Supremacists", *Washington Post*, 19 December 1998, A8; Thomas B. Edsall, "Another Republican Retreats From Council of Conservative Citizens", *Washington Post*, 7 March 1999, A12.

110 "Editorial: Recent Events and Activities", archived from the original, https://web.archive.org/web/20000818230559fw_/http://www.americabnp.net:80/editorial.html (accessed 15 April 2020).

111 www.splcenter.org/fighting-hate/intelligence-report/2015/counsel-citizens (accessed 15 April 2020).

112 See Patricia Anne Simpson and Helga Druxes (eds), *Digital Media Strategies of the Far-Right in Europe and the United States* (Lanham, MD: Lexington Books, 2015),

esp. 21–36, for a discussion of how the American far right transitioned from print to digital media.

113 Online meeting reports reference from August 1999–April 2000, archived from the original, https://web.archive.org/web/20010312174307fw_/http://www.americabnp.net:80/august.htm; https://web.archive.org/web/20010312175049fw_/http://www.americabnp.net:80/january.htm; https://web.archive.org/web/20010312174613fw_/http://www.americabnp.net:80/february.htm; https://web.archive.org/web/20010415072513fw_/http://www.americabnp.net:80/march.htm;https://web.archive.org/web/20010312173817fw_/http://www.americabnp.net:80/april.htm (all accessed 13 November 2018).

114 "Editorial: Recent Events and Activities", 15 August 2000, archived from the original, https://web.archive.org/web/20000818230559fw_/http://www.americabnp.net:80/editorial.html; www.splcenter.org/fighting-hate/intelligence-report/1999/national-alliance-reveals-new-leaders-including-military-unity-coordinator (accessed 13 November 2018).

115 *Heritage and Destiny*, summer 2000, 1; "April Meeting" report, April 2000, archived from the original, https://web.archive.org/web/20010312173817fw_/http://www.americabnp.net:80/april.htm (accessed 13 November 2018).

116 Edsall, "Conservative Group Accused of Ties to White Supremacists".

117 Paul Waugh, "BNP Leader Faces Jail over 'Funding from US'", *Independent*, 1 September 2001, www.independent.co.uk/news/uk/politics/bnp-leader-faces-jail-over-funding-from-us-9201154.html (accessed 15 April 2020).

118 http://conservative-headlines.com/2010/07/90-of-black-owned-farms-in-south-africa-are-a-failure/; http://conservative-headlines.com/2010/12/white-south-african-family-killed-execution-style-black-killers-vow-deaths/; http://conservative-headlines.com/2011/01/major-groups-in-south-africa-openly-calling-for-mass-murder-of-white-people/ (accessed 9 August 2017).

119 *Citizens' Informer* 45.1 (January–April, 2012), https://io.wp.com/topconservative-news.com/wp-content/uploads/2012/03/front_page.jpg; http://conservative-headlines.com/2011/05/extreme-affirmative-action-in-south-africa/; http://conservative-headlines.com/2011/06/black-on-white-murders-reach-genocidal-levels-in-south-africa/; http://conservative-headlines.com/2011/10/two-white-teen-girls-kidnapped-and-set-on-fire-in-south-africa/ (accessed 9 August 2017).

120 Roof, "Manifesto", 1.

121 Sid Secular, Letter from the Editor, *Citizens' Informer* 49.4 (October–December 2016), 5, http://conservative-headlines.org/citizens-informer-archive/ (accessed 15 April 2020).

122   www.theatlantic.com/politics/archive/2017/08/trump-defends-white-nationa list-protesters-some-very-fine-people-on-both-sides/537012/ (accessed 15 April 2020).

123   Nicole Lewis, "From Idea to Action: White Supremacy's New Visibility", *Washington Post*, 24 August 2017, www.washingtonpost.com/news/post-nation/wp/2017/08/24/from-idea-to-action-white-supremacys-new-visibility/?noredirect=on (accessed 15 April 2020).

124   Ibid.

125   Jon Swaine, "Leader of Group Cited in 'Dylann Roof Manifesto' Donated to Top Republicans", *Guardian*, 22 June 2015, www.theguardian.com/us-news/2015/jun/21/dylann-roof-manifesto-charlston-shootings-republicans (accessed 15 April 2020).

126   http://conservative-headlines.org/statement-of-principles/ (accessed 15 April 2020).

The far right in the Anglosphere

8

White Australia alone?
The international links of the
Australian far right in the Cold War era[1]

Evan Smith

IN THE 1960s, as Australia underwent significant social change at the tail end of Sir Robert Menzies' prime ministership, the far right started to slowly re-emerge, having been quite dormant in the immediate post-war years as the conservative Liberal–Country Party pursued an anti-communist agenda and the continuance of the "White Australia Policy", the highly restrictive immigration control system that had been in place since Federation in 1901. With the beginnings of the political and cultural radicalism of the late 1960s in Australia, predominantly the movement against the Vietnam War, the far right started to mobilize to combat this social change and to push against the incremental reforms of the Liberal government after Menzies' retirement in 1966 (such as the gradual weakening of the "White Australia Policy" and the backing of the referendum on Aboriginal rights in 1967). This reaction against the domestic politics of the Liberals (which saw a succession of four prime ministers between 1966 and 1972) played out against the global political backdrop of the Cold War and the process of decolonization across Africa and Asia. The fight against communism and for a white Australia was seen as part of a wider worldwide struggle against communism and multiracial democracy that supposedly linked "white" people in Europe, North America, and settler-colonial societies in the southern hemisphere (such as South Africa, Rhodesia, Australia, and

New Zealand). Similar to other far right movements across the Anglophone world, there was a feeling that traditional right-wing political parties, such as the Conservatives in the UK, the Republicans in the US, and the National Party in New Zealand, had betrayed their support base, and in Australia, as elsewhere, the far right started organizing to reverse the perceived slide towards liberalism in the Cold War era.

Between the 1960s and the 1980s, the Australian far right, in its various guises, attempted to situate itself within a transnational network of white supremacists, national socialists, and radical nationalists. The chief political and ideological influences of the Australian far right came from Britain and the United States, but there was also inspiration from continental Europe. This chapter will explore how these international influences impacted upon the development of the far right in Australia, with often a divide between those who looked to the United States and those who looked to Britain, which oscillated throughout the Cold War era. It will show how the Australian far right took these international influences and tried to incorporate them into an explicitly "Australian" nationalist framework, portraying these groups as the legacies of Australia's racialized and often violent settler-colonial history.

While these groups were often on the margins of political life in Australia during the post-war era, there were times when they made some direct political impact (such as the Australian League of Rights' entryism into the Country/National Party)[2] or when their violence became a cause for concern (such as the Australian National Socialist Party in the early 1970s or National Action and the Australian Nationalist Movement in the 1980s–1990s).[3] Possibly more important than their impact on domestic politics was the fact that these groups plugged into an international white supremacist and anti-communist network,[4] which reinforced the notion of Australia as being within a global system of white supremacist solidarity.

National Socialism and Australia in the 1960s

Aside from the short-lived Australian Union of Fascists and National Socialists (modelled on Oswald Mosley's British Union of Fascists and

National Socialists) in the late 1930s,[5] there was no explicit Nazi Party in Australia until the early-to-mid-1960s. The Australian Nationalist Workers Party (ANWP) was established in the mid-1950s and the Australian National Socialist Party (ANSP) was then formed in 1962. The far right in Australia had been marginalized by the events of the Second World War and only started to reappear in the late 1950s and early 1960s, as a result of sociopolitical shifts in the domestic sphere, as well as events overseas. The "White Australia Policy", which had placed strict controls upon migrants from outside the British Isles and northern Europe since Federation and enjoyed bipartisan support within government circles, remained in place after 1945. However, an ongoing concern about Australia's population growth and post-war labour shortages saw the system tinkered with by the Menzies government in the 1950s. This saw a large number of southern European migrants come to the country, and a limited number of migrants from Asia were also allowed entry.[6] Maintenance of the "White Australia Policy" was at the heart of the Australian far right and there was strong opposition to any watering down of immigration controls. For example, the programme of the ANWP (also known as the National Australian Workers Party) stated, "We stand 100% behind the White Australia policy."[7] As Josiah Brownell shows in his chapter in this volume on "white" migration to Rhodesia, the meaning of "white" within the "White Australia Policy" was malleable and unstable, which caused tensions within the far right in Australia over perceptions of "whiteness", "Europeanness", and "Britishness" that had been central to Australian national identity since Federation in 1901.

Intertwining concerns about international communism and the break-up of the European empires created further anxieties for the far right in Australia, which saw Australia threatened by Asian communism (a widespread and mainstream right-wing fear in the 1950s and 1960s) and their white brethren in southern Africa vulnerable to Soviet-backed African national liberation movements. In an era of apartheid in South Africa and white minority rule in Rhodesia, there were increasing links between white supremacists in southern Africa and Australia (as well as in New

Zealand, Britain, and North America). For example, Frank Rosser, one of the leading members of the Australian National Socialist Party, had lived in Rhodesia and worked as a mercenary in the Congo in the early 1960s before emigrating to Australia.[8]

Originally founded by Ted Cawthorn and Don Lindsay in South Australia in 1962, the ANSP eventually established its headquarters in Sydney the following year when Arthur Smith joined the party and became its leader. After initial interest from the media and the authorities (which led to a raid on the ANSP's Sydney headquarters in 1964), the party faded in the mid-1960s after Smith served a short jail term and then relocated to Tasmania. In 1967, Cawthorn and Hungarian émigré Ferenc (Frank) Molnar formed the rival National Socialist Party of Australia (NSPA), which was based in Canberra. Succeeding Smith, Eric Wenberg helped orchestrate a merger between the two parties in 1968 which lasted in this form until the early 1970s (although a rump continued as the ANSP during the same period).

Kathleen Belew has demonstrated how the Vietnam War had a deep impact on the American far right.[9] Australia's involvement in the war (as well as the large-scale anti-war movement) also had a significant effect on the far right. For the Australian far right, the Vietnam War was a battle to save the nation from Asian communism and there were a number of confrontations between small bands of neo-Nazis and anti-war protestors in the late 1960s and early 1970s. These confrontations generated publicity for the National Socialist Party of Australia and there was a belief that the NSPA's counter-demonstrations in favour of the Vietnam War could be a possible recruiting tool.[10] NSPA members also disrupted anti-apartheid protests, as part of their solidarity with southern Africa, and joined protests by Eastern Europeans (such as those staged by Ukrainian and Hungarian anti-communists) against the Soviet Union. For the National Socialists in Australia during the Cold War era, solidarity with other white supremacists, extreme nationalists, and hardline anti-communists was an important means of building up the country's tiny far right forces, linking them to similar movements across the globe.

International Nazism in the Anglophone world

The Australian far right groups were heavily influenced by Colin Jordan's National Socialist Movement in Britain and George Lincoln Rockwell's American Nazi Party in the United States, both of which were founding members of the World Union of National Socialists in the early 1960s. Prior to joining the Australian National Socialist Party, Smith had been in contact with Rockwell while a member of the Australian Nationalist Workers Party, and had attempted to bring Rockwell to Australia in 1961. Rockwell was denied a visa, though Smith later admitted that the ANWP did not in any case have the funds to pay for his trip.[11]

Throughout the 1960s, those in the National Socialist parties in Australia maintained contact with Jordan and Rockwell. Andrew Moore has shown that several Australians corresponded with Jordan in the 1960s, and from these two international figures the Australian Nazis "derived an adulation for Hitler, a denial in the [H]olocaust of six million Jews and related, crudely fashioned anti-Semitism".[12] When the Australian Security Intelligence Organisation (ASIO) interviewed NSPA member Leslie Leisemann in 1965, Leisemann said that Jordan "was doing a good job in England and the youth are with him", while commenting with regard to a recent split in Rockwell's American Nazi Party that "I don't know whether he can handle it or not but if he goes down the whole world goes down."[13] ASIO also noted the previous year that there had been "no formal affiliation" between the Australian Nazis and overseas parties, with an application from the ANSP to join the World Union of National Socialists being unsuccessful in 1963–64.[14] It was not until after Rockwell's death that the NSPA became affiliated to the World Union of National Socialists.

Eric Wenberg, a member of the ANSP and then the NSPA, travelled to the United States in 1967 to make links with Rockwell and his American Nazi Party.[15] After Rockwell was assassinated in August 1967 by a former member of his organization, Wenberg disrupted the trial of the killer by trying to punch him and was deported from the United States with a certain amount of notoriety.[16] When assessing the risk that Wenberg posed after his deportation from the US, ASIO suggested:

> While WENBERG may seek some advantage from his recent press publicity on his return to Australia, there is no evidence to suggest that the National Socialist Party of Australia consists of other than a very small number of individuals of questionable mental stability who profess Nazi beliefs. They are essentially at variance with each other, and their activities have not extended beyond the sporadic distribution of Nazi propaganda emanating originally from the United States and the United Kingdom.[17]

Cawthorn and Molnar launched the *Australian National Socialist Journal* in the summer of 1968, which demonstrated its links to the Rockwell and Jordan groups overseas. The first issue of the *ANSJ* featured a lengthy review of Rockwell's book *White Power*, describing him as "the most out-standing and courageous National Socialist to appear since the catastrophe of 1945".[18] The review stated that Rockwell's message was "for White Men everywhere", and urged National Socialists in Australia to "procure 'White Power' and benefit from [its] deep wisdom and inspiring insight".[19]

In a revised version of the journal, after Molnar was pushed out of the party and Wenberg (along with several others) became an assistant editor, there was an increased focus on Rockwell and his idea of "white power". A quote from Rockwell adorned the inside cover and a four-page article by the late Rockwell was published in the first issue of the new *ANSJ*, entitled "In Hoc Signo Vinces" (roughly translated as "under this sign, you will conquer") after one of Rockwell's books.[20] The first issue also carried a letter of congratulations from the World Union of National Socialists leader William Pierce (who later became infamous as the leader of the National Alliance in the United States and the author of the white supremacist tract, *The Turner Diaries*).[21] The second issue published a longer letter from Rockwell's successor, Matt Koehl, who wrote that he believed that the journal could "become an important instrument in forging Aryan racial solidarity" and thanked the journal for making the American Nazis aware of Henry Lawson.[22] Lawson was an Australian writer from the turn of the twentieth century who was involved in the establishment of the journal *The Bulletin*, which promoted the idea of a distinct Australian national identity, as well as a defence of the "White Australia Policy" after 1901 (a quote from Lawson adorned the masthead of the far right journal *Audacity* in the late 1970s and early 1980s).[23] The same issue of the *ANSJ* published a piece from the United States on the National Socialist White People's Party (NSWPP) after Rockwell's death and the reconfiguring of the party under Koehl, as well as a piece on American Nazis fighting anti-Vietnam War protestors in Chicago penned by a rival of Koehl's, Frank Collin, who had split from the NSWPP in the late 1960s.[24] The same issue concluded with another instalment from Rockwell's "In Hoc Signo Vinces" and also ran an advertisement for Rockwell's *White Power* book on the back page.[25]

While the National Socialist Party of Australia clearly modelled itself on Rockwell's and Jordan's organizations, as well as worshipping Hitler and the German Nazi Party, the party's literature also tried to frame it within an Australian context and portray the NSPA as the true inheritor of the country's violent and racist settler-colonial past. As Stuart Ward highlights in his chapter for this volume, the racial politics of this settler-colonial tradition have been replicated over the last century and are still at work today, and the far right through its various incarnations has referred back to this tradition.

In the *ANSJ* there were articles on Henry Lawson and the Eureka Stockade. The Eureka Stockade was a miners' rebellion in 1854 in the Victorian goldmines, primarily against the imposition of a prohibitive miners' licence, but it has been viewed as part of a broader fight for social and political rights in colonial Australia. Eureka had traditionally been used a symbol of the Australian labour movement, but the far right in the 1970s and 1980s attempted to incorporate the event into its historical narratives as an assertion of Australian national independence.[26] Eric Wenberg wrote of Eureka:

Those heroes at Eureka symbolise a new era in our Nation. What those men fought for 116 years ago, we, as National Socialists will now finish … We National Socialists join hands with our brothers who fell so many years ago; in dying, their strength and duty to the Cause overcame their fear of death, and with this death they have shown to us a more noble duty which overshadows all else.[27]

In an editorial, Cawthorn argued that the NSPA must be "unquestionably AUSTRALIAN" and that an "Australian National Socialism" must be allowed to "evolve its own characteristics", remonstrating:

If we National Socialists, who seek to be the very embodiment of the new Australian nationalism, adopt the external characteristics of another country and another people, we will not only negate our own ideology but alienate the very people we will be looking to for our most steadfast support in the years to come.[28]

A similar sentiment was expressed in the NSPA newsletter in 1968 when discussing the World Union of National Socialists and the NSWPP in the United States. Presumably written by Cawthorn, the newsletter suggested that while "a NS victory in Australia would be much more difficult in isolation than with the simultaneous or near simultaneous victory of our fellow National Socialists in the US or in other countries", it was to be remembered that "a NS victory in America, for example, will not automatically ensure a victory in Australia".[29]

The second iteration of the *ANSJ* published a letter asking why the NSPA didn't produce a magazine like the NSWPP's *Stormtrooper*,[30] which was much more of a tabloid magazine than the "theoretical" *ANSJ*. After Cawthorn stepped down from active duties in the party and Wenberg travelled to Rhodesia, Cass Young and Michael McCormick took charge of the NSPA and produced *The Stormtrooper Magazine*, which was a crude cut-and-paste publication (even less professional looking than its US counterpart). In an internal bulletin of the NSPA, Young acknowledged that some would accuse the NSPA of "following America too closely", but argued that he had "found the average Australian to be apathetic, but, very curious" and suggested that the aesthetics of the magazine would "arouse enough curiosity to boost its sales".[31] As Paul Jackson has written, the World Union of National Socialists "acted as a vehicle for Australian neo-Nazis to discover, and then echo, the presentational style of the American Nazi Party".[32]

The magazine lasted for about eight issues and ran for most of 1972. Each issue contained a section that looked at other parties in the World Union of National Socialists, with coverage given to the NSWPP in the United States, Jordan's British Movement in the UK, the National Socialist Party of New Zealand, and the National Socialist Irish Workers' Party, including contact details for each organization. The back pages of the magazine advertised literature from the United States, including copies of the NSWPP's *White Power* magazine. The front cover of the fifth issue read "Aryan Solidarity" and displayed the symbols of a number of fascist, Nazi, and far right groups from across Europe and North America. Interestingly it included the symbol of Oswald Mosley's Union Movement (which was viewed with scepticism by many of the World Union of National Socialists-affiliated fascists) and the British National Party, which had been subsumed into the National Front in 1967.

At times, the coverage was mutual. The *WUNS Bulletin* in 1972 gave a glowing account of the NSPA in the lead-up to the Australian federal election, in which the party was running ten candidates, claiming that Cawthorn was reporting "a very satisfactory electoral effort".[33] The same story reported on the NSPA training "in methods of self-defence to protect themselves from the growing Jewish violence", after Cass Young's house was attacked by protestors.[34] The bulletin also published an obituary of Wenberg, who had been killed in a car crash in Rhodesia, stating that he was "establishing important contacts for the Movement at the time of his death in Rhodesia".[35]

Despite the flurry of activity in 1972, peaking with the contesting of several seats in the federal election (won by Labor's Gough Whitlam), the party did not survive for much longer. Tensions between the various state branches led to a lack of cohesion at the national level, and over the next two years the NSPA faded away. While some members retired from political activity with the break-up of the party in the mid-1970s, others became involved in the National Front of Australia or the various "radical nationalist" groups associated with Jim Saleam (a young and upcoming NSPA member) in the late 1970s. Saleam has remained a central figure on the Australian far right, co-founding National Action in the early 1980s and leading the Australia First Party from the mid-to-late 2000s, as well as serving a prison sentence for an attack on an African National Congress representative in Australia, Eddie Funde, in 1989. But before the "radical nationalists" associated with National Action and its short-lived predecessors in the late 1970s and early 1980s, the more Anglocentric sections of the far right came to prominence, such as the Australian League of Rights (ALOR) and the National Front of Australia (NFA).

The Australian League of Rights and empire loyalism

In contrast to the explicitly fascist NSPA, the Australian League of Rights was a populist far right organization that existed throughout the post-war era, combining anti-Semitism, anti-communism, anti-immigrationism, and empire loyalism. The ALOR existed on the fringes of the hard right of the Liberal Party and the Country (later National) Party, and used these associations to project the optics of respectability upon their conspiracy-laden worldview. Andrew Moore notes that the 1991 government report into racial violence in Australia described the ALOR as "undoubtedly the most influential and effective, as well as the best organised and most substantially financed, racist organisation in Australia".[36] Despite garnering attention from ASIO since the 1960s, the League were seen as less of a threat than the neo-Nazi parties, with ASIO boss Charles Spry writing to Liberal–Country Party Attorney General Billy Snedden in 1965 that there was "no evidence that the Australian League of Rights is anything other than a reputable organisation".[37]

The ALOR emerged from the Social Credit Movement of the interwar period, and was founded in the late 1940s by Eric Butler in Adelaide, South Australia. Butler claimed that international capitalism was a Jewish conspiracy and that both Nazism and communism were controlled by the "international Jew".[38] Andrew Campbell has shown that in the 1960s, the League's programme promoted "opposition to communism; supported the Vietnam War; loyalty to the monarchy, and the British Empire; opposed 'liberalism' and moral permissiveness".[39] The ALOR was particularly concerned about decolonization and the spread of communism in Africa and openly defended apartheid South Africa and Ian Smith's regime in Rhodesia throughout the 1960s and 1970s.

From the 1950s onwards, Butler established links with the League of Empire Loyalists (LEL), a pressure group linked to the hard right of the British Conservative Party. Started by the former British Union of Fascists' director of propaganda A.K. Chesterton in 1954, the LEL was against decolonization and Commonwealth immigration to Britain. The LEL made a name for itself by disrupting Conservative Party meetings, particularly at the annual Tory conference. Beside these protest spectacles the LEL probably would have been forgotten, except that it became the conduit for most of the leading figures of the British far right for the next twenty years. Alongside Chesterton and the aforementioned Colin Jordan, future National Front (NF) leaders John Tyndall, Martin Webster, John Bean, and Andrew Fountaine went through the group in the 1950s before they all left.

Butler belonged to an Australian chapter of the League of Empire Loyalists, travelling to London in 1962 to meet with Chesterton.[40] Like the ALOR, the LEL had a particular following in South Australia, and in 1958 the South Australian Police's Special Branch noted connections between those involved in the Social Credit Movement (such as Butler) and the local version of the LEL.[41] The aims of the LEL, the Special Branch reported, were:

1 To maintain the name of the British Commonwealth of Nations.
2 To restore the British Empire as such.
3 To engineer, where possible, the separation of the British Commonwealth from the United Nations.
4 To awaken the public to the gradual dissolution of the Empire and to take steps to prevent such dissolution.
5 To avert the establishment of a "World Police Force".[42]

From the time that the LEL formed in July 1954, the ALOR's publications, *New Times* and *On Target*, reported positively on Chesterton's organization and often reprinted material from Chesterton's own publication, *Candour*. Announcing the formation of the LEL, *New Times* (then the journal of the Victorian League of Rights) declared:

> The Victorian League of Rights announces that it welcomes the move in England and is keen to co-operate with the League of Loyalists. The spirit of genuine patriotism is not dead yet. The world monopolists are finding their task much harder than they possibly thought.[43]

Chesterton's LEL merged with the British National Party, the Racial Preservation Society, and the Greater Britain Movement, as well as several other smaller groups, to form the National Front in 1967. The ALOR's publications did not report on the NF as frequently as it had the LEL, but Butler did keep some links with the NF (even after Chesterton left in 1970). In 1974, *Spearhead*, the journal of the NF, published a speech that Butler had given in London. Butler talked about "Political Zionism" and the "centralised control" of the Common Market in the wake of the 1973 oil crisis, which fitted into the worldview of the NF, but he did not make any mention of the Anglosphere and the ties between Britain and the settler colonies, even though this was a favourite topic of both parties.[44]

At the same time as pursuing these links through Chesterton, the LEL, and the NF, Butler was putting together his own network of international Leagues of Rights, with sister LORs in New Zealand, Canada, and Britain, as well as an overarching Crown Commonwealth League of Rights. The leader of the British League of Rights (BLOR), Donald A. Martin, had worked with Butler in Australia for over a decade before returning to the UK,[45] although Martin did make return trips to Australia to address ALOR meetings.[46] On the back cover of a copy of Butler's pamphlet *Censored History*, an advertisement for the BLOR stated that the organization had the following objectives:

Loyalty to the Christian concept of God and the Crown; Fostering the strengthening of ties between the member nations of the British Crown Commonwealth; Support of private property and genuine competitive enterprise; Defence of the Rule of Law; Opposition to all policies of totalitarianism, irrespective of their label.[47]

However, both *Searchlight* and *Patterns of Prejudice* demonstrated that the BLOR, like its sister organization, was deeply anti-Semitic, promoting anti-Semitic literature (including a wealth of Holocaust denial material) and establishing links with anti-Semitic groups in the United States, such as the Liberty Lobby.[48] The Liberty Lobby, started by William Carto in the late 1950s and the publisher of Holocaust denial literature, including the infamous *Journal of Historical Review*, sent a letter of congratulation to the ALOR in 1982 for its annual dinner, calling the Australian League "one of the most effective and respected citizen organizations in the world".[49] The ALOR also sold copies of the *Journal of Historical Review* from its Melbourne offices.[50]

By the late 1970s, the ALOR was seen by a younger generation of far right activists as an anachronism from a bygone era. Although it had its origins in the LEL, the NF in Britain seemed to many on the far right across the British Commonwealth to be the dynamic and broad movement needed for the political landscape of the crisis-ridden 1970s.

The National Front of Australia

The establishment of the National Front of Australia (NFA) in 1978 was part of a wider plan to create a Commonwealth National Front (CNF) among the settler-colonial countries. This was partly an idea put forward by John Tyndall, now leader of the National Front, but also by those on the far right in the settler colonies who were searching for direction. An interlinked CNF suited the ambitions of the NF in Britain, looking for positives as the anti-racist movement against it was building, and it suited those in Australia, New Zealand, and Canada who were attempting to tap into a more dynamic (and clearly identifiable) political movement from the centre of the former empire. As Paul Stocker has shown, a revival of the British Empire, with particular links to the former Dominions, was a key part of post-war British fascism.[51] The programme of the NF in the mid-1970s declared:

> The National Front believes that Britain's destiny lies with the British Commonwealth and resolves every effort should be made to repair the damage done by recent governments to Commonwealth unity.
>
> It believes, however, that the present multi-racial conception of Commonwealth is unrealistic, and that the Commonwealth should be reformed into a partnership of White countries with its main nucleus being the United Kingdom, Canada, Australia and New Zealand. Every effort should be made to persuade South Africa and Rhodesia to rejoin the Commonwealth.[52]

The month before the establishment of the NFA, Jeremy May (an NF member who had previously resided in Australia) wrote an article in *Spearhead* entitled "Towards a National Front of Australia". The NF saw Australia as "a vast and fascinating country with tremendous social and economic potential" and while the country was "almost completely self-sufficient in economic resources", it was perceived that Australia was at the mercy of foreign investment and international liberalism. May pointed to the ending of the "White Australia Policy" as a particular symbol of Australia's despair, lamenting the "invading hordes" from southern Europe, the Middle East, and Asia. Furthermore, May focused on Australia's "complete absence of protection for almost the entire length of the country's vast coastline" as another example of the country's weakness, with the naval defences, described as a "bathtub flotilla", unable to prevent "Chinese drug racketeers, Pacific Islanders and, most recently, Vietnamese refugees" from reaching its shores.[53]

Despite this, Australia was still seen as a bastion of the old white Commonwealth at a time when South Africa and Rhodesia seemed on the verge of collapse. May warned *Spearhead's* readers:

Let us be clear on one point. Should South Africa ever fall to the forces which threaten to engulf Western civilisation, we can be sure that Australia will be next on the list. Liberalism is a luxury which Australia simply cannot afford, if only for geographical reasons. No protection money will ever be sufficient to dissuade the teeming Asiatic billions from erupting into the island continent once they get their chance.[54]

May declared that the only way to "safeguard the nation from this fate" was the creation of the National Front of Australia, which he described as "an urgent and imperative necessity". "Native Australians", by which May meant white Australians with a British background, "are a proud, strong-minded and independent people", who also maintained their links to Britain. It was up to the NFA to "ensure that this distinctive national identity ... is encouraged, enforced and politically activated".[55]

May worked with a Melbourne law student named Rosemary Sisson to form the NFA. Sisson began her work towards building a National Front in Australia by publishing a mimeographed journal called *Australian Nationalist* in early 1978. The first issue called for a united Australian nationalist party and bemoaned the fact that the nationalist movement at that time was "almost hopelessly and irretrievably fragmented into mutually suspicious, competitive, and absurdly idiosyncratic, exclusive little groups".[56] But Sisson declared:

IT IS IMPERATIVE THAT WE REGROUP AND UNITE! Only though unity and the strength this gives us can we begin to tap and realise the incalculable political potential of national patriotism within this country.[57]

Sisson pointed to the British NF as the example "forever before our eyes" of the unification of several different far right groups.[58] *The Australian Nationalist* expressed a pro-British Commonwealth nationalism and its influences were very much drawn from the British fascist movement, rather than the American far right.

On Saturday 2 June 1978, a group of people gathered in a room of the Southern Cross Hotel in Melbourne city centre to launch the National Front of Australia. According to an ASIO informant, nine people attended the meeting, including several well-known far right activists, a 16-year-old schoolboy and an undercover reporter for the newspaper *The Age*.[59] Seven out of the nine were already known to the authorities in some regard. The schoolboy was David Greason, who later wrote an exposé of the Australia far right in the 1970s and 1980s in his memoir *I Was a Teenage Fascist*.[60] The meeting was led by Sisson, who had travelled to the UK in 1977 to seek permission from Tyndall to establish a National Front in Australia. According to ASIO, Tyndall had appointed Sisson to be chair of the NFA until a directing body was created.

In June 1978, the *Australian Nationalist* became *Frontline: Magazine of the National Fronts of Australia and New Zealand*, with the debut issue dedicated to the formation of the NFA. Quoting the opening address by Sisson, the meeting supposedly "mark[ed] an important event in the political history of Australia" by forming a new political party that "represents the future of the Australian people" and would "revive national pride".[61] The magazine also carried the text of a tape-recorded speech by Tyndall played at the meeting, in which Tyndall described Australia as a *terra nullius* transformed by British settlers into a bulwark of white civilization on the edges of the British Empire: "Australia was not so very long ago a wilderness inhabited by a few savages, and it took some very hardy, determined, self-reliant and tough pioneers to carve a great country and a great civilization out of that wilderness ..."[62] Tyndall enthused about the formation of the Commonwealth National Front, remarking that the "realisation of the National Front spanning the whole British Commonwealth has always been a dream to me", and with the establishment of the NFA, "the sight of this dream being fulfilled is enormous encouragement to me". Tyndall asserted that the NFA was not subordinate to the British NF and there were to be "equal partnerships" between the NF in the UK and those in Australia, New Zealand, and South Africa.[63] An article in *Frontline* stated that the CNF was to coordinate activities among the various National Fronts across the

Commonwealth, but would allow discretion to each NF to function as it desired. The article explained:

Subject to their adherence to a common set of basic principles and objectives, National Front organisations in various countries are free to determine their own rules of association, to make their own executive decisions and to determine themselves all policies relating to their own countries' domestic political affairs.

The above will include the right to determine whether the National Front in a particular country will function as a fully fledged political party, seeking power in its own right by the ballot box, or whether it will function merely as a pressure group or society for the furtherance of National Front ideals.[64]

The magazine also carried a letter of congratulations from the National Front of New Zealand's leader David Crawford, which described the NF as "the vanguard of the most impelling force ever to strike your country in the last 100 years".[65] Crawford mentioned that National Fronts now existed in Australia, New Zealand, South Africa, and Canada. The journal *Patterns of Prejudice* noted the announcement of the Commonwealth National Front in mid-1978, but stated that the only National Front that had been set up by that time was in New Zealand[66] – although by March 1979, ASIO believed that the NFNZ was "almost finished".[67] The Canadian National Front never seemed to get off the ground, and the National Front in South Africa was subsumed by the Afrikaner Herstigte Nasionale Party and the paramilitary Wit Kommando, after its leading figures resigned and one (Ray Hill) returned to the UK as an anti-fascist mole for *Searchlight* magazine.[68]

Beside the production of *Frontline*, there was little evidence of the NFA engaging in much political activity after the initial flurry of excitement around its founding in mid-1978. By 1980, *Patterns of Prejudice* was reporting that the NFA had between 100 and 300 members, but had been subject to infighting,[69] particularly as Sisson made trips to the UK to meet with Alan Birtley, an NF member jailed for weapons and explosives offences. In the UK general election in May 1979, the British NF contested more than 300 seats and was wiped out at the polls, receiving barely more than 1 per cent of the vote.[70] Similar electoral contests by the NFA led to the same results, with Sisson and Viktor Robb both failing dismally in the race for a Senate seat in Queensland during the 1980 federal election. This led to a number of defections to rival far right organizations, primarily those being developed by Jim Saleam and others with historical ties to the NSPA.

The British NF, which was seen as the beacon of the Commonwealth National Front, also collapsed after the 1979 election into warring factions. Tyndall formed the New National Front in 1980, and in 1982 transformed this into the British National Party (BNP). The remnants of the NF in the 1980s divided into several factions,[71] which competed with the more outwardly neo-Nazi British Movement and the BNP for support in the Thatcher years, primarily among football hooligans and skinheads.[72] Both factions of the NF flirted with Strasserism (emphasising the "left-wing" and "anti-capitalist" aspects of National Socialism), with one wing, led by Nick Griffin, Patrick Harrington, Joe Pearce, and Derek Holland, combining this with the idea of the "political soldier" and eschewing the electoralism of the NF of the 1970s.

As the British NF imploded, the NFA strongly supported the Tyndall wing, probably due to the links between Tyndall and Sisson. In the August 1980 edition of *Frontline*, the journal talked of "certain dissident factions" looking to take control of the NF after the 1979 election and announced to Australian readers the formation of Tyndall's New National Front (NNF). The NFA described the NNF as "a valiant effort to draw together the best elements of British nationalism into an instrument capable once again of offering effective opposition to the nation's tormentors".[73] From the following month onwards until the mid-1980s, *Frontline* regularly reproduced articles from Tyndall's *Spearhead* and, at times, advertised the local distribution of *Spearhead* via NFA contacts. When Tyndall formed the BNP in 1982, *Frontline* gave positive coverage to that organization as well – so much so that there was a regular "British National Party News" section in nearly every issue in 1984. However, by this time the NFA was not much more than those who produced *Frontline*, and the momentum of the Australian far right had swung to other groups who promoted a more "radical" Australian nationalism that shunned the pro-Britishness of the NFA.

Radical nationalism and National Action

Opposing the "Anglo-Nazism" of the National Front of Australia were a group of radical nationalists (such as Frank Salter, Jim Saleam, and Eddy Azzopardi) that centred around a number of small organizations and newspapers which eventually led to the formation of National Action in the early 1980s. National Resistance started as a far right student group in Sydney in the late 1970s, which soon changed its name to the (Australian) National Alliance (ANA). National Resistance first produced a newspaper called *Advance*, which became the newspaper of the ANA, before it changed its name to *Audacity* in 1978.

National Resistance portrayed itself as separate from the rest of the far right groups in Australia, emphasising a "radical" Australian nationalism that warned against both "foreign" communism (particularly Chinese communism) and capitalism (particularly US imperialism). A December 1977 edition of *Advance* stated:

NATIONAL RESISTANCE possesses a NEW nationalist perspective. It has dared to raise the Eureka Banner from its symbolic representation. It therefore challenges the Mao-line Peking-paid communists who are misusing the Eureka symbol.[74]

After National Resistance became the Australian National Alliance in early 1978, *Advance* declared that the ANA stood for "a new nation" and opposed those on the right who wanted "a modified, but still backward Old Order".[75] The ANA set itself against the Anglophilia of the Australian League of Rights and the National Front of Australia. When the NFA was formed in mid-1978, the ANA attacked it for its alleged attempt to transplant the programme of the British National Front on to Australian conditions, suggesting that the "National Front of Australia ... will probably become just a noisy League of Rights". The ANA claimed that the NFA "object[ed] to the Eureka flag and the spirit of independence" of the ANA and contended that the NFA "would accuse the National Alliance of having an anti-British sentiment".[76] In an article in *Quadrant* in 1981, Ted Murphy explained that the ANA (by now the Progressive Nationalist Party) "frequently expressed solidarity with white nations other than Australia but it always regarded the interests of Australia as paramount". Murphy argued that while the ANA "praised [the NF] as beneficial for Britain", the Front was "nevertheless criticized for having a colonialist attitude towards Australia".[77]

On the surface, it looked as if the ANA was rejecting the traditional influence of the British and American far right on the Australian movement, but David Greason wrote that those in the ANA were still influenced by the journals of the US far right, such as *Thunderbolt*, *National Vanguard*, and *Instauration*. Greason asserted, "We couldn't have got half of our illustrations for *Audacity* if we hadn't subscribed to the outpourings of the US far-right press."[78] The appeal of the American far right was that there was less of a colonial relationship, and unlike the NFA's subordination to the British NF, the American far right only served as inspiration for the ANA and its later incarnations, rather than offering a formal relationship. Since the days of the Australian Nationalist Workers Party in the late 1950s, sections of the Australian far right (such as the rival Nazi parties and later the ANA) had emphasized the Australian exceptionalism of their nationalism, separate from the British influence found in the ALOR and then the NFA. While seeing themselves as part of a globalized network of white European nations, the ANA also stressed that Australian nationalism needed to be demonstrably distinct from its overseas variants. Like the National Socialist Party of Australia, this was partly done by using a racialized version of Australian history, such as the Eureka Stockade, the "White Australia Policy", or the Pacific War, to establish connections between the ANA and the nation's settler-colonial past.

In 1981, the ANA merged with the Progressive Conservative Party and the Immigration Control Association to form the Progressive Nationalist

Party (PNP), still using the newspaper *Audacity*. At this time, the PNP started to look towards the shift occurring within the European far right and developments in the NF in Britain. While the NFA supported Tyndall and the New National Front, the PNP looked to the National Front, especially the Strasserism and "political soldier" lines being promoted by the NF journal *Nationalism Today*. Around this journal coalesced future British National Party leader Nick Griffin, Joe Pearce, Derek Holland, and Patrick Harrington, who were seen by the PNP as having "succeeded in bringing a radical fresh approach to the British nationalist scene". The PNP enthused: "Since the expulsion of both Conservatives and Anglo-Nazis from the British National Front, it has made real moves towards a realignment of its ideology towards what a British nationalism should be – as opposed to the Anglo-Nazism of the old NF."[79]

In April 1982, the PNP evolved into National Action (NA). Troy Whitford has written that NA "saw itself predominantly as a militant propaganda unit aiming to capitalise on the anti-immigration sentiments expressed in opinion polls and in public debates". For the most part, it rejected electoral politics, focusing on a cadre-like party structure with a "strong authoritarian leadership".[80] Despite its size, NA gained a reputation for violence throughout the 1980s, as evidenced by the 1991 National Inquiry into Racist Violence.[81]

The structure and outlook of NA had strong similarities with the "political soldier" wing of the NF in Britain and the "Third Positionists" in Europe. Third Positionism had evolved in France and Italy in the post-war period, combining anti-capitalism with "a Europeanized ultra-nationalism", and was taken up in the NF in Britain by Griffin, Pearce, and Holland.[82] This shifted the focus of the English-speaking far right from building networks in the Anglosphere to European-wide solidarity. In late 1984, *Audacity* published an editorial from *Nationalism Today* on the European Economic Community, which ridiculed the promotion by the Tyndall-era NF (and its Australian counterpart) of a white Commonwealth led by Britain, labelling it a "pipedream" that was "clearly unattainable and absurd to realistic Nationalists". Alternatively, the NF journal proposed: "the greatest danger of all – the foreign occupation of Europe – can only be ended by co-ordinated action chiefly by Britain, Germany, Italy and France. It may be possible for Britain to forge closer links with our kinfolk overseas, but only once they have Nationalist governments."[83]

National Action endorsed this viewpoint, arguing that a "patriotic" government needed to be installed in Australia first, and white European solidarity was an extension of this national agitation. Peter Coleman wrote a companion piece to this republished *Nationalism Today* editorial, positing that "contacts with likeminded groups in foreign countries" were important for the future, and declaring: "In the advent of Australian Nationalists coming to power, we would require considerable support, from any quarter. WE MUST THINK LONG-RANGE. Our work IS Australian, but it has a wider dimension."[84]

Nationalism Today also published articles on the work of NA in Australia, reinforcing the relationship between NA and the NF. David Greason wrote an article for the NF journal in 1982 announcing the formation of NA, and in 1984 the journal republished an article from *Audacity* on NA's self-described radical nationalism.[85] Written by Dave Merrett, the article again attempted to define NA's vision of Australian nationalism as something distinct: "Australian Nationalism is a progressive idea, it is radical. WE do not seek the 're-form' of the present system by expelling a minority racial group, and perhaps giving a face-lift to the current power structure. Australia means more than a new flag or constitution."[86]

While supportive of NA, there were some differences between the NF and NA. The NF's Derek Holland criticized NA for not perceiving "the essential threat that Zionism presents to nationalism and cultural differentiation everywhere", advising the Australian party "to pay more attention to the subject".[87] Although anti-Semitism was not as explicit in NA publications as in the publications of the National Socialist Party of Australia or the Australian League of Rights, anti-Semitism, coded as "anti-Zionism", could still be found in the pages of *National Action*.[88]

In early 1987, *National Action* noted that the NF (now the Official National Front) was still seeking to make a "Europe of Nations" network, with similar groups invited from across Europe, as well as NA.[89] Jim Saleam wrote in response to this, suggesting that "[c]onsidering the uniquely EUROPEAN problems" that this proposed network would face, it was "unlikely that National Action would actually join", though he highlighted that NA was interested in the fortunes of the far right abroad. Saleam further elaborated on this:

> While our party is "NATIONAL" in its colouring, its methods, its cultural-political context and its historical tasks, it is a FACT for us that whatever injures the global position of the "European Race", harms Australia as well. It is a FACT that the European countries are being "asked" to integrate politically, economically and "demo-graphically" with the Third World. Movements of resistance to this madness hatched in the collective brain of international liberalism, have grown stronger of late. In this sense, National Action is one of these movements of resistance. We can learn from, and in our own small way teach, other "Racial-Nationalist" movements ...
>
> Each country MUST "create" a party which expressed the cultural disposition of its People. To LEARN from each other, however CAN ONLY speed the moment of victory!![90]

An article in *National Action* in late 1988 further outlined the links between the International Third Positionist groups and NA in Australia. While avowing that NA did not belong entirely to the Third Positionist network, it acknowledged the similarities between NA and the ITP groups, particularly attempting to disassociate them from other neo-Nazi and white supremacist groups that had come before. Third Positionism had apparently rejected the "Ku Kluxism" and "White Power" of previous radical right-wing groups, which had a "preoccupation with 'superiority/inferiority' of races". Appropriating the language of liberation politics (and of apartheid), "the right to DIFFERENCE and IDENTITY for all has become the revolutionary way forward", which meant separate "development" for white Europeans in Europe, as well as in the settler-colonial countries such as Australia. The article declared, "THIRD WAY Nationalism is not an OPTION for us [in Australia]. It's a political necessity."[91]

While NA downplayed its links to the American far right, a breakaway group, the Australian Nationalist Movement (ANM), more readily looked to the US for inspiration. The ANM was founded by Jack Van Tongeren in Perth in the mid-1980s with a more explicit anti-Semitism mixed with the anti-Asian rhetoric it shared with NA.[92] In the late 1980s, the ANM started an anti-Asian and anti-Semitic poster campaign, which escalated to burglary and arson, with Van Tongeren eventually being jailed for his part in the firebombing of several Chinese restaurants.[93] Peter Henderson suggests that the ANM's trajectory towards political violence was inspired by the reading of the US white supremacist text *The Turner Diaries*,[94] which became a blueprint in the US for political violence and terrorism by far right extremists in the 1980s and 1990s. The aforementioned National Inquiry into Racist Violence was established by the Human Rights and Equal Opportunity Commission in 1988 in reaction to a perceived rise in racist attacks, including those conducted by people associated with these far right groups.[95] The inquiry concluded that Australia was not "in danger of a Fascist 'takeover' or racist violence in the form of 'lynchings'", but found that both NA and the ANM had been involved in directing violence against persons and property on the basis of their ethnic identity.[96] Although the membership of these groups was very small, one of the outcomes of the inquiry was increasing recognition that the threat that they presented needed to be taken seriously – an issue that has been contested in Australia since the 1990s.

Conclusion

The influence of the British, American, and European far right on the Australian movement continued into the 1990s. *Searchlight* noted that the US organization White Aryan Resistance was influential in the skinhead music scene in Australia in the early 1990s,[97] with the skinhead scene also taking inspiration from Combat 18 and Blood & Honour in Britain.[98] With the growth of the internet from the late 1990s onwards, the far right in Australia has become more interconnected with its overseas counterparts – a topic that is explored in more detail in Kyle Burke's chapter in this volume.[99] In recent years, various groups in Australia have been inspired by the English Defence League and similar far right movements in Europe.[100] These are the latest examples of a long history of influence of the international far right on groups in Australia, stretching back to the interwar period.

This chapter has traced how the Australian far right, in its various guises, often looked to the far right in Britain and the United States for inspiration, but at the same time attempted to shape this into a distinctly "Australian" form of extreme right-wing politics. This began with the Australian National Socialist Party and the National Socialist Party of Australia in the 1960s, which both looked to George Lincoln Rockwell's American Nazi Party and Colin Jordan's National Socialist Movement, taking an explicit neo-Nazi approach and mixing it with a celebration of Australia's violent settler-colonial past, such as the Eureka Stockade.

The Australian League of Rights rejected the explicit optics of neo-Nazism, but still indulged in racist and anti-Semitic politics from the 1950s, acting more as a right-wing pressure group than a fascist movement. The ALOR primarily promoted loyalty to the British Empire/Commonwealth and were opponents of decolonization, as well as projecting solidarity with South Africa and Rhodesia. Motivated by A. K. Chesterton's League of Empire Loyalists, the ALOR's Eric Butler formed League of Rights groups in Britain, New Zealand, and Canada in the 1960s and 1970s, but also maintained links with anti-Semitic groups in the US, such as the Liberty Lobby.

The National Front of Australia appeared in the late 1970s, attempting to build upon the momentum created by the NF in Britain over the previous decade. Like the ALOR, the NFA was highly supportive of the British Commonwealth as a "whites only" collective of the settler-colonial countries, and tried to transplant the programme of the British NF into the Australian context. Led by Rosemary Sisson, the NFA was strongly tied to John Tyndall's leadership of the NF, and when Tyndall left in the early 1980s to form the New National Front (then the British National Party), the NFA followed suit.

A group of "radical" nationalists endeavoured to develop an alternative to the Anglophilia of the ALOR and the NFA, beginning as National Resistance in 1977 and going through several incarnations until it became National Action in 1982. These groups sought to promote themselves as Australian nationalists first and foremost, but as David Greason has shown, there was still heavy borrowing from the international far right, such as the publications of US white supremacist groups. In the 1980s, NA (and its predecessor the Progressive Nationalist Party) fostered ties with "Third Positionists" in Europe, including the "political soldier" wing of the NF in Britain. The pan-European nationalism put forward by the Third Positionists appealed to NA's emphasis on racial nationalism and separate development for white Europeans in the settler colonies, but NA still emphasized that racial solidarity could only exist within the struggle for an Australian nationalist revolution.

Throughout the Cold War era, the Australian far right tapped into international networks of anti-communists, anti-Semites, white supremacists, and empire loyalists. Links were made primarily with similar groups in the US and Britain, with expressions of solidarity, the transfer of political ideas, and some organizational unity. The far right in Australia has its own history, but this chapter has sought to put this in an international context and highlight how developments in the far right overseas often impacted the Australian movement. Particularly since the Christchurch massacre in March 2019, perpetrated by an Australian in New Zealand and inspired by white supremacist tropes from around the globe, there has been much more focus on how the Australian far right fits into an international network of white supremacism and far right activism. While much of the discussion rightly focuses on present-day links, it is also important to place this within a historical context. This chapter demonstrates that the Cold War period was key to the reconfiguration of the far right in Australia, but just as significant was the influence of fascist and far right forces in Britain and North America, as well as continental Europe and southern Africa. In an era of a resurgent far right, understanding how the far right in Australia fits into this wider dynamic, both historically and in the present, is imperative.

Notes

1 I would like to thank Jimmy Yan, Ebony Nilsson, Jayne Persian, and Daniel Jones at the Searchlight Archive (University of Northampton) for their assistance with obtaining several of these resources. I would like to thank Graham Macklin and Aurelien Mondon for their comments on earlier drafts of the chapter.

2 See Richard Brockett, "The Australian Country Party, the Australian League of Rights and the Rural Crisis of 1968–1972", *The Electronic Journal of Australian and New Zealand History*, 1997, http://pandora.nla.gov.au/pan/10033/20050726-0000/www.jcu.edu.au/aff/history/articles/brockett.htm (accessed 4 August 2019); David Greason, "The League of Rights: A Reply to Brockett, 'The Australian Country Party, the Australian League of Rights and the Rural Crisis of 1968–1972'", *The Electronic Journal of Australian and New Zealand History*, 1997, http://pandora.nla.gov.au/pan/10033/20050726-0000/www.jcu.edu.au/aff/history/articles/greason.htm (accessed 4 August 2019).

3 Steve James, "The Policing of Right-Wing Violence in Australia", *Police Practice and Research* 6.2 (2005): 103–19.

4 See Kyle Burke, *Revolutionaries for the Right: Anticommunist Internationalism and Paramilitary Warfare in the Cold War* (Chapel Hill, NC: University of North Carolina Press, 2018).

5 Evan Smith, "The Pivot of Empire: Australia and the Imperial Fascism of the British Union of Fascists", *History Australia* 14.3 (2017): 378–94.

6 Gwenda Tavan, *The Long, Slow Death of White Australia* (Melbourne: Scribe, 2005), 89–108.

7 National Australian Workers Party, "Our National Programme", n.d., A6119 2244, National Archives of Australia, Canberra (hereafter NAA).

8 David Harcourt, *Everybody Wants to be Fuehrer: National Socialism in Australia and New Zealand* (Cremome, NSW: Angus and Robertson, 1972), 26.

9 Kathleen Belew, *Bring the War Home: The White Power Movement and Paramilitary America* (Cambridge, MA: Harvard University Press, 2018).

10 *National Socialist Bulletin*, August/September 1970, p. 2, A432 1963/2409 PART 1, NAA.

11 Peter Henderson, "Franke Browne and the Neo-Nazis", *Labour History* 89 (November 2005): 73–86 (82).

12 Andrew Moore, *The Right Road: A History of Right-Wing Politics in Australia* (Melbourne: Oxford University Press Australia, 1995), 86–7.

13 "National Socialist Party of Australia—Leslie Leisemann", 27 May 1965, A6119 2305, NAA.

14　"National Socialist Party of Australia", 28 July 1964, A432 1963/2409 PART 1, NAA.

15　Harcourt, *Everybody Wants to be Fuehrer*, 24.

16　*Canberra Times*, 9 September 1967, 10.

17　"Fortnightly Digest: National Socialist Party of Australia", 22 September 1967, A6119 2595, NAA.

18　Trevor Lawson, "Book Review Section", *Australian National Socialist Journal*, summer 1968, 5.

19　Ibid.

20　G. L. Rockwell, "In Hoc Signo Vinces", *Australian National Socialist Journal*, winter 1969, 18–21.

21　*Australian National Socialist Journal*, winter 1969, 1. For a discussion of the role that *The Turner Diaries* has played in the far right in the United States since the 1980s, see Terence Ball and Richard Dagger, "Inside *The Turner Diaries*: Neo-Nazi Scripture", *PS: Political Science & Politics* 30.4 (1997): 717–18.

22　*Australian National Socialist Journal*, summer 1970, 1.

23　Christopher Lee, "An Uncultured Rhymer and His Cultural Critics: Henry Lawson, Class Politics, and Colonial Literature", *Victorian Poetry* 40.1 (2002): 84–104 (89). The quote from Lawson was "The South must look to herself for strength in the storm that is yet to break …"

24　G. T. Parker, "Nothing Can Stop Us Now!!", *Australian National Socialist Journal*, summer 1970, 2–3; Frank Collin, "Viet Nam—Chicago Style", *Australian National Socialist Journal*, summer 1970, 13–15.

25　G. L. Rockwell, "In Hoc Signo Vinces: Part II", *Australian National Socialist Journal*, summer 1970, 23–5.

26　See John King, "Contested Interpretations, Confused Pedigree, Common Symbol: The Eureka Flag and Australian Nationalism, 1970–1985", *Victorian Historical Journal* 75.2 (2004): 145–60; Anne Beggs-Sunter, "Eureka: Gathering 'the Oppressed of All Nations'", *Australian Journal of Colonial History* 10.1 (2008): 15–34.

27　E. R. Wenberg, "Our National Socialist Folk Heritage: The Revolt at Eureka", *Australian National Socialist Journal*, summer 1970, 4–5.

28　E.R.C., "Editorial: Our First Twelve Months", *Australian National Socialist Journal*, winter 1968, 2.

29　*NSPA Newsletter*, September–October 1968, 2.

30　*Australian National Socialist Journal*, summer 1970, 1.

31　*National Socialist Action Report*, March 1972, 1.

32　Paul Jackson, "Dreaming of a National Socialist World: The World Union of National Socialists (WUNS) and the Recurring Vision of Transnational Neo-Nazism", *Fascism* 8 (2019): 275–306 (292).

33 "Australia", *WUNS Bulletin*, July 1972, 2.

34 Ibid.

35 "In Memoriam", *WUNS Bulletin*, July 1972, 11.

36 Cited in Moore, *The Right Road*, 67.

37 Letter from Charles Spry to Billy Snedden, 7 December 1965, A6122 1628, NAA.

38 Andrew A. Campbell, *The Australian League of Rights: A Study in Political Extremism and Subversion* (Collingwood, Vic.: Outback Press, 1978), 32–9.

39 Campbell, *The Australian League of Rights*, 10.

40 "Soft Selling Anti-Semitism: *Searchlight* looks at the League of Rights", *Searchlight* 49 (1979), 3; Moore, *The Right Road*, 66.

41 "League of Empire Loyalists", SAPOL Special Branch report, 11 February 1958, p. 1, D1918 S3039, NAA (Adelaide).

42 "League of Empire Loyalists", 2.

43 "League of Empire Loyalists Formed", *New Times*, 6 July 1954, 6.

44 Eric Butler, "The Plotters Behind the World Crisis", *Spearhead*, June 1974, 12–14.

45 "British Peddlers of 'Anti-Communist' Literature", *Patterns of Prejudice* 17.2 (1983), 39.

46 *Beverly Times* (Queensland), 6 November 1975, 5.

47 Advertisement for British League of Rights, back cover of Eric Butler, *Censored History*.

48 "British Peddlers of 'Anti-Communist' Literature", 6; "Don Martin's Anti-Semitics Circus Comes to Town", *Searchlight*, December 1985, 4.

49 Robert Bartell, "Only Irate Citizenry Have Effected Real Change in Government", *New Times*, November 1982, 4.

50 "World's First Anti-Holocaust Convention", *New Times*, April 1980, 5.

51 Paul Stocker, "The Postwar British Extreme Right and Empire, 1945–1967", *Religion Compass* 9.5 (2015): 162–72.

52 "The National Front", *Britain First*, July 1975, 6.

53 Jeremy May, "Towards a National Front of Australia", *Spearhead*, May 1978, 17.

54 Ibid.

55 Ibid.

56 "Editorial", *The Australian Nationalist*, January 1978, 1, A6122 2553, NAA.

57 Ibid., 2.

58 Ibid.

59 ASIO Intelligence Report, "National Front of Australia", 8 June, 1978, p. 1, A6122 2553, NAA.

60 David Greason, *I Was a Teenage Fascist* (Ringwood, Vic.: McPhee Gribble 1994).

61 "National Front of Australia Formed", *Frontline*, June 1978, 1, A6122 2554, NAA.

62 Ibid., 6.

63 Ibid., 4–5.

64 "The Commonwealth National Front", *Frontline*, June 1978, 3, A6122 2554, NAA.

65 "A Message from the NF New Zealand on the Occasion of the Formation of the National Front of Australia", *Frontline*, June 1978, 8, A6122 2554, NAA.

66 "National Front's 'Global Network'", *Patterns of Prejudice* 12.2 (1978), 12.

67 ASIO Intelligence Report, "National Front of Australia", 23 March 1979, A6122 2554, NAA.

68 "National Front Setback", *Patterns of Prejudice* 12.4 (1978), 11; Ray Hill and Andrew Bell, *The Other Face of Terror: Inside Europe's Neo-Nazi Network* (London: Grafton, 1988), 63–5.

69 "Subversion Down Under", *Patterns of Prejudice* 14.3 (1980), 35.

70 Christopher T. Husbands, "The National Front: What Happens to it Now?", *Marxism Today*, September 1979, 268.

71 Nigel Copsey, *Contemporary British Fascism: The British National Party and the Quest for Legitimacy* (Basingstoke: Palgrave Macmillan, 2004), 36–46.

72 See Anti-Nazi League, *British Movement: Nazis on our Streets* (London: ANL pamphlet, 1981), 12–13; Roger Eatwell, *Fascism: A History* (London: Pimlico, 2003), 343.

73 "National Front News", *Frontline*, August 1980, 7.

74 "Who?", *Advance*, December 1977, 4.

75 "Who?", *Advance*, January/February 1978, 8.

76 "The National Front", *Audacity*, 6, 1978, 5.

77 Ted Murphy, "Australian Fascism", *Quadrant*, November 1981, 6.

78 Greason, *I Was a Teenage Fascist*, 158.

79 "Jailed!", *Audacity*, February/March 1982, 5.

80 Troy Whitford, "A Political History of National Action: Its Fears, Ideas, Tactics and Conflicts", *Rural Society*, April 2011, 217.

81 James, "The Policing of Right-Wing Violence in Australia", 105.

82 Roger Griffin, "Alien Influence? The International Context of the BNP's 'Modernization'", in Nigel Copsey and Graham Macklin (eds), *The British National Party: Contemporary Perspectives* (London: Routledge, 2011), 193–6.

83 Cited in "Our Stand Endorsed", *Audacity*, November 1984, 14.

84 Peter Coleman, "International?", *Audacity*, November 1984, 14.

85 David Greason, "The Invasion of Australia", *Nationalism Today*, June 1982, 12; Dave Merrett, "Are We Radicals?", *Nationalism Today*, September 1984, 13.

86 Merrett, "Are We Radicals?", 13.

87 Derek Holland, "Advance Australia Fair", *Nationalism Today*, May 1985, 18.

88 See "'Nazis'/Zionists Unite?", *National Action*, January 1987, 5; "No to 'War Crimes' Trials", *National Action*, November/December 1988, 12. For a discussion of the use of anti-Zionism as veiled anti-Semitism by the Anglophone far right, see Benjamin Bland, "Holocaust Inversion, anti-Zionism and British Neo-Fascism: The Israel-Palestine Conflict and the Extreme Right in Post-War Britain", *Patterns of Prejudice* 53.1 (2019): 86–97.

89 "International", *National Action*, January 1987, 6.

90 Jim Saleam, "A Nationalist 'International': Our Attitude", *National Action*, January 1987, 6, 14.

91 "The Third Way: Origins of a Term", *National Action*, November/December 1988, 10.

92 James, "The Policing of Right-Wing Violence in Australia", 105.

93 Peter Henderson, "A History of Australian Extreme Right since 1950", PhD diss., University of Western Sydney, 2002, 222–3; James, "The Policing of Right-Wing Violence in Australia", 105.

94 Henderson, "A History of Australian Extreme Right since 1950", 222–3.

95 Stephen Nugent, Meredith Wilkie, and Robyn Iredale, "Racist Violence", *Violence Today* 8 (1989), 2.

96 Human Rights and Equal Opportunity Commission, *Racist Violence: Report of the National Inquiry into Racist Violence in Australia* (Canberra: Australian Government Publishing Service, 1991), 176, 167.

97 "LaRouchites Take Up Bushwhacking", *Searchlight*, October 1991, 13.

98 Ryan Shaffer, *Music, Youth and International Links in Post-War British Fascism: The Transformation of Extremism* (Basingstoke: Palgrave Macmillan, 2017), 129.

99 Danny Ben-Mosche, "'One Nation' and the Australian Far Right", *Patterns of Prejudice* 35.3 (2001): 24–40; Imogen Richards, "A Dialectical Approach to Online Propaganda: Australia's United Patriots Front, Right-Wing Politics, and Islamic State", *Studies in Conflict & Terrorism* 42 (2019): 43–69.

100 Andy Fleming and Aurelien Mondon, "The Radical Right in Australia", in Jens Rydgren (ed.), *The Oxford Handbook of the Radical Right* (Oxford: Oxford University Press, 2018), 660–2.

9

"It's a white fight and we've got to win it": culture, violence, and the transatlantic far right since the 1970s

Kyle Burke

IN THE SUMMER of 1990, some two hundred white supremacists gathered on the remote estate of an Oklahoma farmer for Aryan Fest, a three-day-long concert and rally. Organized by the California group White Aryan Resistance (WAR), Aryan Fest was meant to politicize and radicalize young American skinheads.[1] The leader of WAR, a former Klansman from suburban San Diego named Tom Metzger, had been thrilled by the spread of skinhead subculture across the United States in the late 1980s, seeing in it profound political potential. "I was the first in the country to recognize skinheads and befriend them," he later boasted.[2] Along the West Coast, Metzger's group recruited heavily at skinhead shows, building a loose network of militant followers.[3]

By staging Aryan Fest, Metzger hoped to recruit more skinheads from other parts of the country, transforming them into the shock troops of a growing white power movement. Others thought the same. Neo-Nazi and white supremacist leaders from as far away as Idaho and West Virginia arrived at the Oklahoma compound with boxes of literature, T-shirts, posters, and recorded speeches. Between sets, they took to the stage, reciting well-worn right-wing liturgies about Jewish conspiracies for world domination, the racial inferiority of African Americans, and the deluge of dangerous foreigners arriving on American soil.[4]

The real action, however, was the music. Among the festival's headliners was the British band No Remorse, a major part of England's burgeoning white power music scene. Mixing punk rock with fascist politics, No Remorse had helped propel a flourishing far right mobilization in Britain, pulling young men into the National Front and other groups. Metzger, following suit, believed skinhead music would guide American men into White Aryan Resistance and kindred groups in the United States. But the concert was about more than recruitment. Metzger thought skinhead culture would help unite white supremacists around the world. In the pages of his group's newsletter, he gushed about Aryan Fest's significance, explaining that the show was but the first of many to come, and that it was already making waves in other white enclaves. Within a month, WAR was selling tapes of the concert in Canada, Britain, Germany, and Australia. Soon, Metzger hoped, Aryan Fest cassettes would make their way into "White Russia," where the Soviet government was on the verge of collapse.[5]

As Metzger suggested, WAR and the skinhead bands who played at Aryan Fest were part of a transnational white power movement that spanned large swaths of the globe. Convinced that white men in the United States, Britain, northern Europe, Russia, Australia, and New Zealand shared a common racial, cultural, and religious past—and therefore faced common challenges in the late twentieth century—white power activists disseminated texts, sold records, raised money, and hosted international gatherings. Reworking Nazi doctrines, they vilified immigrants and non-whites as inferior and unassimilable, and ranted about Jewish plots to conquer the world. But those old racist tropes took on new meaning as white supremacists fretted about new geopolitical shifts. In their eyes, the flows of people and capital wrought by decolonization and globalization threatened the end of white societies in the West. Conjuring crude villains, they claimed their countries were being flooded with foreigners who stole jobs and social benefits and schemed to replace existing national cultures with their own. Soon, they predicted, white people, the bedrock of Euro-American civilization, would vanish under this rising tide of multiculturalism and race-mixing. "It's not an American fight or a British fight or a German fight," concluded one English activist. "It is a white fight and we've got to win it."[6]

To wage that international fight, far right leaders and activists in the U.S., Britain, and elsewhere turned to popular culture. For Metzger and others, skinhead music articulated a vision of besieged white masculinity that could bring young, radical men into politics. Concerts like Aryan Fest were useful recruiting grounds, and the music itself could move across national borders and touch minds in places where far right leaders would never go—and in some cases, could never go, due to growing state surveillance. Radio and public access television was another viable medium, and many groups broadcast their messages. Other leaders turned to white power literature, which also traveled more easily than people. Before the advent of the internet, white supremacists utilized books, magazines, radio shows, record labels, and concerts to make a transnational movement.

Theirs was not a formal political movement united around a central organization, but instead a decentered movement with a common language and shared concerns, convictions, and strategies. Circulating within this world and drawing it together was an affinity for violence. Some white power activists targeted perceived foes in their own communities through beatings, stabbings, and arson. But a select few were more ambitious, launching terrorist plots that killed scores of people. Culture played a key role in stoking that violence, for it provided fantasies of white male power and action that shaped how white power partisans saw themselves and the world around them.

* * *

The white power movements that coalesced across the Atlantic in the late 1970s and early 1980s came after decades of failure. In the 1930s, fascist groups in the United States, Britain, and Europe started to see each other as potential allies. Yet they never established a workable program for international collaboration, and their affinity for Nazi Germany marginalized them from mainstream political life during and after World War II.[7]

The dream of a fascist international remained elusive for decades. Its proponents were scattered and contentious, had few resources, and were subject to persistent state scrutiny. The most enduring effort came from George Lincoln Rockwell, leader of the American Nazi Party and author of *White Power*, who founded the World Union of National Socialists in 1959.[8] But when a former member of the American Nazi Party murdered Rockwell in 1967, the World Union of National Socialists lost its driving force. The group limped through the 1970s, passing through the hands of a few different leaders while its already minimal influence further evaporated.[9] Meanwhile, the Ku Klux Klan and other armed white power groups had started to fall apart by the mid-1970s, the result of growing popular antipathy and sustained state pressure.[10]

For Tom Metzger, the disintegration of this older world of white supremacy hit home. An army veteran and television repairman, Metzger had moved through a series of right-wing groups including the John Birch Society and the Minutemen, a guerrilla organization that sought to overthrow the U.S. government in the 1960s. In 1975, he joined David Duke's Knights of the Ku Klux Klan, rising to become Grand Dragon of the California branch. In that role, Metzger led the Klan's Border Watch, hoping to snare migrants entering the country from Mexico. But he and Duke soon had a falling out, and Metzger grew disillusioned with the Klan.[11]

Metzger's struggles in the far right were matched by his dissatisfaction with electoral politics. He saw signs of degeneration everywhere in post-Vietnam America—oil embargoes, energy crises, inflation, stagnation, deindustrialization, and urban decline. Politicians from both major parties seemed incapable of resolving these issues. In his eyes, the establishment had sold out white American men to accommodate racially inferior African Americans, uppity women, sexual deviants, and recently arrived non-white immigrants.[12] He began promoting "pro-white" candidates for office, and even launched his own unsuccessful electoral bid for the U.S. Senate in California.[13]

When conventional politics failed, Metzger decided that only militant action could set things right. In 1983, he founded White Aryan Resistance and its junior wing, the Aryan Youth Movement, in a suburban community north of San Diego. He saw himself as a latter-day Lenin leading a revolutionary vanguard, with a small number of "dedicated people" working through a "fanatical inner-structure," as Metzger put it.[14] The ultimate goal was to "overthrow the U.S. government and eliminate Jews and blacks."[15] In monthly editions of *White Aryan Resistance*, a short, crudely manufactured periodical that Metzger bragged was the "most racist newspaper on earth," he urged his followers to create chaos in the streets.[16] He predicted the government would fail, causing ordinary Americans to take up arms and start killing each other. In time, he said, this race war would destroy the federal government.

To develop this vision, Metzger turned to television. For years he ran a late-night cable-access program, *Race and Reason*, which he billed as a "small island of free speech in a sea of controlled and managed news."[17] A call-in talk show, it featured regular guest appearances from J. B. Stoner, a Klan leader who had bombed a Birmingham church in 1958, and Ben Klassen, founder of the Church of the Creator, who urged whites to launch a "Racial Holy War."[18] Through *Race and Reason*, Metzger created the appearance of a national following, earning him media coverage on shows such as *Geraldo*, *Crossfire*, and the *Oprah Winfrey Show*. In the spotlight, Metzger and a few skinheads spouted vitriol, riled up the audience, and physically attacked the other guests. Setting themselves apart from—and in opposition to—mainstream conservative elites, the men of WAR cultivated a hypermasculine, working-class, anti-authoritarian image.[19]

Metzger's militancy dovetailed with that of William Pierce, an emerging white power intellectual and organizer. A descendent of the southern aristocracy—his great-great-grandfather was the governor of Alabama during the Civil War—Pierce earned a doctorate in physics from the University of Colorado but turned his back on an academic career. A member of the John Birch Society, Pierce worked for the aerospace manufacturer Pratt Whitney, a leading defense contractor, but quit after a few years to join Rockwell's American Nazi Party. As editor of the *National Socialist World*, Pierce built relationships with a handful of like-minded figures from Britain and Europe. Yet he also flirted on the edges of mainstream conservative politics in the late 1960s, helping to line up votes for George Wallace's failed 1968 bid for the presidency, a campaign that galvanized many white supremacists.

Wallace's failure convinced Pierce that a new strategy was needed. He founded the National Alliance in 1974. Like Metzger, Pierce saw his group as a revolutionary vanguard that would guide the *lumpen* white masses into a war to save their race. Believing the electoral game was rigged, Pierce also sought power through paramilitary action, blending an old tradition of white vigilante violence with the kind of guerrilla warfare advocated by leftist national liberation movements. Pierce organized his small band of followers into cells and talked of a cleansing struggle for the United States.[20] As he explained, "All the homosexuals, race mixers, and hard-case collaborators who are too far gone to be re-educated can be rounded up, packed into 10,000 or so railroad cars, and eventually double-timed to an abandoned coal mine in a few days' time."[21]

Pierce's calls for violence resonated most powerfully in his influential 1978 novel, *The Turner Diaries*, published under the pen name Andrew MacDonald. Told from the perspective of a white government looking back on its triumph in the "Great Revolution," the book documents the life of Earl Turner, a hero in the war to save the white race. Recruited into a guerrilla movement known as the Organization, Turner battles a totalitarian U.S. government known as the System which has confiscated Americans' weapons, ended rape laws, and allowed African Americans and Jews to take over the country. For ten years, Turner stages hit-and-run attacks against the System, blowing up the FBI's headquarters in Washington, D.C., and lobbing mortars at Congress. These efforts lead to Turner's induction into a secret leadership, called the Order. After the "Day of the Rope," on which the Order lynches thousands of white media figures, academics, and women for betraying their race, it launches missiles at the Soviet Union, which sparks a nuclear war that cripples the System. Turner delivers the death blow when he flies a plane loaded with a nuclear warhead into the Pentagon.[22] A fantasy tale of white martial manhood, the *Turner Diaries* joined the canon of far right literature alongside Adolf Hitler's *Mein Kampf* and George Lincoln Rockwell's *White Power*.

Advertised in *Soldier of Fortune* magazine and other paramilitary periodicals, the book sold hundreds of thousands of copies over the following years.[23] Its portrayal of the System lent credence to an older right-wing conspiracy theory that said the United States was in fact ruled by the Zionist Occupation Government, or ZOG, a dictatorial Jewish regime that controlled domestic and international affairs from the shadows. Its calls for guerrilla warfare reverberated not only in the United States, but also across the Atlantic.[24]

* * *

As Pierce and Metzger dreamed of violent revolution in the United States, their counterparts in the British far right were gaining ground. Heirs to Oswald Mosley's British Union of Fascists, they had been marginal figures in British public life for decades after World War II. But new developments had brought them fresh support. As the British Empire collapsed, and large numbers of non-white immigrants arrived from the Commonwealth countries, narratives of national decline and cultural disappearance imbued mainstream politics. Those anxieties registered most profoundly in Conservative MP Enoch Powell's famous "Rivers of Blood" speech and its aftermath. Warning that the large-scale immigration of non-whites threatened to send the country down a spiral of insecurity, anarchy, and racial violence, Powell remade Britain's recent past—World War II and the end of the empire—into a "myth of Britain permanently under siege."[25] Powell tapped into and deepened a feeling among many whites that they were victims of elite politicians and foreign peoples whose very presence suggested that the mythic, white England of the past was gone.[26]

In this new climate, the British far right regrouped. At its core was the National Front, a small but growing political force that wanted to reclaim Britain for white people, most notably through the forced repatriation of non-white immigrants. By 1972, the National Front was under the leadership of John Tyndall, an ex-member of the World Union of National Socialists who had founded several fascist and neo-Nazi groups over the years. His National Socialist Movement, active in the early 1960s, advocated Nazi doctrines and organized its members into a paramilitary unit called Spearhead—acts which earned Tyndall a six-month prison sentence.[27] After prison, Tyndall found his way into the National Front, and eventually seized power from rival leaders. At the helm, Tyndall led the National Front into its strongest period of growth, drawing some 17,500 members in 1972 and 1973. He enticed recruits by hammering on three interrelated issues: non-white immigration, national decline, and a disappearing British cultural identity. The violence of the Irish Republican Army, which brought its bombing campaign to London and other cities, gave his appeals a deeper sense of urgency. Decolonization, it seemed, had come home in the form of guerrilla war on the mainland. By the late 1970s, as inflation and unemployment skyrocketed, the National Front had earned a visible presence in British political life, winning 120,000 votes in the Greater London Council elections of 1977.[28]

But elections were only part of the National Front's strategy. To forge a common identity and gain publicity, it trotted out the myths and symbols of the Empire. The National Front staged elaborate processions in which a legion of men carried British flags alongside the banners of Northern Ireland, South Africa, and Rhodesia. Mimicking mass Nazi spectacles, the marches were often marked by violence.[29] Tyndall also began seeking allies abroad. He rekindled his friendship with William Pierce, whom he had met through the World Union of National Socialists. In 1979, Tyndall came to the United States, spending a week at the National Alliance's fortified compound in West Virginia.[30]

As the National Front became Britain's most prominent far right party, cultural developments suggested its brand of politics might appeal to a new generation. Chief among them was the rise of the skinhead subculture and its explicitly racist offshoots. Although most skinheads resisted any straightforward political affiliation—and some had links to anarchist and leftist groups—a few bands found their voice on the right. Incorporating fascist, anti-immigrant, and racist motifs into their lyrics, they exhorted rebellion against the same enemies the National Front targeted—elite politicians, non-whites, and foreigners.[31]

Skinhead culture and far right politics found common ground via an aesthetic of hypermasculine violence. Yet the skinhead scene did not simply breed fascists or neo-Nazis. Rather, neo-Nazis and fascists sought it out to build grassroots support. The far-right British Movement was the first to do so. Members began recruiting heavily at skinhead shows, building a hardcore set of followers who liked to go "Paki-bashing," targeting South Asian immigrants in brutal assaults.[32] The National Front followed suit. The effort came not from the top ranks of the National Front—John Tyndall despised skinheads—but instead from local organizers. They had been to the concerts, and they knew people in the scene.[33] As Leeds district organizer Eddy Morrison explained, skinhead music was a "powerful weapon for anyone who could turn it politically."[34] As part of the National Front's new youth wing, founded in 1977, Morrison and others traveled to shows, distributed pamphlets, and talked politics with concertgoers. This effort extended into other arenas of working-class life where National Front recruiters found large numbers of young men and large quantities of alcohol, particularly at football matches. By the early 1980s, the National Front had made inroads into several football hooligan "firms" for major clubs like Chelsea, Arsenal, Leeds, and Millwall.[35]

Of course, it helped that a few musicians already shared the National Front's worldview. One was Ian Stuart Donaldson—often referred to simply as Ian Stuart—the leader of Skrewdriver, perhaps the most successful skinhead band of the 1980s. An avowed admirer of Hitler, Mussolini, Oswald Mosley, and Robert E. Lee, Stuart served as a paid youth organizer for the National Front in the late 1970s and early 1980s, turning his band's shows into recruiting grounds.[36] Having dabbled in right-wing political thought for a few years, he adopted the National Front's party line full sail, arguing that Britain had fallen apart in the 1970s. For him, this "degeneration of society" had occurred under both Conservative and Labour governments, "speeded up by the massive immigration into this country of so many inferior cultures, who introduce such 'benefits' as drugs, mugging, rioting [and] looting."[37] The National Front promised to turn the tide, and music would help guide the way.[38] Stuart's lyrics laid this out in plain terms. In his song "Hail the New Dawn," a reworking of the British Union of Fascists' anthem, he anticipated the white race's ultimate victory:

> The streets are still, the final battle has ended
> Flushed with the fight, we proudly hail the dawn
> See over the streets, the White man's emblem is waving
> Triumphant standards of a race reborn[39]

In another song, Skrewdriver's trademark "White Power," titled after George Lincoln Rockwell's notorious book, Stuart howled:

> I stand and watch my country, going down the drain
> We are all at fault, we are all to blame
> We're letting them take over, we just let 'em come
> Once we had an Empire, and now we've got a slum
>
> White Power! For England
> White Power! Today
> White Power! For Britain
> Before it gets too late[40]

For listeners, there was little ambiguity about what he meant. The same held for other bands, like No Remorse and Skullhead, which also spread overtly racist and fascist political messages in their music and interviews.

In 1979, the National Front embarked upon a more concerted effort to claim skinhead culture with the formation of the Rock against Communism (RAC) movement. A response to the Rock against Racism movement—which sponsored hundreds of gigs in the late 1970s and early 1980s, often under the aegis of the Socialist Workers Party and other leftist groups—RAC sought to steer skinhead music away from anarchism and radical progressive politics to become *the* soundtrack of British fascism. The far right activists linked through RAC-sponsored shows recruited fledgling white power bands and published record reviews in the National Front's *Bulldog* and other magazines.

As its fascist politics became clearer, skinhead music was forced underground in the early 1980s. Promoters started to organize shows in secret to avoid disruption from the Anti-Nazi League and other groups. The National Front chose to set up its own label, the White Noise Club, helping turn fascist punk into a "self-contained micro scene," increasingly isolated from other strains of punk culture, especially those associated with leftist and anarchist politics.[41] Away from the usual circuit of bars and clubs, the White Noise Club sponsored concerts featuring white power bands from across the United Kingdom, France, Germany, and Scandinavia.[42] At one major White Noise festival, held in 1987 at a Suffolk farm owned by the parents of future British National Party leader Nick Griffin, Skrewdriver headlined along with several bands from Europe.[43]

That same year, Ian Stuart founded Blood & Honour, a neo-Nazi organization "independent from any recognized far-right party."[44] Named after the motto of the Hitler Youth, Blood & Honour hoped to be the new home for white power music. Through it, Stuart sought to bring "together racist groups that previously had been at odds" while also disseminating white power music internationally. Putting out records, publishing a slick magazine, and sponsoring international tours, Blood & Honour joined the National Front and other groups in spreading the skinhead movement to both sides of the Atlantic.[45]

* * *

Despite the limited appeal and fierce rivalries that defined the British skinhead scene, white power music began to arrive in the United States in the mid-1980s. The National Front led the way through the White Noise Club, which produced and distributed some 10,000 records, published a magazine, and organized overseas tours for skinhead groups.[46] One National Front organizer explained the purpose in all this was to "build a network of connections with like-minded groups and organizations around the world to operate internationally."[47] Through White Noise and other channels, Americans were grafted onto British skinhead subculture. They copied the styles, purchased the records, and started their own magazines. British skinhead culture provided an aesthetic for an "authentic" white working class. Soon American skinhead bands were traveling to Griffin's estate to play festivals put on by the National Front or gigs organized by Stuart's Blood & Honour.

As in Britain, American skinheads were quick to embrace violence. In Chicago, for instance, white power activist Clark Martell imported and sold Skrewdriver records. He soon recruited a few dozen young men for his Chicago Area Skinheads, a gang devoted to street violence. They beat up several Latina women, broke into homes, spray-painted swastika graffiti, and attacked parade-goers at the city's annual Gay and Lesbian Pride parade. Seeing his gang as a kind of militia, Martell spent a few weeks in 1986 training at the camp of Robert Miles, a Michigan Klan leader who wrote articles in *White Aryan Resistance* denouncing what he called the Zionist Occupation Government and urging whites to form a separate state in the Pacific Northwest.[48]

Across the country, from Florida to Washington, small skinhead groups popped up. By 1988, the Anti-Defamation League estimated there were two thousand skinheads in the U.S. Their small numbers belied their power. "Virtually everywhere they are," Anti-Defamation League researchers said, "they're engaged in criminal activity."[49] They also merged with older white supremacist groups. In Bradenton, Florida, for instance, local skinheads staged a march with the city's Ku Klux Klan chapter, protesting an NAACP demonstration at a Confederate monument.[50]

The skinheads' emergence in the United States delighted far right leaders like Tom Metzger, who thought they would serve as stormtroopers in the unfolding racial struggle.[51] To him, white power music was the best way to politicize skinheads—"the most powerful message in the country today for the white race."[52] Metzger, who was fifty years old in 1988, started selling tapes and vinyl from the National Front's White Noise label and Germany's Rock-O-Rama records, as well as videos of Skrewdriver's performance at Nick Griffin's family property, in which Ian Stuart praised Metzger on stage.[53] In 1989, Metzger put on an "Aryan Woodstock" in Napa County, drawing bands from as far as Milwaukee and Philadelphia.[54] The following year, one of Metzger's affiliates hosted the first Aryan Fest in Oklahoma, which would become an annual fixture, attracting more and more bands from the United Kingdom, Germany, and elsewhere.[55]

William Pierce saw promise in the skinheads too. In the pages of *White Aryan Resistance*, he explained, "we will win the war only by killing our enemies, not by any clever, indirect schemes which involve no personal risk." Skinheads could spearhead that campaign through low-level, vigilante assaults: "someone who cracks the enemy's skull in the street with a baseball bat, rips his face open with a bicycle chain, or breaks his legs across a curbstone." For that was a "healthy red-blooded response to the current situation in America's cities."[56]

Indeed, communal violence was the core of skinhead culture. Many young men who joined the gangs felt rejected from their families, their communities, and the broader currents of American life. Their skinhead brethren provided a sense of belonging, and the violence offered a feeling of power. On the streets of San Diego, Portland, Chicago, Tampa, and many other cities, skinhead gangs terrorized their enemies, sparking headlines in major newspapers across the country. By 1990, several skinheads had been prosecuted for assault, arson, and murder, causing local police forces and the FBI to direct more attention to their activities.[57]

As American skinheads grew more organized and more violent, the broader U.S. white power movement took on new paramilitary dimensions. Driving that shift was Louis Beam, a Vietnam veteran and Klansman from Texas. Beam had outlined the strategy of "leaderless resistance" in an influential tract called *Essays by a Klansman*, later translated into a half-dozen languages. Rather than unite disparate bands under a single leader, Beam urged white supremacists to form an underground of independent cells, capable of working toward a common cause, but self-reliant enough to withstand the collapse of other cells. Modeled on how Beam understood communist undergrounds, as well as the guerrilla heroics of *The Turner Diaries*, "leaderless resistance" signaled the far right's shift toward a more decentered, and more destructive, form of paramilitary violence.[58] This thinking refracted the wars of the decolonizing world into domestic terrorism. Tom Metzger loved it. "Much of what we will have to learn has actually been well articulated by the leftist national liberation movements," said one writer in *White Aryan Resistance.* "What that entails is a resistance battle which partakes of guerrilla warfare techniques in every possible aspect."[59]

Guided by these fantasies, two WAR members helped found the neo-Nazi terror group known as the Order. Inspired by the group of the same name in Pierce's *Turner Diaries,* the Order started robbing shops and armored security cars in 1983, seeking funds for war against the federal government. The bounty from these heists, totaling more than $4 million, circulated across the American white power movement. Tom Metzger received some $300,000. Others affiliated with WAR, like William Pierce, received smaller sums. This money helped mobilize—and militarize—white power groups across the United States, even though the Order collapsed in 1986.[60]

To Metzger, the Order embodied the kind of armed action that he wished to see from skinheads and others in the white power movement. To mythologize the group and guide his supporters toward violence, Metzger regularly featured interviews and writings from incarcerated members of the Order—"Prisoners of War," as he called them—in the pages of WAR's eponymous newspaper.[61] Through WAR and other groups, one incarcerated member of the Order, David Lane, would popularize what would become the most influential white power slogan, known simply as the Fourteen Words: "We must secure the existence of our people and a future for white children."[62]

Fearing the loose bands of skinheads affiliated with Metzger might follow the Order's example, the FBI stepped up its investigation of White Aryan Resistance. Through informants, observers, and a rigorous collection of WAR's printed material, the FBI deduced that it posed a serious threat to civil order.[63] As federal authorities chipped away at WAR, Metzger faced dogged pursuit from civil rights organizations. In 1990, WAR nearly collapsed after three skinheads in Portland murdered an Ethiopian student, Mulugeta Seraw. The Southern Poverty Law Center won a civil lawsuit that laid the ultimate responsibility at Metzger's feet.

A few weeks before the murder, Metzger had sent a recruiter to Portland to organize local skinheads, and press them toward street violence. The court ordered WAR to forfeit its headquarters and pay $12 million in damages to Seraw's family, which nearly bankrupted the organization.[64]

Afterwards, Metzger and those around him turned underground, continuing to believe that only a violent uprising could set things right. From the WAR offices in suburban San Diego—renamed Robert Mathews Hall, in honor of the Order's dead leader—Metzger maintained a phone hotline on which he recorded messages exhorting listeners to violence. Meanwhile, *White Aryan Resistance* published a four-part series entitled "Whitey Revolutionary," telling readers how to become guerrillas. By picking up arms, they would rekindle the martial masculinity that had made the United States a white man's country, joining the pantheon of Aryan heroes. As one writer in *White Aryan Resistance* put it, "Young terrorists, or freedom fighters, gain eternal glory by joining the fight, and reverence toward them is amplified by martyrdom or sainthood if they perish in the course of violent duty."[65]

A few took the message to heart. In 1993, 17-year-old Richard Campos committed a string of firebombings in Sacramento. He targeted a city councilman's house, a synagogue, NAACP offices, the Japanese American Citizens League, and a state anti-discrimination agency. Campos was not a formal member of WAR, but investigators discovered he called Metzger's phone hotline thirty-four times in the month before the bombings. Arrested and indicted, Campos credited the attacks to the Aryan Liberation Front, a terrorist group of which he was the sole member.[66]

The reverie of leaderless resistance also registered in Metzger's growing fascination with Islamists. When Ramzi Yousef's cell bombed the World Trade Center in 1993, Metzger was impressed. "A handful of Arab Semites did more damage in one operation than the entire racial right-wing has accomplished in decades," he wrote. For too long, "misguided young Aryans" had been throwing "their lives away on absolute suicide missions" or doing "decades of prison time for having machine guns they will never fire and grenades they will never throw." Meanwhile a "few so-called inferior ragheads" caused massive "panic with one operation.

Had these people been a bit more sophisticated, the entire center would have collapsed in a pile of New Order rubble."[67]

* * *

In the late 1980s and early 1990s, cultural connections—and the violent fantasies they animated—helped American and British white supremacists find new allies elsewhere in the world. The reunification of Germany and the collapse of both the Soviet Union and apartheid South Africa signaled to white supremacists in the United States and Britain that new frontiers were now open. They imagined themselves as world leaders, presiding over a great awakening of white racial consciousness.

In Germany, neo-Nazi skinhead groups made remarkable progress in the late 1980s and early 1990s, especially in the East, where decades of communist rule produced a stagnant economy and lots of underemployed and unemployed young men. Feeling their fortunes declining in the reunified federal state, they recalled the Nazi era, borrowing old dogmas to explain new realities—globalization and immigration. Believing recent arrivals were taking their jobs, abusing social services, and poisoning the German body politic, skinheads targeted minorities in escalating attacks.[68] In 1992, the movement burst into the national consciousness as hundreds of neo-Nazis in the coastal city of Rostock launched a three-day riot, beating Turkish asylum seekers and throwing petrol bombs at their residences.[69] A few years later, No Remorse, the British skinhead band who had headlined Aryan Fest in Oklahoma, commemorated the assault in a song called "Barbeque in Rostock." Its opening verse:

> Didn't want their town filled with scum,
> So they got together and made petrol bombs.
> Then one cold, starry night,
> They set them filthy Turks alight![70]

The Rostock riot—and other attacks like it—mirrored the violence of U.S. and British skinheads, but on a dramatically larger scale. As a result,

German skinheads gained a special luster on the international stage. The culture shifted, too. Mythical imagery associated with Nazi Germany had long featured in the songs and styles of American and British skinhead bands—Skrewdriver's Ian Stuart liked to lead chants of "Sieg Heil" on stage, for instance—but the growing involvement of German bands in the transatlantic music scene brought it to the fore. Symbols and legends from Norse mythology and Odinism, in particular, circulated through white power music, reaching audiences in the United States and Britain. They also graced album covers, posters, and T-shirts. Meanwhile, *White Aryan Resistance* published articles trying to convert its Christian readers to the more authentic pagan religions of their ancient Aryan forebears.[71]

The collapse of the Soviet Union was perhaps the most exciting development for white power groups in the West. For many far right leaders, the Cold War had divided white peoples in the West and East for too long. As Tom Metzger explained, the struggle between capitalism and communism was, in reality, just another facet of a Jewish conspiracy for world domination. A "nuclear war would not be good for the white race," he explained, for it would "destroy the entire northern hemisphere, the ancestral home of the Caucasian people," which is what the Jews had supposedly wanted all along.[72] However, the end of the Cold War meant the far right no longer had to make fighting communism a central aim. And so Metzger and those around him shoehorned leftist critiques of capitalism into their racial worldview. They mined Karl Marx's writings for alleged anti-Jewish passages while praising Eugene Debs and other early twentieth-century socialists for supposedly standing up to greedy "race traitors." Wealthy whites—bankers, bosses, and businessmen—were just as much an enemy as Jews and non-whites, Metzger argued. They sold out their race by undercutting the economic security of the white working class.[73] Hoping to capitalize on the post-Cold War moment, Metzger sent a subordinate to Russia to meet dozens of far right groups from Moscow to Vladivostok.[74]

If the dissolution of the Soviet Union offered hope to white supremacists, then the fall of South Africa was terrifying. For Americans and Britons, South Africa was the last place where white people still occupied the social position that biology had bequeathed and colonization had secured. Years before, in 1978, many in the Anglo-American far right watched in horror as the short-lived white supremacist rogue state of Rhodesia collapsed to the brutal regime of Robert Mugabe.[75] Now they feared the same would happen in South Africa if apartheid ended and the government instituted the one-man, one-vote policy. There was little to cheer for in South Africa, apart from a beleaguered group of whites pledging to fight to the last: the neo-Nazi Afrikaner Resistance Movement, a paramilitary group dedicated to the creation of an independent Afrikaner republic, which drew some of its support from skinheads. Back in Britain, Ian Stuart incorporated the Afrikaner Resistance Movement's flag, a modified version of the Nazi swastika, into Blood & Honour's magazine masthead.[76]

The growth of skinhead culture on the world stage in the 1990s—and the ways in which it helped white power leaders stitch together an imagined community—caused some to seek more direct connection with their allies abroad. It was not easy. For instance, Tom Metzger and his son John visited Canada in 1992, but Canadian police arrested and deported the pair for attempting to incite racial hatred. When the Metzgers traveled to Berlin in 1994, local authorities quickly sent them back to the United States—though not before the Americans staged a rally with members of the Deutsche Volksunion (German Peoples' Union), a leading far right party that attracted neo-Nazis and skinheads.[77]

While state scrutiny often stifled face-to-face political organizing, the rise of the internet widened and deepened the cultural collaboration that music, magazines, and books had enabled in the 1980s. By the mid-1990s, white power groups had built a social network of websites and message boards which, like the skinhead music industry, enabled them to push their ideas globally without leaving their home countries. As one member of WAR put it, cyberspace allowed white supremacists to "spread ourselves across the planet" since no one could "arrest our thoughts."[78] Former Klansman Don Black, who spent three years in prison in the 1980s for his role in a botched attempt by white supremacists to invade the tiny Caribbean island of Dominica, set up one of the first websites in 1995. Named Stormfront, Black's website featured the writings of William Pierce, Louis Beam, Tom Metzger, and others. It became perhaps the most popular white supremacist online community, with hundreds of thousands of registered members around the world.[79] By 1998, the Southern Poverty Law Center counted 258 sites devoted to white power. Several U.S. groups also used their servers to host the sites of their allies abroad, especially those in Germany, since federal laws there made it illegal to run neo-Nazi websites.[80]

Through Stormfront and other sites, French and German translations of *The Turner Diaries* spread across the white power social network in the mid-1990s, helping William Pierce secure European-based publishers for his works. "Because of his books," said one expert, Pierce became "undoubtedly the most well-known American right-wing figure in Europe."[81] In turn, Pierce devoted more resources to skinhead music. In 1999, he put up $250,000 to buy Resistance Records, founded a few years earlier by Canadian neo-Nazi musician George Burdi of the band RaHoWa, short for Racial Holy War.[82] Pierce believed it would win new converts and secure his group's financial future. With a new website for the label, Pierce hoped to "add an increasing number of younger members in the 18 to 25 age range, to our ranks," as part of his vanguard strategy, a way to build a cadre of committed youth. "What we have to do is encourage in every way we can the growth of the racially conscious portion of the Skinhead community," he said. "We have to give young people back their sense of identity."[83]

For Pierce and many other likeminded leaders, white power music was itself a form of leaderless resistance. It spread far beyond those actively involved in its production and distribution. And it imbued young men with narratives of white martial power, urging them take up arms—both metaphorically and actually—against their perceived enemies. As Pierce explained in 1999,

> Music speaks to us at a deeper level than books or political rhetoric; music speaks directly to the soul. Resistance Records will be the music of our people's renewal and rebirth … It will be music of defiance and rage against the enemies of our people. It will be the music of the great cleansing revolution which is coming.[84]

Pierce's Resistance Records, itself a subsidiary of the National Alliance, was only one node in a much larger web, what some called the Skinhead International. By 1995, according to researchers from the Anti-Defamation League, the "neo-Nazi skinhead movement" was "active in no fewer than 33 countries on six continents." The United States, Britain, and Germany formed the core, but skinhead "shock troops" had spread from Austria to Argentina, Belgium to Brazil, Slovakia to South Africa. Many had ties to formal far right parties, often serving as recruiters or foot soldiers in street demonstrations. Others, following the path of leaderless resistance, aimed to destabilize society "through the direct application of violence and intimidation." Whatever their endgame—if indeed they had one—many of the skinhead gangs functioned as fraternities of sorts, offering young men a sense of camaraderie and clout. They also suggested that they were indeed part of an international—even global—movement, despite their generally scant numbers.[85]

* * *

As white power music and culture served as the connective tissue for a growing far right mobilization around the world in the early 1990s, the British National Party (BNP) became the most prominent group in Britain. Formed by John Tyndall in 1982 after a split with the National Front, the BNP rehashed old attacks against non-white immigrants as well as free-trade acolytes, homosexuals, mainstream parties, and the Irish Republican Army.[86] Cultivating an air of belligerent masculinity in the face of cowardice and acquiescence, the BNP first tried to harness white power culture for political gain. It was often hard. For all the rock concerts, rallies, and amateur football matches it sponsored, the BNP struggled mightily to gain votes in the early 1990s. Tyndall and other BNP leaders were torn between radicalism and respectability. They wanted to win elections and yet clung to skinhead paramilitary groups such as Combat 18—the 1 and the 8 stood for the first and eighth letters of the alphabet, A and H, the initials of Adolf Hitler. Splintering from Ian Stuart's Blood & Honour after the singer's death, Combat 18 served for a time as the BNP's armed wing, protecting its meetings from anti-fascist protestors. It also controlled a "lucrative and illegal music business," putting on shows and selling pirated recordings, which provided a small but steady stream of cash.[87]

Spiraling beyond the BNP's control, Combat 18 rejected the path of electoral politics and embraced leaderless resistance. Inspired by *The Turner Diaries*—Combat 18's magazine was called *The Order*, after the guerrilla group in Pierce's novel—some members launched organized attacks on leftists, immigrants, and other foes.[88] Other targets included members of the BNP, deemed by Combat 18 to be insufficiently committed to racial revolution. As Zoe Hyman's chapter in this volume reveals, in the American South there was a long-standing tension between the ideology of white supremacy— or the abiding belief in political violence to protect white supremacy—and electoral efforts to appear legitimate and respectable in the post-civil rights era. We see this, too, in Britain. Tyndall feared Combat 18 would jeopardize the BNP's electoral future, so he turned to the American far right and its leading ideologue, William Pierce. In November 1995, he brought the National Alliance leader to speak at the BNP's annual rally, where Pierce downplayed his long-standing support for paramilitary action.[89] Pushed to the margins, members of Combat 18 continued to press for "war against the government and the people invading this fucking land."[90]

Seeking a more viable electoral path, the BNP leadership started to see violent skinheads—and white power culture—as a liability both at home and abroad. Instead of promoting skinhead music in the United States, as the National Front had once done, the BNP sought something more powerful and permanent: an organized and reliable source of direct financial support. The effort took shape as the American Friends of the British National Party (AFBNP), organized by emerging leader Nick Griffin and Mark Cotterill, a veteran activist who had also staged skinhead concerts and other public spectacles in the 1980s.[91] Cotterill had migrated to the United States in 1995, first staying with Pierce on the National Alliance's fortified compound in West Virginia before moving to the Washington suburbs.[92] He founded the AFBNP, which Griffin then brought into the party fold as its first overseas affiliate. Both hoped it would operate like the Friends of Sinn Féin, a U.S.-based group that raised money for the Irish political party. Cotterill then sought out David Duke, the notorious leader who had worked for two decades to put a friendly face on the Klan. With Duke's guidance, he arranged meetings in bars and hotel conference centers from New Jersey to Florida. He flew the Union Jack alongside the Confederate flag and Nazi banners, paying homage to the "martyrs who had died for Britain, the Confederacy and the Racial Nationalist Cause." By 2001, he counted a hundred dues-paying members.[93]

"It is now time to give Americans of British heritage" the "opportunity to hear a real racial-nationalist message from the old country," one Scottish organizer said. "That message is coming from the BNP and the BNP only."[94] To make that message resonate with Americans, Cotterill brought Griffin to the United States for a six-day fundraising tour in the fall of 2001. Griffin's presence caught the attention of investigators from the Southern Poverty Law Center, Britain's *Searchlight* magazine, and the federal government. After a brief investigation, agents from the Department of Justice concluded that the AFBNP violated the 1938 U.S. Foreign Agent Registration Act, which stipulates that any agent of a foreign power or party must register as such. Forced to deregister his group, Cotterill left the United States in 2002. On his way out, he received a ten-year exclusion order from the U.S. government. Although its financial impact was minuscule, the AFBNP had helped solidify connections between the American and British far right as the BNP overhauled its image and launched a successful electoral campaign in the early 2000s.[95]

While the BNP leadership pivoted away from violent fantasies, some of its supporters did not. They remained committed to leaderless resistance. Indeed, Louis Beam's writing had long circulated among British groups such as Combat 18, helping them turn low-level acts of vigilante violence into something more. In the U.S., the actions of Oklahoma City bomber Timothy McVeigh modeled a much more deadly approach. McVeigh was an avid fan of the *Turner Diaries*—police found pages of the book in his car when he was arrested after the blast that killed 169 people. Seeking retribution for strong-armed federal actions against militant white Americans at Waco and Ruby Ridge, McVeigh hoped to start a guerrilla war against what he too called the Zionist Occupation Government.[96] Far right figures in Britain found inspiration in McVeigh's act of leaderless resistance. When the U.S. government executed McVeigh in June 2001, members of the BNP, Blood & Honour, and other far right groups in Britain pledged to mark his execution with a "night of blood." For them, McVeigh was a martyr. He had sacrificed his life in the struggle to save the white race.[97]

Meanwhile, some members of the British far right launched their own campaigns of terror. In 1999, Combat 18 spearheaded a mail bombing campaign in several cities.[98] That same year, David Copeland, a former BNP member who was "obsessed with Hitler and bombs," spent two weeks planting explosives around London's black, Asian, and gay communities. Three people died, and hundreds were injured. Like McVeigh, his goal was to start a "race war," plunging the country into "murder, mayhem and chaos" from which a new white state would rise. It should be noted that this white terror in Britain was seen, at the time, as a direct reaction to efforts to combat racism and promote multiculturalism under a new Labour government.[99] In February 1999, a major government inquiry into the London Metropolitan Police's mishandling of the 1993 racist murder of 18-year-old Stephen Lawrence revealed the profound "institutional racism" of the police; the resulting Macpherson Report was widely recognized as marking a watershed moment in public understanding. Arrested by London police, Copeland stood trial in June 2000, receiving six concurrent life sentences. From the U.S., Tom Metzger praised Copeland's act of "ethnic cleansing," saying he was one of many "lone wolves on the move all over the world."[100]

With leaderless resistance serving as a call to arms on both sides of the Atlantic in the late twentieth century, white power activists tried to build an overarching racial ideology to bind them together. The result was what many called pan-Aryanism. Reviving dormant racial doctrines from the late nineteenth century, white power groups in the U.S., Britain, and elsewhere claimed they shared an ancestral lineage going back thousands of years—although just who counted as Aryan often varied, since different racial ideologues had different criteria. Some brought in Old Norse or Odinist mythology, while others harnessed the anti-Semitic Christian Identity theology, which said white, European-descended people were the actual lost tribes of Israel, Jews were the seeds of Satan, and non-whites were inferior "mud peoples." Such a mishmash of ideas made little sense to outsiders. But as an ideological program, pan-Aryanism was less about the past and more about the future. It emphasized that "white revolutionaries must adopt a global strategy to succeed," as William Pierce explained. "We must understand that we are in a planet-wide race war, and survival of our race depends on our winning this war."[101]

* * *

At the end of the twentieth century, after four decades of collaboration, white power activists in the United States and Britain shared a transnational movement which, ironically, grew larger and more powerful as it decentralized. No one attempted to build a single overarching organization along the lines of the World Union of National Socialists. Instead, white power activists guided each other through a complex web of cultural connections, transforming the tenor and trajectory of the far right in the United States, Britain, and beyond. Through music, books, magazines, radio and television programs, they fashioned a common language and embraced similar modes of action. Their global framing of whiteness—embodied in the pan-Aryan ideal and glimpsed in the shared struggles of white people from Germany to Russia to South Africa—strengthened their conviction that the problems facing their race in the twenty-first century required a global solution. They spoke in the idioms of war and revolution, and enacted paramilitary campaigns against their perceived enemies. By 2016, buoyed by successful electoral campaigns and grassroots organizing in a number of countries, white power activists in the United States, Britain, and elsewhere appeared more confident than they did at any point since 1945.

The BNP made significant strides in the 2000s, as Islamophobia swept the country in the wake of the 9/11 and 7/7 attacks. Nick Griffin tried to overhaul the image of the BNP and push skinheads and other advocates of violence further to the margins. As he explained in 2006, "We're not raving, racist skinheads who want to kill everyone ... we are perfectly able to have cordial relations with other groups."[102] To promote this impression, he started a new record label for the BNP. Called Great White Records, it sold folk albums that advocated roughly the same messages the skinhead bands did, but in a more mellow style. Griffin and his family even sang on some tracks. By any measure, it failed. "People who are nationalistically inclined don't want to listen to that," said one BNP activist. More importantly, the rise of the internet had made it less profitable to run a white supremacist record label, regardless of genre. People no longer needed magazines and mail order clubs to satiate their appetite for racist music.[103]

Still, the BNP's bid for respectability worked. As many in the Labour, Conservative, and Liberal Democratic parties employed anti-immigrant tropes, it legitimized the BNP's virulent hostility to non-whites.[104] Although the BNP suffered an electoral collapse in 2010, its shift away from white power culture—at least in part—had opened space for other ultra-nationalist, anti-immigrant groups like the United Kingdom Independence Party, which spearheaded the campaign to take Britain out of the European Union.[105]

In the U.S., white power groups re-entered politics in a way not seen since the 1960s. Having struggled to organize outside the two-party system, they tried to make the Republican Party conform to their vision. In an era of exploding economic inequality—disappearing jobs, wages, pensions, savings, and housing capital—they drew strength from widespread Islamophobia and anti-immigrant sentiment among conservatives. Emboldened by shifts within the Republican Party, the new crop of white nationalist leaders preferred a more buttoned-up approach. Learning from white-collar Klansman David Duke, who pioneered that strategy over the previous decades, they wanted to be seen as serious people, not peripheral players. They sponsored workshops and policy institutes, offering more subtle appeals to white nationalism. They still made the old pleas to save the white race, backed up by dubious figures and statistics, but they usually avoided vitriolic language—in part because the huge network of white power websites and image boards provided plenty of space to talk about bombs, bullets, and bloodshed. Calling their movement the "alt-right," these new white power activists and ideologues stoked white Americans' antipathy toward President Barack Obama and channeled it into Republican electoral politics, joining forces with the Tea Party and other groups who wanted, in the oft-used phrase, to "take our country back."[106]

But even as white supremacists softened their tone and sought formal political power, paramilitarism remained firmly entrenched in the cultural world of white power. The ranks of the skinhead movement swelled. Today, the Hammerskin Nation, a union of skinhead groups, claims twenty local or regional chapters in the United States and another ten overseas—and still comprises a core constituency for the far right.[107] Echoing Tom Metzger, Louis Beam, and Ian Stuart, members of the Hammerskin Nation affirm that white power music and skinhead culture are the most viable ways to transform young men into dedicated activists. "Kids grow up without any form of self-identity," wrote one Hammerskin. "They are given two choices, either go with the 'norm' of multi-culturalism and race mixing or be deemed an outcast, a minority. Let's take hold of the Racist minority and welcome them into the movement."[108] Today, the Hammerskin Nation describes itself "a leaderless group of men and women who have adopted the White Power Skinhead lifestyle." Doing so is a "way of achieving goals which we have all set for ourselves ... summed up with one phrase consisting of 14 words."[109]

Over the last decade, dozens of right-leaning Americans have imbibed and enacted fantasies of leaderless resistance, often encountered online or through cultural media.[110] In 2015, Dylann Roof, a 21-year-old man from South Carolina, gunned down nine African American parishioners at a Charleston church. A loner, he had spent much of his young life on the internet, visiting Stormfront and the website of the Council of Conservative Citizens. Although he struggled to make strong connections with others in digital forums, he nevertheless came to see himself as a member of a global white nationalist community. He traced his family's racial lineage back to Europe and the British Isles. He learned the mythology of the white supremacist states of South Africa and Rhodesia, causing him to wear a jacket emblazoned with the banners of both. He also ran a webpage called the Last Rhodesian, on which he published a manifesto calling for a race war. His contribution to white power culture is now widely circulated on Stormfront and other sites.[111]

A similar story has unfolded in Britain and Europe. Paramilitarism and white power culture have fused and circulated through digital social networks, music, magazines, and books. That, in turn, has propelled new waves of far right political organizing. Since forming in 2008, the English Defence League has battled what it perceives as the spread of Islam and multiculturalism. Grouped into regional, militaristic divisions, the English Defence League includes many skinheads who join demonstrations, often turning against their opponents or the police.[112] And some members have plotted lone-wolf acts, like activist Simon Beach, arrested in 2011 for trying to burn down a mosque in Stoke-on-Trent.[113]

Around Europe, copycat groups have also appeared—the Serbian Defence League, the Norwegian Defence League, and the like. On an English Defence League message board, one Norwegian man pledged his gratitude. "In these dark times," he wrote, "all of Europe is looking to you" for "inspiration, courage and even hope that we might turn this evil trend of islamisation all across our continent."[114] His name was Anders Breivik. He had spent months shuttered in a bedroom at his mother's house, immersing himself in white power culture as a member of Stormfront and follower of the English Defence League on Facebook. He was also a fan of white power music, listening repeatedly to a cover of RaHoWa's "Ode to a Dying People," which features the line "White man, fight the flight towards the grave."[115] Through this cultural world, rather than face-to-face politics, Breivik inducted himself into the movement. On July 22, 2011, he set off a car bomb in downtown Oslo before massacring dozens of teenagers at an island retreat, actions that left seventy-nine people dead and more than three hundred wounded.[116] At his trial and since, Breivik has consistently sought to portray his act of terror as part of an international struggle, hoping to inspire others.[117]

And he has. Five years after his assault, Thomas Mair, a 52-year-old unemployed gardener living on a council estate in Birstall, Yorkshire, enacted his own version of leaderless resistance. On June 16, 2016—days before the Brexit vote—he gunned down Labour MP Jo Cox in broad daylight as she prepared to meet constituents at a library. Cox had urged Britons to remain in the European Union; her position led to Mair's attack. Police found at Mair's home a cache of white supremacist literature, including news clippings about the Breivik attack and a small library purchased from William Pierce's National Alliance including the classic text of the armed right: *The Turner Diaries*. A few weeks after the murder, Pierce's old contact Mark Cotterill, now back in the UK working for the England First party, explained that he was not shocked by the violence. If anything, he was "surprised there haven't been more Mairs—so many people want to do something."[118]

Recent attacks, such as the 2019 massacre at a mosque in Christchurch, New Zealand, have borne out this same pattern. Australian Brenton Tarrant, the perpetrator of that assault, was deeply versed in the myths, symbols, and narratives of the white power movement, even though he had few personal connections to likeminded leaders and activists. His manifesto, called "The Great Replacement," borrowed its title and thesis from a book written by French right-winger Renaud Camus in 2012. On his way to kill, he steeled himself by listening to the marches of the Waffen-SS and the British Grenadiers and the song "Remove Kebab," which originated among Serbian militias who slaughtered Muslims during the Yugoslav wars of the early 1990s. On his rifle, Tarrant had scrawled the number 14, referencing the Fourteen Words popularized by American white supremacist David Lane: "We must secure the existence of our people and a future for white children." He didn't see himself as a leader, "just a partisan."[119]

Such links highlight the continued collaboration—material, ideological, and cultural—among white power activists in the United States, Britain, and the wider world. For more than forty years, they have reached across national borders, transforming disparate groups into a formidable transnational movement in pursuit of political power. To buttress this movement, they used music, print and broadcast media, and the internet to cultivate cultures of violence and terror among adherents, from jack-booted racist skinheads to seemingly faceless "leaderless" resisters, who understood themselves as part of a world struggle for racial survival. If we are to make sense of these white power groups in the era of Donald Trump and Brexit, then we must account for this deadly cooperation.

Notes

1   "Aryan Fest, '89," *White Aryan Resistance* 9.3 (1989), Radicalism Collection, Michigan State University Library Special Collections, East Lansing, Michigan (hereafter MSU).

2   Southern Poverty Law Center, Hate Watch, "Extremist Profile: Tom Metzger," www.splcenter.org/fighting-hate/extremist-files/individual/tom-metzger (accessed August 3, 2017).

3   "Former Klansman Tom Metzger and Bill Riccio Encourage Skinheads to Cooperate," *Southern Poverty Law Center Intelligence Report*, fall 2006.

4   Tom Metzger, "Editorial," *White Aryan Resistance* 9.3 (1989), Radicalism Collection, MSU.

5   Ibid.

6   Mark Cotterill, leader of the American Friends of the British National Party, a support group for the fascist British National Party, quoted in "Hands across the Water," *Southern Poverty Law Center Intelligence Report*, fall 2001.

7   On transatlantic fascist networks in the interwar era, see Eric Hobsbawm, *The Age of Extremes: A History of the World, 1914–1991* (New York: Vintage, 1994), 109–41; Markku Rustsila, "International Anticommunism before the Cold War: Success and Failure in the Building of a Transnational Right," and Arnd Bauerkämper, "Interwar Fascism in Europe and Beyond: Toward a Transnational Radical Right," in Martin Durham and Margaret Power (eds.), *New Perspectives on the Transnational Right* (New York: Palgrave Macmillan, 2010), 11–38 and 39–66. On American sympathizers and collaborators with Nazi Germany in the 1930s, see Leo Ribuffo, *Old Christian Right: The Protestant Far Right from the Great Depression to the Cold War* (Philadelphia, PA: Temple University Press, 1983); and Arnie Bernstein, *Swastika Nation: Fritz Kuhn and the Rise and Fall of the German American Bund* (New York: St. Martin's Press, 2014).

8   For its founding principles, see Program of the World Union of National Socialists, "National Socialist Worldview," no date, circa 1959, P300373, Political

Pamphlets Collection, Northwestern University Library Special Collections, Evanston, IL.

9 See Paul Jackson, "Accumulative Extremism: The Post-War Tradition in Anglo-American Neo-Nazi Activism," in Paul Jackson and Anton Shekhovtsov (eds.), *The Post-War Anglo-American Right: A Special Relationship of Hate* (New York: Palgrave Macmillan, 2014), 13–16.

10 On the decline of the Klan in the 1960s, see Wyn Craig Wade, *The Fiery Cross: The Ku Klux Klan in America* (New York: Simon and Schuster, 1987), 307–67; John Drabble, "The FBI, COINTELPRO-WHITE HATE and the Decline of Ku Klux Klan Organizations in Mississippi, 1964–1971," *Journal of Mississippi History* 66.4 (2004): 353–401; and David Cunningham, *Klansville, USA: The Rise and Fall of the Civil-Rights Era Ku Klux Klan* (Oxford: Oxford University Press, 2013).

11 Southern Poverty Law Center, Hate Watch, "Extremist Profile: Tom Metzger," www.splcenter.org/fighting-hate/extremist-files/individual/tom-metzger (accessed August 3, 2017).

12 Metzger's views are explored in depth in Elinor Langer, "The American Neo-Nazi Movement Today," *The Nation*, July 16/23, 1990.

13 Southern Poverty Law Center, Hate Watch, "Extremist Profile: Tom Metzger," www.splcenter.org/fighting-hate/extremist-files/individual/tom-metzger (accessed August 3, 2017).

14 Tom Metzger, quoted in Langer, "The American Neo-Nazi Movement Today," 89.

15 This comes from an FBI field report, assembled by the bureau's San Diego office. See FBI, San Diego SAC, Domestic Security-Terrorism, "White Aryan Resistance, also known as White American Resistance," May 19, 1988, 4, in the FBI's Freedom of Information Act Reading Room (hereafter FBI-FOIA).

16 From at least 1984 onwards, monthly editions of *White Aryan Resistance* bore this message under its banner.

17 Metzger quoted on *Race and Reason* no. 309, interview with Ben Klassen, online at www.youtube.com/watch?v=DkEOVPQY-lo (accessed November 28, 2017).

18 Judith Michaelson, "Hate on the Air: A Question of Access," *Los Angeles Times*, August 10, 1988. On Klassen, see Bruce Henderson, "Church Preaches Hatred, Faces Challenge on Tax Status," *The Sun* (Baltimore), August 30, 1990.

19 Langer, "The American Neo-Nazi Movement Today," 86.

20 These details come from Southern Poverty Law Center, "Extremist Profile: William Pierce," www.splcenter.org/fighting-hate/extremist-files/individual/william-pierce (accessed August 1, 2017); Leonard Zeskind, *Blood and Politics:*

The History of the White Nationalist Movement from the Margins to the Mainstream (New York: Farrar, Straus, and Giroux, 2009), 17–26; Martin Durham, *White Rage: The Extreme Right in American Politics* (London: Routledge, 2007), 27–8; and the hagiographic Pierce biography, Robert S. Griffin, *The Fame of a Dead Man's Deeds* (Washington, DC: National Vanguard Books, 2001).

21 · Pierce quoted in Morris Dees, *Gathering Storm: America's Militia Threat* (New York: HarperCollins, 1996), 138.

22 See Andrew MacDonald [William Pierce], *The Turner Diaries* (Washington DC: National Alliance, 1978). See also James William Gibson, *Warrior Dreams: Violence and Manhood in Post-Vietnam America* (New York: Hill and Wang, 1994), 200–7.

23 On the *Turner Diaries*' sales figures, see John Sutherland, "Gospels of Hate that Slip through the Net," *Guardian*, April 3, 2000, www.theguardian.com/uk/2000/apr/03/race.mcveigh (accessed November 28, 2017); and J. M. Berger, "The Turner Legacy: The Storied Origins and Impact of White Nationalism's Deadly Bible," International Centre for Counterterrorism—The Hague, September 2016, https://icct.nl/wp-content/uploads/2016/09/ICCT-Berger-The-Turner-Legacy-September2016-2.pdf (accessed November 28, 2017).

24 "National Alliance Leader, William Pierce, Looks to Build Far Right Alliances," *Southern Poverty Law Center Intelligence Report*, March 1999.

25 Camilla Schofield, *Enoch Powell and the Making of Postcolonial Britain* (Cambridge: Cambridge University Press, 2013), 210.

26 On Powell, race, and memories of empire in postcolonial Britain, see Bill Schwarz, *The White Man's World* (Oxford: Oxford University Press, 2011).

27 Nigel Copsey, *Contemporary British Fascism: The British National Party and the Quest for Legitimacy* (Basingstoke: Palgrave Macmillan, 2008 [2004]), 8–15; and G. Gable, "Britain's Nazi Underground," in L. Cheles, R. Ferguson, and M. Vaughn (eds.), *The Far Right in Western Europe* (London: Longman, 1995), 258–9.

28 Max Hanna, "The National Front and Other Right-Wing Organizations," *Journal of Ethnic and Migration Studies* 3.1–2 (1974), 49–55. On the National Front's political program, see National Front Policy Committee, *It's Our Country—Let's Win It Back! The Manifesto of the National Front* (London: National Front, 1979), Radicalism Collection, MSU.

29 On the National Front's use of streets and parades, see Thomas Linehan, "Cultures of Space: Spatialising the National Front," in Nigel Copsey and John E. Richardson (eds.), *Cultures of Post-War British Fascism* (London: Routledge, 2015), 49–67.

30 See Jackson, "Accumulative Extremism," 17–18.

31 See Timothy S. Brown, "Subcultures, Pop Cultures, and Politics: Skinheads and 'Nazi Rock' in England and Germany," *Journal of Social History* 38.1 (2004): 157–78; Dick Hebdige, "This is England! And they don't live here!," in *Skinhead* (London: Omnibus, 1982), 26–35; and Dick Hebdige, *Subculture: The Meaning of Style* (London: Routledge, 2002), 59–60.

32 See Richard Thurlow, *Fascism in Britain: From Oswald Mosley to the National Front* (London: I.B. Tauris, 1998), 252.

33 See Ryan Shaffer, "British, European, and White: Cultural Constructions of Identity in Postwar British Fascist Music," in Copsey and Richardson (eds.), *Cultures of Post-War British Fascism*, 143.

34 Eddy Morrison, quoted in Robert Forbes and Eddie Stanton, *The White Nationalist Skinhead Movement: U.S. and UK, 1979–1993* (London: Feral House, 2015), 10.

35 Nick Lowles, "Far Out with the Far Right," in Mark Perryman (ed.), *Hooligan Wars: Causes and Effects of Football Violence* (Edinburgh: Mainstream Publishing, 2001), 108–21.

36 Ryan Shaffer, "Radicals in Harmony: Skinhead Music, International Networks and the Transformation of British Fascism, 1967 to Present," Ph.D. diss., State University of New York at Stony Brook, 2013, 85.

37 Ian Stuart, quoted in Forbes and Stanton, *The White Nationalist Skinhead Movement*, 89.

38 See interview with Ian Stuart in Stephen Duncombe and Maxwell Tremblay (eds.), *White Riot: Punk Rock and the Politics of Race* (London: Verso, 2011), 130–3.

39 Skrewdriver, "Hail the New Dawn," *Hail the New Dawn*, Rock-O-Rama Records, 1984.

40 The song was released as a single in 1983. Skrewdriver, "White Power," Rock-O-Rama Records.

41 Matthew Worley, *No Future: Punk, Politics, and British Youth Culture, 1976–1984* (Cambridge: Cambridge University Press, 2017), 153–8 (157).

42 The first Rock against Communism show was held at Conway Hall in London's Red Lion Square in 1979, and featured White Boss and the Dentists. Some 200–300 youths showed up, not only members of the National Front but also of other far right groups such as the British Movement. See Ryan Shaffer, "The Soundtrack of Neo-Fascism: Youth and Music in the National Front," *Patterns of Prejudice* 17.4–5 (2013): 458–82 (468); and Forbes and Stanton, *The White Nationalist Skinhead Movement*, 22.

43 See Shaffer, "Radicals in Harmony," 183–4; and Bill Buford, *Among the Thugs* (New York: Vintage, 1990), 149–50.

44 Worley, *No Future*, 157.

293

45 After Stuart's death in a 1993 car accident, Blood & Honour splintered into rival factions, each claiming to represent his legacy. See Brown, "Subcultures, Pop Cultures, and Politics," 164–5; and Southern Poverty Law Center, Hate Watch, "Blood and Honour," www.splcenter.org/fighting-hate/extremist-files/group/blood-honour (accessed November 28, 2017).

46 Shaffer, "The Soundtrack of Neo-Fascism," 472–5.

47 Shaffer, "British, European, and White," 144–5.

48 See Bill Wyman, "Skinheads," *Chicago Reader*, March 23, 1989; "White Supremacists Indicted in Attack," *Chicago Tribune*, February 20, 1988; Matt O'Connor, "Skinhead Gets 11 Years in Beating," *Chicago Tribune*, June 1989; and Robert Miles, "From the Mountain," *White Aryan Resistance* 9.3 (1989), Radicalism Collection, MSU.

49 Katherine Bishop, "Neo-Nazi Activity Is Arising Among U.S. Youth," *New York Times*, June 15, 1988.

50 "Klan, 'Skinheads' March," *Philadelphia Tribune*, May 6, 1988.

51 As the FBI noted in 1989, a growing number of "skinheads are currently associated with WAR." FBI, San Diego SAC, Domestic Security-Terrorism, "White Aryan Resistance, also known as White American Resistance," May 19, 1988, 4, FBI-FOIA.

52 Metzger, quoted in Durham, *White Rage*, 31.

53 Shaffer, "The Soundtrack of Neo-Fascism," 476. Metzger subscribed to Stuart's Blood & Honour newsletter, and also published advertisements for Skrewdriver in WAR's newspaper, which is probably how they came to know each other. See "Pan-Aryanism Binds Hate Groups in America and Europe," *Southern Poverty Law Center Intelligence Report*, fall 2001.

54 See Katherine Bishop, "Judge Blocks Neo-Nazi 'Woodstock' in California," *Los Angeles Times*, March 4, 1989; and Andrew Pollack, "Boredom and Rain End Racist Rally," *New York Times*, March 6, 1989.

55 "Aryan Fest, '89," *White Aryan Resistance* 9.3 (1989); Tom Metzger, "Editorial," *White Aryan Resistance* 9.3 (1989), Radicalism Collection, MSU.

56 Dr. William Pierce, "Guest Commentary," *White Aryan Resistance* 9.3 (1989), Radicalism Collection, MSU.

57 On the prosecution of various skinheads for violence, see Langer, "The American Neo-Nazi Movement Today"; "Skinhead Attacks Worry Police," *Philadelphia Tribune*, June 7, 1988; Katherine Bishop, "Neo-Nazi Activity Arising Among U.S. Youth," *New York Times*, June 13, 1988; John Spano, "Threat from Skinhead Gangs Reported on Rise," *Los Angeles Times*, October 27, 1988; Rudolph Unger, "Skinhead Leader Guilty in Beating of Ex-member," *Chicago Tribune* April 28,

1989; "Skinhead Gets Life Sentence for Fatal Racist Attack," *Los Angeles Times*, June 6, 1989; Stanley Bailey, "Skinhead Threat Grows," *Philadelphia Tribune*, October 13, 1989; John Lucadamo, "'Skinhead' Sentenced in Attack," *Chicago Tribune*, December 6, 1990; Jack Newton and John Lucadamo, "Skinhead Flouts His Upbringing," *Chicago Tribune*, December 30, 1992; Peter Applebome, "Skinhead Violence Grows," *New York Times*, July 18, 1993; Jim Newton, "Skinhead Suspects Admit to Bombing, Court is Told," *Los Angeles Times*, September 8, 1993.

58　On Louis Beam and "leaderless resistance," see Kathleen Belew, *Bring the War Home: The White Power Movement and Paramilitary America* (Cambridge, MA: Harvard University Press, 2018); and Zeskind, *Blood and Politics*, 88–93.

59　John Newell, "Past Lessons & Today's Reality," *White Aryan Resistance* 9.3 (1989), Radicalism Collection, MSU.

60　See Belew, *Bring the War Home*, 133.

61　Elinor Langer, *A Hundred Little Hitlers: The Death of a Black Man, the Trial of a White Racist, and the Rise of the Neo-Nazi Movement in America* (New York: Picador, 2004), 156–7 (156).

62　Ibid., 164.

63　See the FBI's declassified file on White Aryan Resistance, FBI-FOIA, vault.fbi.gov/white-aryan-resistance/white-aryan-resistance-part-1-of-1/view (accessed May 3, 2020).

64　See Morris Dees and Steve Fiffer, *Hate on Trial: The Case against America's Most Dangerous Neo-Nazi* (New York: Villard Books, 1993).

65　Quote from the anonymously authored article, White Revolutionary, "The Potential Terrorist," *White Aryan Resistance*, November 1995. See also John Baumgardner, "The Resistance," *White Aryan Resistance*, September 1994; "A Soldier of the Order Speaks," *White Aryan Resistance*, December 1994; Edward Kerling, "Whitey Revolutionary—An Incredible Journey," *White Aryan Resistance*, December 1995; Edward Kerling, "Whitey Revolutionary," *White Aryan Resistance*, March 1996; Edward Kerling, "Whitey Revolutionary," *White Aryan Resistance*, April 1996; Edward Kerling, "Whitey Revolutionary," *White Aryan Resistance*, May 1996; James Mason, "The Revolutionary Position," *White Aryan Resistance*, August 1996; "Beware the Lone Wolf," *White Aryan Resistance*, September 1998; Shawn Young, "Revoltus Tyrrannus," *White Aryan Resistance*, April 2000, University of Michigan Library Special Collections, University of Michigan, Ann Arbor, MI (hereafter UM).

66　"Former Klansman Tom Metzger and Bill Riccio Encourage Skinheads to Cooperate," *Southern Poverty Law Center Intelligence Report*, fall 2006.

67 Tom Metzger, "Editorial," *White Aryan Resistance*, May 1994, UM.

68 See Martin A. Lee, "An Overview of Far Right Politics in Europe," *Southern Poverty Law Center Intelligence Report*, fall 2001; Brent Hagtvet, "Right-Wing Extremism in Europe," *Journal of Peace Research* 31.1 (1994): 241–6.

69 Panikos Panayi, "Racial Violence in the New Germany 1990–93," *Contemporary European History* 3.3 (1994): 265–87, special issue, "Race and Violence in Germany and Europe."

70 No Remorse, "Barbeque in Rostock," *Barbeque in Rostock*, ISD Records, 1996.

71 For instance, Bob Matthews, founder of the neo-Nazi terrorist group called the Order, subscribed to a variant of Odinism. "A New Brand of Racist Religion on the March," *Southern Poverty Law Center Intelligence Report*, winter 1998.

72 Tom Metzger, quoted in James Ridgeway, *Blood in the Face: The Ku Klux Klan, Nazi Skinheads, and the Rise of a New White Culture* (New York: Thunder's Mouth Press, 1990), 169.

73 See "White Worker," *White American Resistance*, special issue, no date, circa 1984; Edward Kerling, "Karl Marx the Racist," *White Aryan Resistance*, October 1994; and John Jewell, "Another Look at Stalin," *White Aryan Resistance*, February 1995, UM.

74 See "Russian Nationalist & Separatist Organizations," *White Aryan Resistance*, June 1994; "Russian Nationalist & Separatist Organizations," *White Aryan Resistance*, July 1994; "Russian Nationalist & Separatist Organizations," *White Aryan Resistance*, August 1994; and "Russian Nationalist & Separatist Organizations," *White Aryan Resistance*, September 1994, UM.

75 See Kyle Burke, *Revolutionaries for the Right: Anticommunist Internationalism and Paramilitary Warfare in the Cold War* (Chapel Hill, NC: University of North Carolina Press, 2018), ch. 4.

76 For WAR's views on South Africa, see Tom Metzger, "Editorial," *White Aryan Resistance*, April 1994; "Update on South Africa," *White Aryan Resistance*, April 1994; Tom Metzger, "Editorial," *White Aryan Resistance*, May 1994; "A Black Separatist's View of South Africa," *White Aryan Resistance*, September 1994, John Jewell, "South African White Revolt," *White Aryan Resistance*, October 1994; "Analysis of African Policy," *White Aryan Resistance*, April 1995; "What's Up With South Africa?" *White Aryan Resistance*, February 1997; and Letter from South Africa, *White Aryan Resistance*, March 1998, UM. For the BNP's treatment of South Africa, see "War on Whites Hits South Africa," *British Nationalist*, April 1993; "South Africa Slides into Chaos," *British Nationalist*, August 1996; and "South Africa," *British Nationalist*, December 1996, Radicalism Collection, MSU. For skinheads in the Afrikaner Resistance Movement, see Anti-Defamation

League, *The Skinhead International: A Worldwide Survey of Neo-Nazi Skinheads* (New York: Anti-Defamation League, 1995), 65. For Blood & Honour and the Afrikaner Resistance Movement, see Forbes and Stanton, *The White Nationalist Skinhead Movement*, 255.

77 "WAR on Germany," and John Metzger, "Metzger Invades Germany," *White Aryan Resistance*, May 1994, UM.

78 Carl Abrahamson, "Declaration of Independence of Cyberspace," *White Aryan Resistance*, March 1996. See also "Reports from W.A.R. and the Aryan Network," *White Aryan Resistance*, October 2000, UM.

79 Wyatt Kaldenberg, "The Nazi Net," *White Aryan Resistance*, September 1995, UM.

80 See Mark Potok, "The Spreading Flood of Hate," *Southern Poverty Law Center Intelligence Report*, winter 1998; "Number of Hate Sites Increase Online," *Southern Poverty Law Center Intelligence Report*, winter 1998; and "Stormfront Standing Strong as Hate Sites Expand," *Southern Poverty Law Center Intelligence Report*, winter 1999.

81 "National Alliance Leader, William Pierce, Looks to Build Far Right Alliances," *Southern Poverty Law Center Intelligence Report*, March 1999.

82 Anti-Defamation League, "Deafening Hate: The Revival of Resistance Records," 2012, www.adl.org/sites/default/files/documents/assets/pdf/combating-hate/Deafening-Hate-The-Revival-of-Resistance-Records.pdf (accessed August 22, 2017).

83 "National Alliance Leader Hopes to Acquire Hate Label, Resistance Records," *Southern Poverty Law Center Intelligence Report*, fall 1999.

84 William Pierce, quoted in Nancy S. Love, *Trendy Fascism: White Power Music and the Future of Democracy* (Albany, NY: State University of New York Press, 2016), 2.

85 Anti-Defamation League, *The Skinhead International*, 1–2.

86 "What We Stand For," *British Nationalist*, August/September 1992, Radicalism Collection, MSU. On the origins of the BNP and its relation to the National Front, see Copsey, *Contemporary British Fascism*, 24–5; and Daniel Trilling, *Bloody Nasty People: The Rise of Britain's Far Right* (London: Verso, 2012), 54–60.

87 Nick Ryan, "Combat 18: Memoirs of a Street-Fighting Man," *Independent* (London), February 1, 1998.

88 See Copsey, *Contemporary British Fascism*, 65–6; and Trilling, *Bloody Nasty People*, 68–70.

89 See Copsey, *Contemporary British Fascism*, 67–8. The BNP sold videos of Pierce's speech for many years afterward. See, for instance, advertisement for

"Latest Video: Rally '95," *British Nationalist*, March 1996, Radicalism Collection, MSU.

90 Ryan, "Combat 18: Memoirs of a Street-Fighting Man."

91 See Roger Eatwell, "The Esoteric Ideology of the National Front in the 1980s," in Mike Cronin (ed.), *The Failure of British Fascism: The Far Right and the Fight for Political Recognition* (Basingstoke: Palgrave Macmillan, 1996), 108–9.

92 About the National Alliance compound, Cotterill later said, "I had three of the most interesting and enjoyable days of my life there." Cotterill, quoted in "Hands across the Water," *Southern Poverty Law Center Intelligence Report*, fall 2001.

93 The AFBNP claimed that it raised over $85,000 from American donors, but the actual amount was around $20,000. See "Financing Fascism," *Southern Poverty Law Center Intelligence Report*, winter 2001; and Ryan Shaffer, *Music, Youth, and International Links in Post-War British Fascism: The Transformation of Extremism* (Cham, Switzerland: Palgrave Macmillan, 2017), 233.

94 "Hands across the Water," *Southern Poverty Law Center Intelligence Report*, fall 2001.

95 Ryan Shaffer, "Foreign Friends and British Fascism: Understanding the American Friends of the British National Party," *Contemporary British History* 34.1 (2020): 118–39.

96 McVeigh had absorbed the theory of leaderless resistance through the writings of Louis Beam and William Pierce. See Stuart A. Wright, *Patriots, Politics, and the Oklahoma City Bombing* (Cambridge: Cambridge University Press, 2007), 170–2.

97 Tracy McVeigh, "UK Extremists Make Martyr of McVeigh," *Observer*, May 27, 2001.

98 "Combat 18 'Claims Nail Bomb Attack,'" *BBC News*, April 19, 1999, http://news.bbc.co.uk/2/hi/uk_news/323295.stm (accessed July 22, 2019).

99 Vron Ware and Les Back, *Out of Whiteness: Color, Politics, and Culture* (Chicago: University of Chicago Press, 2002), 4.

100 Tom Metzger, "Editorial," *White Aryan Resistance*, July 2000. See also "Bomber Tells English Court, 'I'm a Nazi,'" *White Aryan Resistance*, October 2000, UM.

101 Pierce, quoted in "Pan-Aryanism Binds Hate Groups in America and Europe," *Southern Poverty Law Center Intelligence Report*, fall 2001.

102 Ian Cobain, "Racism, Recruitment and How the BNP Believes it is Just 'One Crisis Away from Power,'" *Guardian*, December 21, 2006, www.theguardian.com/uk/2006/dec/22/politics.thefarright (accessed July 23, 2019).

103 See Shaffer, "British, European, and White," 156.

104 See Trilling, *Bloody Nasty People*, 103–51; Copsey, *Contemporary British Fascism*, 125–50.

105 See Georgia Graham, "Nigel Farage: I Am Proud to Have Taken a Third of the BNP's Support," *Telegraph*, March 31, 2014; and Tim Wigmore, "What Killed the BNP?" *New Statesman*, January 12, 2016, www.newstatesman.com/politics/staggers/2016/01/what-killed-bnp (accessed August 24, 2017).

106 See Leonard Zeskind, "The Tea Party Movement at the Crossroads of Nation and State," in Jackson and Shekhovtsov (eds.), *The Post-War Anglo-American Right*, 104–21; Josh Harkinson, "Meet the White Nationalist Leader Trying to Ride the Trump Train to Lasting Power," *Mother Jones.com*, www.motherjones.com/politics/2016/10/richard-spencer-trump-alt-right-white-nationalist/ (accessed September 6, 2017); and Matthew Sheffield, "Rise of the Alt-Right: How Mainstream Conservatives' Obsession with Purity Fueled a New Right-wing Radicalism," *Salon.com*, www.salon.com/2016/12/14/rise-of-the-alt-right-how-mainstream-conservatives-empowered-racism-and-engineered-their-own-destruction/ (accessed September 6, 2017).

107 Anti-Defamation League, "Hammerskin Nation," www.adl.org/education/resources/profiles/hammerskin-nation?xpicked=3&item=15 (accessed November 28, 2017).

108 Anti-Defamation League, "Profile: The Hammerskin Nation," www.adl.org/education/resources/profiles/hammerskin-nation (accessed June 17, 2019).

109 David Leonard and Richard King, "Understanding the Wisconsin Terror Attack," *Ebony*, August 7, 2012.

110 For a summary and analysis of many of these attacks, see Southern Poverty Law Center, "Age of the Wolf: A Study in the Rise of Leaderless Resistance Terrorism," February 2015, www.splcenter.org/sites/default/files/d6_legacy_files/downloads/publication/lone_wolf_special_report_0.pdf (accessed August 24, 2017).

111 John Ismay, "Rhodesia's Dead—But White Supremacists Have Given It New Life Online," *New York Times Magazine*, April 10, 2018, www.nytimes.com/2018/04/10/magazine/rhodesia-zimbabwe-white-supremacists.html (accessed April 15, 2020).

112 On the EDL, see Hilary Pilkington, *Loud and Proud: Passion and Politics in the English Defence League* (Manchester: Manchester University Press, 2016); Joel Busher, *The Making of Anti-Muslim Protest: Grassroots Activism in the English Defence League* (London: Routledge, 2016); and James Treadwell and Jon Garland, "Masculinity, Marginalization and Violence: A Case Study of the English Defence League," *The British Journal of Criminology* 51.4 (2011): 621–34.

113 "Stoke-on-Trent Arsonists Jailed," *BBC News*, December 8, 2011, www.bbc.com/news/uk-england-stoke-staffordshire-16098897 (accessed August 24, 2017).

114 Anders Breivik, quoted in Trilling, *Bloody Nasty People*, 189–90.

115 Love, *Trendy Fascism*, 4.

116 The best account of Breivik's massacre is Åsne Seierstad, *One of Us: The Story of Anders Breivik and the Massacre in Norway*, trans. Sarah Death (New York: Farrar, Straus, and Giroux, 2013).

117 "Norway Mass Killer Anders Behring Breivik Studied al Qaeda, Oklahoma City Bombing before Rampage," *CBS News*, April 2, 2012, www.cbsnews.com/ news/norway-mass-killer-anders-behring-breivik-studied-al-qaeda-oklahoma-city-bombing-before-rampage (accessed May 15, 2017); Scott Shane, "Killings in Norway Spotlight Anti-Muslim Thought in U.S.," *New York Times*, July 24, 2011. Spencer likes to talk of "an ethno-state that would be a gathering point for all Europeans." See C. J. Ciaramella, "Some Well-dressed White Nationalists Gathered in DC Last Weekend," *Vice News*, October 29, 2013, www.vice. com/en_us/article/some-well-dressed-white-nationalists-gathered-in-dc-last-week end (accessed June 6, 2017).

118 Tom Burgis, "Thomas Mair: The Making of a Neo-Nazi Killer," *Financial Times*, November 23, 2016.

119 "New Zealand Shooting Gunman's Rifles Covered in White Supremacist Symbols Popular Online," *CBS News*, March 15, 2019, www.cbsnews.com/news/new-zea land-shooting-gunman-rifles-white-supremacist-symbols-memes/ (accessed July 23, 2019); Tarrant's manifesto, "The Great Replacement," can be found at www. europeanfreedom.com/2019/03/16/the-great-replacement-the-manifesto-of-br enton-tarrant-the-new-zealand-mosque-shooter/ (accessed July 23, 2019).

Postscript:
Islamophobia and the struggle against white supremacy

Omar Khan

I N THIS POSTSCRIPT I reflect on my tenure as director of the Runnymede Trust, which ended in late May 2020, just as the Black Lives Matter movement helped to spur wider global understanding of and activism against racism. Runnymede is a race equality think tank founded in 1968, the same year as Enoch Powell's "Rivers of Blood" speech, to which it was partly a response. The 1968 founding of Runnymede marks an important moment in the transatlantic effort to fight the global colour line; it is part of what Zoe Hyman refers to in this volume as the geographically "wide" civil rights movement. This book focuses on the reactionary backlash against the post-war struggle for equality, manifest in both the civil rights movement and the connected history of anti-colonialism. It shows how, as *explicitly* racist policies were challenged and reformulated, white nationalist ideas became increasingly coded into pronouncements about heritage, "law and order", and national security. This challenges readers to think not just about the recent resurgence of racist political parties, but also about how we think about racism today and the limits of our anti-racist strategies.

Among many other contributions, Runnymede is well known for its work on Islamophobia. Islamophobia is fundamental to understanding the global imagination of white nationalists, but it also reveals some of the blockages and misunderstandings that continue to hinder the struggle against racism. Twenty years after publishing *Islamophobia: a challenge for us all* in 1997, the Runnymede Trust published a second report on the topic in 2017. One of the unexpected conclusions of that 2017 report was that there was a need for a definition of Islamophobia to help further public understanding. The short definition we provided for Islamophobia was "anti-Muslim racism".[1] This focus on a definition was felt necessary because there remains some confusion or resistance to the idea that Islamophobia is a form of *racism*. There are good faith and bad faith versions of this criticism, but we were particularly concerned not just with white nationalist or far right framings, but with a certain kind of liberal, and sometimes anti-racist, resistance to seeing Islamophobia as a form of racism, as well as how policymakers' resistance to that definition impeded a better response to anti-Muslim racism, and indeed all forms of racism.

In other words, the question of a definition of Islamophobia reveals wider challenges for public and elite understandings of racism, and how and why responding to racism has remained too narrow. Consider the main alternative term advanced by policymakers (and some researchers and think tanks) in the UK: anti-Muslim bigotry. While it is a positive development that UK decision makers take forms of prejudice against Muslims seriously, this phrase reveals a wider problem in public and policy understandings of racism. On this view of Islamophobia as anti-Muslim bigotry, the problem of Islamophobia is located in individual attitudes. This leads to a focus on more "extreme" forms of Islamophobia committed by the far right, or on street-level violence. It is, of course, important that the state seeks to protect all citizens from violence, but this focus on far right attitudes and behaviours presents those attitudes as pathological rather than as having any wider or deeper sources or manifestations in Britain or other countries.

Instead racism, including anti-Muslim racism, should be seen as having deep roots in our collective culture, intellectual traditions, and institutions. Perhaps most striking is the contrast here with standard anti-racist thinking that the state itself is implicated in (if not responsible for) the reproduction of racism not just as an ideology but in terms of outcomes in the world. It is probably not incidental that "counter-terrorism" policies are definitionally deemed not to be racially discriminatory by a state that defines discrimination only in terms of bigoted citizens acting in extreme ways. With this approach, there is no account of where "bigoted" attitudes come from, or how they are reproduced. Some bad apples just become rotten.

What this suggests is that racism is a question of personal intent, but also that racism is in some ways natural. If we put aside the structural and historic ways in which racism was produced and reproduced, we are then left with the suggestion that people naturally develop bigotry and dislike of other people because of their race. This is both a pessimistic account of human nature but also a dangerous concordance with the view that race is in some sense "real". When we then hear objections that "Islam is a religion, not a race", the obvious conclusion is that only "real races" experience racism. While most people may not have thought deeply about biological racism, there does appear to be a "common sense" view that races or ethnic groups really just are different people at a fundamental level, that racial inequalities are reasonably explained by the proclivities, behaviours, and attitudes of different "racial groups", and that this is just the way of the world. This bolsters the work of white nationalist activists, who regularly argue that their political vision merely recognizes this reality. But reflecting on the case of Islamophobia and its critics reveals a wider concern: poor public literacy on race and racism.

Focusing on individual intent rather than structural inequalities and outcomes is not just a problem when it comes to anti-Muslim racism. During the Windrush injustice, when Caribbean people who had lived in Britain for decades were detained, deported, and denied public services, the official response was that this was accidental. The "apologies" offered to those who experienced these injustices was that it was not the government's intent to affect Caribbean people. But when it comes to understanding discrimination, intent isn't always relevant. And this isn't just a question of academic thinking on racism: in British law, direct discrimination does not require proving intent, while *indirect* discrimination was introduced over forty years ago in the 1976 Race Relations Act in large part because victims of racism found it difficult to prove intent. If the public and policymakers better understood racial discrimination in structural rather than individual terms, they would better understand where it comes from, how it is reproduced, why the forms it takes vary but also tap into centuries-old tropes and stereotypes, but also why the response to it needs a wider, societal-level response as suggested by the Black Lives Matter movement.

In addition to the generally poor literacy on race and racism, there is a specific issue with Islam as a religion. This manifests in different ways. The first are free-speech-focused concerns, which suggest that Islamophobia is a term intended to shut down speech about Islam. The emphasis on criticising religion has the effect of deflecting conversations about where anti-Muslim racism comes from and its wider impact on people's lives; this almost obsessive focus on criticising religion also obscures how the link between hate speech and racist acts is shared with all forms of racism. The problem of hate speech is not about *religion* per se, nor are most people much motivated by or literate in theological or doctrinal disputes.[2] More generally, and even among some activists who challenge Islamophobia, this reflects a mistaken argument that Islamophobia is different from other forms of racism *because* of the focus on religion or culture or beliefs. Such an argument is mistaken because *all* forms of racism have a "cultural" component. More specifically, racism has always been justified because of the particular attitudes or behaviours of a specific group; all individuals of a "racial group" are assumed to have a tendency towards behaviours that are deemed pathological and that hence explain or justify racial inequalities (if not racial discrimination). Josiah Brownell in this volume offers a stark case study of how Rhodesia's racist immigration policies were framed around the supposed economic behaviours of African people, even when these same people were middle class and highly educated.

Far right groups have exploited the confusion about "cultural" vs "colour" based racism. They have suggested that they aren't really racist because racism is about prejudice on the grounds of skin colour, while Islamophobia is justifiable because it's about criticising people for their beliefs or actions. Foregrounding Islamophobia in this way is a clever tactic, as it appeals to a wider audience, and allows them to hide or smuggle in their wider beliefs about inherent cultural difference and racial hierarchy.

Claims about irreconcilable cultural difference, that Muslims cannot ever be European or British, and that pluralistic societies always descend into violence are of course familiar among white nationalists. The notion that Europe or Britain should be defined by race and religion is no longer a marginal view. Advocates of ethno-nationalist "illiberal democracy" explicitly reject values such as equality and rights; they found their voice – and support in some governments – during the refugee crisis. The inability to agree on a European-wide settlement scheme for Syrian refugees, and Britain's unwillingness to offer sanctuary, exposed the limits of cooperation and humanitarianism, especially when tainted by Islamophobic views about Muslims specifically.

White nationalists focus on Muslims not just because they hold elaborate, long-standing views about Muslims as a "demographic threat", but because they know the British public holds more negative views about Muslims. For example, a 2016 survey found that a majority of respondents believed that Islam is "not compatible with British values", while the proportion who would be comfortable with a family member marrying a Muslim is much lower (around half) than it is for other groups.[3] A recent (2019) *Hope not Hate* report found that "the attitude of conservative voters to Muslims has got considerably worse over the last few years".[4] There are regular stories about "no-go" areas in Britain, despite the fact that the areas being referred to have a *minority* of Muslim residents, that the largest local authority (Tower Hamlets) Muslim population is only 34.5%, that many such areas are seeing a *decline* in the proportion of Muslim residents, and that white British people have the highest levels of residential segregation in the country.[5]

White nationalists are not coy about their racism and object to even small minorities of Muslims, or ethnic minorities generally, living in the UK. Their view is both that some racial groups are inherently different and inferior, and that racial conflict is inevitable. However carefully phrased, those who refer to "Eurabia", "great replacement", or "demographic threats" are directly affirming white nationalist beliefs, and it is concerning how far those views, tapping into widespread Islamophobia, have proliferated in "mainstream" publications and newspapers.

The resistance to the Black Lives Matter movement has revealed how white nationalists don't simply object to Muslims, and how it's not just white nationalists who hold to long-standing racist views about Black people and their demands for justice and rights. The lazy caricatures of the movement and the otherwise curious focus on trivial demands about television programmes should be understood in terms of centuries-old delegitimation tactics that suggest that Black people are violent, irrational, and anti-national, tactics that are themselves steeped in racist presumptions about the moral and intellectual capacities of Black people.

Here it is also worth highlighting the ongoing anti-Semitism among white nationalists, in Europe as well as the United States. When I first started working for Runnymede in 1999, I was perplexed by arguments that Runnymede was founded by Jews to encourage the migration and equal rights of African and Asian people, and so to undermine the British nation. That conspiracy theory is now more common, and also shows how a supposedly "positive" racist argument – that Jewish people have greater intelligence – combines with centuries-old anti-Semitic tropes, while at the same time suggesting implicitly or explicitly that people of colour are themselves too unintelligent or strategically astute to organise and challenge racism directly.

This leads me to the final reflection, namely on the challenge of building a wider anti-racist movement. The current moment has arisen in large part from the brutal murder of George Floyd by police in Minneapolis, and it brings into focus the specific forms that anti-Black racism takes not just in the US but in the UK and more widely. It is both unwise and insulting to deflect immediately or crassly from the specific anti-Black racism that is now inspiring so many people around the globe into a general conversation about all forms of racism everywhere. At the same time this appearance (and often reality) of a deflection raises a wider phenomenon: when discussing or responding to racism as it exists in the world, we are usually if not always responding to a *specific* form of racism. When we are asked to show solidarity with a group, the issue is even clearer: we are asked to show solidarity because of the particular, specific racism that group has just experienced. At such a moment, it is important to listen to that group, to reflect on the particular form of racism that is being experienced, and to focus on responses or solutions that deal with that form of racism. At some point, and I'm speaking cautiously in May 2020, we will need to make a wider move towards tackling all forms of racism, not just because that's what anti-racist or human rights principles require, but because it is the best practical way of building sustained social action against racism. This should, however, be based more on bottom-up links across communities, *as well as* focusing on shared interests and experiences, including by responding to other forms of injustice.

I was first asked to write this postscript on Islamophobia before George Floyd was murdered, and before the Black Lives Matter movement took off globally. While I have focused on why Islamophobia is a form of racism, I have also sought to explain why that formulation – and resistance to thinking of Islamophobia as anti-Muslim racism – has wider significance. It is important that Muslims and non-Muslims reflect more on what anti-Muslim racism is, and fight to challenge it; so far, the struggle against Islamophobia in Britain has lacked not just an understanding of racism but a wide and deep enough social response. Tackling racism, including anti-Muslim racism, requires *both* understanding, listening, and responding to specific forms of racism, *and* building arguments, coalitions, and policies to challenge and ultimately dismantle all forms of injustice.

Notes

1 https://www.runnymedetrust.org/uploads/Islamophobia%20Report%202018%20FINAL.pdf (accessed 7 July 2020).
2 It's important to concede or recognise that religion is not just a difficult area for the free-speech liberal, but also for many secular leftists.

3 http://www.bbc.co.uk/newsbeat/article/36346886/uk-attitudes-towards-islam-concerning-after-survey-of-2000-people (accessed 7 July 2020).

4 https://www.hopenothate.org.uk/2019/02/17/state-of-hate-2019-conservative-party-islamophobia/ (accessed 7 July 2020).

5 https://www.runnymedetrust.org/blog/segregation-isnt-white-minority (accessed 7 July 2020).

Index